1970

THE HERO
AS
FAILURE

"... *denn was ist reizender als die Täuschung?*"
—Thomas Mann, *Joseph in Aegypten*

THE HERO
AS
FAILURE

Balzac and the Rubempré Cycle

BERNARD N. SCHILLING

THE UNIVERSITY OF CHICAGO PRESS/Chicago and London

Library of Congress Catalog Card Number 68-27293

THE UNIVERSITY OF CHICAGO PRESS, CHICAGO 60637

The University of Chicago Press, Ltd., London W.C.1

To the Memory of My Father
A True
"*Médecin de campagne*"

Acknowledgments

On completing a work of this kind one is tempted to apply Churchill's memorable tribute in reverse: never has anyone owed so much to so many. I have worked chiefly in two libraries at home, and am greatly obliged to Rush Rhees Library at the University of Rochester and to the Sterling Memorial Library at Yale for the use of their collections and their excellent services. In Paris, I incurred obligations to five different institutions. At the Bibliothèque Nationale, Mlle Marthe Chaumié was good enough to initiate me into the workings of this ancient edifice, and at the Bibliothèque de l'Arsenal, I was the beneficiary of the Conservateur en Chef, M. Guignard and his erudite colleague Mme Le Gal, who gave me access to rare materials. Professor Louis Bonnerot of the Sorbonne was good enough to introduce me to the Conservateur en Chef of the Bibliothèque de la Sorbonne, M. Germain Calmette, who granted me use of the Salle des Professeurs and its many privileges. All Balzacians are of course in debt to M. André Billy, and I in particular for his leadership in establishing the Salle de Documentation Balzacienne in the Musée Balzac. Here, by the "escalier dérobé" once used by Balzac to escape his creditors, one may descend to a solid collection of books and articles amid excellent working conditions. My sincere thanks are due to M. Patrice Boussel and Mlle Jacqueline Sarment for their courteous reception and assistance.

Finally, I was indeed fortunate to be installed in a room of my own at the Centre Universitaire International, where my work was immensely facilitated and brought to a happy conclusion with the indispensable aid of Mlle Françoise Chaumais and Mlle Françoise Sudre.

Meanwhile I was greatly encouraged and supported by Mlle Marcelle Minet and Mme Henry Puget throughout my stay in Paris, while I enjoyed the constant aid of Cecil Lang and Jules Brody at all stages of my work. G. Robert Stange and Leon-François Hoffman also offered a number of valuable suggestions, and Mme Michel Rybalka was good enough to review the manuscript in detail. Miss Ruth Harper was, as always, patient and willing in preparing a final version for the press.

Special thanks are due to the John Simon Guggenheim Memorial Foundation for the grant of a fellowship that made possible the year in Paris during which this study was written.

The Dedication records a lifelong obligation at many levels. It expresses above all my gratitude for the memorable day on which my father made me a gift of his twenty-four-volume set of Balzac. Here, amid the red and gold splendor of the "Édition Définitive," I first beheld the pages of *Illusions perdues*, *César Birotteau*, and *Le Médecin de campagne*.

BERNARD N. SCHILLING

Contents

Introduction

The following essay will often refer to the *Bildungsroman*, a term easier to illustrate than to define. This German but now international term established itself in the nineteenth century with Goethe and Wilhelm Meister's search for a place in life, becoming the dominant genre of German fiction. In France and England it pursued a modified course. For Balzac and Dickens the hero's life work is, rather, fixed by circumstances and his own nature. Their protagonists demand success in the world here and now, the gaining of ambitions, the fulfillment of expectation. But *Bildungsroman* contains notions of *Erziehung* and *Entwicklung* that lead to completion of the *Bildung*. A process of education for the ignorant young *ingénu*, of learning things not known before, leads to a development through increase in knowledge of the world and oneself, in depth of character, ending finally in the complete *Bildung*, a cultivated maturity. Thus after the lessons have been learned and the *Bildungsmächte* or formative influences have done their work, character has developed until the hero has found his place in the world and is ready to play the role called for by his experience.

A similar development is not always clear for Balzac's hero, and indeed the protagonist of *Illusions perdues* fails for want of this threefold process, despite the theme of "la réalité victorieuse du rêve," in M. Barrière's phrase. Yet the hero of the *roman d'appren-*

1

tissage, d'éducation, d'initiation in France strives equally to "know himself and the world," as required by Matthew Arnold of every cultivated man. He is typically a youth who sets forth in life determined to "arrive." Movement means change, and he who stays where he is remains the same, like Eugénie Grandet and the families of Rastignac and Lucien de Rubempré. So in France the hero leaves the provinces for the Parisian scene to effect the change in his condition, inspired by his talent, his vanity or illusory ambition. In time he undergoes formative influences, he makes the comparisons that reveal to him, for the first time, men and things as they are. "Pour la première fois" echoes throughout the *Comédie humaine,* and aids in creating the sense of vivid immediacy in Balzac. The hero sees others and himself anew; he works, suffers, loves and is loved, is tempted, sins or resists, and proceeds at last to his destiny. Whether he ends in triumph like the Joseph of Mann's tetralogy, in ambiguous uncertainty like Pip in *Great Expectations,* or in abject failure like Balzac's Lucien, he learns that reality and appearance are not the same: he ends without illusions, and any account of his adventures may be called, like the great poem now before us, *Illusions perdues.*

Balzac's title suggests, too, that the experience of Lucien is universal; his initiation, his painful choices and fatal decisions are the material of every life and the essence of every novel. Proust reads the title literally: lost illusions are simply the universal lessons of experience that correct human error. Freud has noted the tendency of all men to be deluded when reality conflicts with wishes, to seek an unattainable happiness through fulfillment of hopes and ambitions, to measure by false standards that seek wealth, power, and success, while undervaluing what is truly precious in life. Inevitably then, as Mr. Levin remarks, the process of disillusion in literature is "realism" and "every great novelist since Cervantes has played his own variation on the theme that Balzac epitomized in *Illusions perdues.*"

In the *Comédie,* men seem to form in lines facing in the direction of typical human experience. A single man takes his place in the queue that contains his kind; but when the time comes, he steps forward and repeats the actions of all others like him who have gone before and will follow again. Balzac's somber, undeceived pessimism, wherein knowledge of life destroys illusion, nonetheless permits his characters their essential freedom, a freedom to be what they are, which accounts for their enormous energy. Balzac interferes far less than Dickens in the fate of his creations; after his typical preparation, indeed, he cannot intrude because it is too late, and he accepts, as he must, the disasters that are bound to follow. The reader stands beside Balzac, watching a movement toward an end that cannot be other than this. In Lucien's career, we know at a certain moment that he is doomed, that his *avenir* is an illusion, his ambition hopeless.

Our knowledge of what is to come in a given work gains enormously the more we have read in the *Comédie* itself, as we are made to see how small is Balzac's world, how readily grasped and accepted. *Illusions* itself is the great *carrefour* of the Balzacian realm, reaching out in all directions to explore French society of the nineteenth century in action. Its importance is clear if we recall certain facts and relationships. M. Bardèche sees the Rubempré cycle as forming with *Le Père Goriot* a kind of trilogy, wherein Vautrin appears and proceeds to his last incarnation. *Le Père Goriot* first invokes the city, society, and money "the Parcae of the Balzacian world"; it raises the questions that receive their answers in the fate of Lucien. His career binds together two contrasted societies in Angoulême, a bohemian world in Paris, the idealistic group of the Cénacle, and the beau monde of the Marquise d'Espard—representing all classes and professions from the summit to the bottom of society. *Illusions* further contains fully developed all that has preceded it in the *Comédie* touching the hero himself and the setting of his adventures. The mere fact of its physical centrality in Balzac's career would insure this. We take *Les Chouans*, the first of Balzac's novels to bear his own name, as the effective start of his literary career, 1829. Balzac needed seven years to write *Illusions* itself, 1836–43, beginning seven years after *Les Chouans*. He died in 1850, just seven years after completing it. The work is in the center, then, of a period of great masterpieces, if we narrow this further to the years from *Eugénie Grandet* in 1833, to the magnificent *Le Cousin Pons* and *Splendeurs et misères des courtisanes* in 1847.

Looking within the *Comédie*, we see that *Illusions* explores fully the question which, in Balzac's view, dominated modern France as a moral and historical phenomenon: the opposition between Paris and the provinces. As Lucien himself has been anticipated variously by the line of protagonists from Raphaël Valentin through Rastignac and Victurnien d'Esgrignon, so has Balzac already shown us the realities of Paris now so powerfully gathered together. We must have in mind these Parisian meanings not only to appreciate the setting of Part II, but to see clearly how Lucien's *avenir* is an illusion, how futile is the ambition to conquer Paris, to be great in such a context. From our reading we know the many Parises and their implications as Lucien does not: the dark Paris of uncertain identities, of concealment, of ambiguous alleys and fearful corners in the fog and gaslit dimness; the Paris of heartless love-intrigue, of caprice and maneuver, of lavish entertainment by a cold aristocracy, of the fashionable ball that must be attended and the enormous influence of women; the Paris, too, of gold and pleasure and the means of obtaining them; the Paris of allure for young ambition, with abysses of temptation, of corruption and doom for the weak, but quick and stunning success for the bold and well-equipped. Knowing all these, we see coming the fate of Lucien, his dreams of success pitiable in a world certain to defeat so fragile a human spirit. We may then indulge in a Balzacian *sourire*, mingling pity and disdain from our superior knowledge and the maturity gained vicariously from the *Comédie* and its fearful lessons.

This essential preparation seems to compel us to follow Balzac's own typical structure: a legato opening, long preparation and careful review of the past, clear study of scene and character with the strategies of their presentation—pursuit of all relevant lines that converge upon Lucien, his fate and the world in which it is to unfold: all of this after Balzac's own fashion, until at last the action itself, concentrating upon the hero, moves relentlessly to its end.

The centrality of *Illusions* encourages us to read Balzac from within, to find our evidence for his meaning, not from his own life and the contemporary world, but from the fiction he created. His "realism" will not trouble us if we take his imagined world to be more "real" than the society of which he was the declared secretary or photographic historian, if we read him as a "divine" or poetic creator, that is. That Balzac presents a "truth" more faithful to the world than life itself, that the so-called "real" world is incoherent and must be brought into form and order by the "God" Balzac, that he was as Croce said "a poet in the best sense of the word," that he was a mystic and a seer, unifying his world by an essentially poetic vision wherein the poetry is inseparable from "la précision documentaire" in M. de Sacy's phrase—such has been the view of a faint line of criticism from Balzac's own time to the present. Despite melodramatic exaggeration, the presence of many stock romantic trappings and terms, and the use of rambling, incoherent sentences, Balzac writes with extraordinary imaginative power, achieving a vivid concreteness, and creating metaphors of great force, which "illuminate and transmute," writes R. A. Sayce, "the material objects described." Taking up the well-known phrase from Baudelaire, that Balzac was a "visionnaire passionné," M. Albert Béguin also delivers Balzac from the realists in showing that his creation is poetic and mythical, that his world is a fiction composed of words, using the novel form as containing all other literary forms, and so presenting him with limitless possibilities. The French critical tradition, whose strengths and omissions are so well described by Mr. Levin, is

thereby reminded of its emphasis on background and source study
to the neglect of the means taken by Balzac to achieve his vision.
How well this approach has been used in France one may discover
from the accumulating volumes of *L'Année Balzacienne*, which goes
steadily onward with a kind of exuberant, obstinate independence,
not one article in twenty addressing itself to questions of art or
style. But since this form of study has produced such results, we
need not repeat it here, being content to draw gratefully upon it
when relevant or helpful. Preceding students have been greatly
fascinated by Balzac's life as it appears in the *Comédie*, by the manner in which he cultivated it as a field from which to draw
numerous details, persons, events, relationships. The identification of all these and the drawing of parallels between life and
work have yielded much of interest and value, but we should
consider what Balzac's imagination has done with such material.
We are not required to identify actual journalists or members of
the "Cénacle" as Balzac presents them, although he tempts us by
his own constant intrusion into the narrative with reminders of
his fidelity to the actual world around him. He seems bent on ful-
filling the requirements of "realism" as seen in Mr. Weinberg's
excellent summary. He is at great pains to provide contemporary
background, showing that events and persons in the story correspond to known facts. But it does not in the least help us to know
how closely his criminal world, for example, corresponds to that
which he documents for us with a scrupulous exactness.

Thus we shall have to resist him when Balzac, making no
distinction between fiction and pamphlets as vehicles of ideas,
allows the essayist, moralist, social historian, philosopher, journalist, or political and religious analyst to intrude upon the novelist
to the detriment of his "real" world, the one he imagines, not the
one he is copying. Still, the interpolated essays, digressions, and
intrusions are there, and we cannot behave as if they did not exist
or were of no benefit in our search for Balzac's meaning. We are
best advised to treat them as part of the imagined fiction of the

Comédie, the same as an event, character, or description in the story itself. Anything within a given work is then taken as evidence of its meaning, whereas an essay separately written by Balzac on the same subject will not be invoked to show his meaning in the work under discussion. The metaphorical structure of the *Comédie* itself will yield us sufficient riches so long as we take his imagined world as the real one, not inquiring whether it corresponds to the world of fact.

In *La Duchesse de Langeais*, for example, Balzac introduces a long historical essay in order to explain how a certain kind of young woman was produced by the Faubourg Saint-Germain. This finally becomes functional as Balzac follows a threefold order, of decreasing generalization: fifteen pages analyse the social, political, and moral climate; then a description of the kind of woman produced by such an ephemeral life; finally we have the duchess, Antoinette herself. Let us grant the narrator his need to explain how the heroine became a certain kind of woman. But in the novel itself the conditions described may be quite imaginary, so that we do not ask whether the Faubourg Saint-Germain of historical fact was like this or not. The background that produced Antoinette, we are sure, is as the narrator says it is, although this background may be fully as imaginary as the adventures that made Antoinette's lover Montriveau the kind of man he is. When we use the word "Balzac" therefore, we mean generally the artist-narrator, and if we are faithful to him and to his enlarged, intensified vision, we shall enjoy "cette paralysie du sens critique" in M. Bardèche's reading, and will cease to ask for truth to the way life is in fact lived. We shall find that Balzac has many ways of commenting on the action without stopping to write a separate discourse. As essayist, Balzac is most effective when his commentary is not detached from but is part of the action, when his characteristic enlargements, similes, and other comparisons or brief *sententiae* in the midst of an action clarify its meaning or function. Then, too, Balzac like Dickens is a master of the immediate presence of objects, whereby things become allied with human beings, taking on the qualities of those who use them, and becoming a social force in binding people together through their presence, their being seen and used in common. A typical Balzacian scene will be essay enough for us on the world that contains it.

In Balzac's world as he imagined it, the work is greater than the man, who accomplishes something more than he intends. We may even decide, if we choose the right examples, that Balzac was a great writer, despite the objections of contemporaries for whom he was "le grand coupable," guilty of all the possible literary sins. One may declare almost anything to be true of the *Comédie* by carefully avoiding the quotations that prove the opposite, and certainly one may decide from the worst examples that Balzac was careless and uneven. We have been repeatedly assured by Flaubert, Edmond Scherer, and others that Balzac simply could not write, that he did not even know the French language and its proper idiom, and more recently, by M. André Wurmser in a work of swollen, repetitious, often petulant Marxist journalism, that Balzac had no literary vocation and was not really a man of letters at all. Such pessimism must yield to a reading that searches for the strategies that give to the work before us so much of its beauty and power.

A great teacher, Charles G. Osgood, has invited us ideally: "Let us sit down together with a great poem and plenty of time." This invitation is also a directive "toward Balzac" in Mr. Levin's phrase, toward the essential, the true Balzac, the poet of our common destiny. "Les *Illusions perdues*," M. Adam says justly, "sont beaucoup mieux qu'un roman. Elles sont . . . œuvre de poésie, elles méritent que nous les appelions un poème." He finds the style itself "aussi audacieusement métaphorique que le plus grand style proustien," so that by the power of its images the work becomes an allegory of good and evil. Let us see, then, what Balzac has done with the literary form that for him contained all others, with a genre also attempted by Dickens and Thomas Mann, among the few novelists who can be compared with Balzac without blasphemy.

At this point we should describe our manner of proceeding, lest the reader form expectations that seem to be left unsatisfied. After a glance at French history and the influence of Napoleon, we present in the chapter "Strategies" a set of terms, images, symbols, motifs, which eventually are shown to be pervasive throughout the novels discussed under "Lineage," throughout the Rubempré cycle, and from there into the *Comédie* as a whole. All that is said in Chapter 2, then, is repeated, illustrated, and enlarged upon in all that follows. Each of the nine units chosen is given brief, introductory treatment and is deliberately left unfinished for the sake of later cumulative effect, only to be resumed in the extended analysis of events, their meaning in the career of Lucien, what they reveal of his character, and the reasons for his failure. The reader will find this far more than a summary of the plot, whole areas of which are omitted entirely as not fully bearing on the hero, and as not illustrating Balzac's use of his controlling "strategies." It is after all within the great novels themselves that the "strategies" do their work and achieve their powerful effect. Therefore we try mainly to show at what points in the action involving the hero the various terms reappear, how they are used, and how Balzac relies upon them to interpret and unify his created world. The Balzacian realm has certain unmistakable qualities that tend to be repeated, and we have chosen to show this by a linear account of a prolonged action centered upon the figure of Lucien. Thus the reader is often reminded that *Illusions* might well be the title of the entire *Comédie*, written on the same theme, as Albert Cook has remarked in *The Meaning of Fiction:* "The whole is a polyphony of disillusions which orchestrates and counterpoints each single disillusion."

The reader will see that we imitate Balzac, for our summary of the action is also a commentary upon it by means of the recurring terms, reference to the "lineage" figures and other parts of the

Comédie. While it may be an exaggeration to say that Balzac's work has the "intimacy of a sonnet cycle," we try to show how closely knit his world in fact is, how the Rubempré cycle is indeed one of its main *carrefours.* Besides the constant reference back and forth to the young men and the works mentioned in "Lineage," in our review of events there are some twenty-five other works from the *Comédie* referred to by title whenever the action calls them to mind; others are employed indirectly through various allusions. Our summary pauses frequently as well for analysis of the hero's character and the reasons for his failure, for various devices whereby Balzac draws the action and the portrait of Lucien together, for restatement of the "strategies" to show how they contain again a summary of the action and Balzac's commentary on its meaning. The repetition of these terms and emphasis on their symbolic intent allow steady review of the preceding action, of key events and their influence.

The chapter and subhead titles show how frequently the theme of temptation emerges throughout. The brief comment on "Clothes" in Chapter 2 is continued later, off and on, all the time, so that in the middle hundred pages some thirteen allusions to clothes are made. We finally pause to round out the full meaning of the symbol in detail, showing the relationship among clothes, the physical beauty of Lucien, and his fatal illusions. Similarly, after the mention of "voiture" at intervals some fifteen times, we pause for a more extended comment on its implications. The various epithets for Lucien are likewise allowed to gather force until they converge at last upon *poète*, greatly intensifying the effect of this term. Paris and all that it stands for appears on almost every page, either by name or by its influence. Again, apart from the brief section called "L'Abîme," there are some ten references to the abyss. The frequency of allusion to Rastignac accounts for the length of his treatment in "Lineage"; the reader is intended to recall especially Eugène's step into the abyss, from which he is miraculously delivered: "Il fallait un miracle pour le tirer de l'abîme où il avait déjà mis le pied. . . ." Balzac repeats the smile image throughout, using it as a turning point in the action to reveal Lucien's knowledge of Esther and to emphasize the diabolism of Vautrin. Indeed, "le sourire" is carried to the final page of the cycle, lest we should fail to grasp its importance. As for the future tense and *avenir*, the signature of Lucien's illusions, it is repeated with its host of related terms more frequently than any other Balzacian symbol, until the day that has no tomorrow and Lucien is no more.

These are the reasons why the parts of Chapter 2 are kept brief and fragmented: to reach their fulfillment in the ensuing review of Lucien's career. With their recurrence the several terms take on accumulated energy, until the reader is persuaded that they are inseparable from the fate of Lucien and all that it implies. The final pages then look back to draw various lines together, leading to the inevitability of the hero's failure.

1

Napoleon and the
Youth of France

When Balzac began to write *Illusions perdues* in June, 1836, he had in mind a more limited study of defeated young ambition than that which emerged seven years later in the completed masterpiece. The subject grew as he wrote until it embraced the nineteenth century itself and the tragic history of youth "depuis trente ans," as Balzac himself says, the clash between youthful ardor, sincerity and confident hope, and the ludicrous pitiable result. M. Poulet has shown that in the *Comédie humaine* there is everywhere a future charged either with promise or menace, as the world seems to offer for the first time the fulfillment of a dream held equally by the ruthless arriviste and the idealistic Saint-Simonian. All the social utopias of the nineteenth century are based equally upon this *avenir*, and in Balzac the young men seem endowed with an "énergie du futur," "cette poésie de l'avenir," in M. Duvignaud's phrase. *Avenir* is proper to the age, then, and while we seek to avoid reliance on the contemporary terms used by Balzac, we must know when it was that he looked at the world and found it to be what writers of ancient and Renaissance times had before him. But the nineteenth century made his terms what they were; he uses money, business, and the move to power by material possessions because these were at hand in the France of his time. His end, to see the world as it was, he had in common with literary predecessors, but the nineteenth century made possible the vast metaphors whereby Balzac could read the world; thus he owes much to an age that compelled his despair, persuading him finally that life contradicts the demands of the very reason, justice, and virtue which it invites and seems to render possible.

Unlike Napoleon and our chosen hero, we must win toward attainable goals and so remain nearer Balzac's original intention. We shall follow the career of a single youth, Lucien, as the type of ambition that left the provinces to seek fortune in Paris. Mr. Watt has shown this theme as inseparable from the novel form, until "triumph in the big city has become the Holy Grail in the individual's secular pilgrimage." Lucien's adventures are presented in the form of a post-Napoleonic novel, whose first masterpiece was Stendhal's *Le Rouge et le Noir*. Lucien is one of thousands of young provincials who follow the same path, drawn by longings "comme jadis les courtisans à Versailles," as M. Girard remarks. M. Jules Vallès has watched these "grands hommes de province à Paris," so many doomed to defeat, even to crime and punishment, the very spectacle of lost illusions. Many things account for their spiritual condition, but we shall leave to one side the influence of Wertherism, Byronism, Chattertonian despair, and similar traces of Romantic melancholy or "mal du siècle." Lucien may then be seen as an example of young hope following on the changes wrought by the Revolution, which in turn gave opportunities that had never existed before—all further inspired by the example of Napoleon, who made anything seem possible, while the great city of Paris lay there seeming to await, to invite the conquest of energetic youth.

The years between twenty and twenty-five, to be sure, have always been a period of hope, discovery, impatience, and temptation. Any young man may see a conflict between his passion and energy, and the structure of society based on established hierarchy, with the summit occupied by the old and those who have already "arrived." A young man looks up toward the obstacles that he must surmount; a long, slow future unfolds, with no assurance of final success. He sees, too, that all of those above him have not obeyed the rules of law and morality; he is therefore tempted to shorten the way to success, to make a rapid fortune while still young. In France after Napoleon the ambitious youth pursues the movement of all French illusion toward Paris, which in turn becomes the central lure of the *Comédie* itself. Among the occupations formerly closed that now became democratized was literature itself, and Balzac describes the fever of *arrivisme*, the flight of an unsettled generation into literary pursuits now open to anyone who could do nothing practical, inviting, as Mr. Brombert says, "moneyless young men of humble birth . . . into literary and artistic careers." Balzac sees Paris at once as the enemy and the beneficiary of the entire nation: provincial society is constantly impoverished as the best of its nobility, industry and talent depart to seek fortune in Paris, a process already advanced, as Tocqueville saw, by 1789, when "Paris had mastered France." Even when a merchant has made a fortune elsewhere, he thinks only of spending it in Paris. All superiority and energy gather in a single place, resulting in destructive combat with ruinous waste and loss.

The fearful nature of this combat is one of the young man's first lessons, he who has cherished the democratic illusion of a career open to all talent. But Tocqueville had seen that if success is available to everyone, the chance for the single individual is reduced, leading to the dualism of battle and the pervasive figures of military combat employed by Balzac in *Le Père Goriot* and *Illusions* with somber effect. In the drive for success, the chance for happiness is lost as the young man moves to the very goal that he imagined would insure it. The first illusion, then, to be lost by Balzac, the reader, and his protagonist, is the democratic one, for democracy, which was to create opportunity, only forces a dehumanizing battle and intensifies the very struggle that it was supposed to solve.

Balzac writes as the modern city begins to take its present form: enormously enlarged in size and population, totally changed in appearance and activity, the city becomes the scene of adventure and tragedy where the hero must survive all of the epic dangers and enemies and where every human passion finds an outlet. It is the new epic scene where at any moment anything is possible. These qualities cling to the myth of the great city of tradition, but they concentrate themselves in Paris, whose importance has increased with its role in the French Revolution, the imposition of its will on the provinces, and the gathering to itself of the entire administration of France. Here then is the realm that the young hero must conquer, unaware of the "force herculéenne" demanded by the struggle before him.

So the hero comes, obsessed "par une brutale envie de parvenir," which means the quick accumulation of money, leading to the possession of all that money can buy: servants, carriages, women, power. For money as such, not only as a classical metaphor of corrupt human wishes, now enabled a man to accomplish what had never before been possible, to achieve elevation, honor, and the power to make or undo the law. This reign of personal interest follows on the Revolution and the success of Napoleon, creating the chance for a single man to rise in the world by his own effort, making possible in turn the development by Stendhal and Balzac of their version of the *Bildungsroman* genre. Now one might set out from anywhere and attain the highest level of French life. The journey becomes essential, then, to the hero's growth and change, a journey toward Paris and upward in the world never before so full of promise. There must be a way up and access thereto, so that literature may imagine the human consequences for ambitious youth. And Napoleon himself had shown by example not only what the single youth could accomplish; he had, by his *Code*, legalized and stabilized the society produced by the Revolution, providing new chances for education, and opening, in a literal sense, the world. Rapidity marked his own rise and his actions, and rapidity of advancement seized the young imagination. Like the medieval initiation of Christ, Napoleon was adored as the glorious conqueror of the whole of Europe, the man of genius, the great statesman and founder of modern France. The intoxicating effect of his example inspired a glowing passage in a letter from one of Balzac's female correspondents; she recalls her

> années de jeunesse, d'illusions, de joie; menteuses espérances, qui me peigniez l'avenir enivrant, parfumé. . . . J'aimais, j'adorais Napoléon! mon imagination me le peignait comme un dieu . . . je fléchissais le genou devant lui, sans réfléchir de quel torrent de larmes surgissait cet éblouissant éclat.

The fact of rapidity was again inspiring when, in a few years' time, a young man could become a general under Napoleon. Small wonder that Julien Sorel, despite his own sensitive and most un-Napoleonic nature, cries out "que Napoléon était bien l'homme envoyé de Dieu pour les jeunes Français!" But not all the young had the qualities of energy and will needed to follow Napoleon's example, which was ruinous to the mediocrities misled into leaving the security of home. Lucien Leuwen's mother laments the frantic ambition at all levels, so that "un garçon cordonnier veut devenir un Napoléon." When Lucien de Rubempré tries to launch his literary career in Paris, an old captain under Napoleon warns him against the example of all the conscripts who desired to become marshals of France. And who but Vautrin, with the devil's knowledge of everything, warns Lucien that he is in too much of a hurry because of Napoleon: "simple écolier, vous avez voulu passer trop tôt maître. C'est le défaut des Français dans votre époque. Ils ont été gâtés tous par l'exemple de Napoléon."

Napoleon was indeed a glorious model, but in departing at last "il a laissé un grand rêve brutal" in persuading youth that all was possible, that all was youth's due. Ironically he, who left nothing to chance, inspired thousands of young aspirants to take disastrous chances, which put them at the mercy of malicious fortune. Was he not a form of tempter as well, offering a seeming value now in exchange for something timeless and beyond price, the soul of youth? He tempts youth to the sin of pride, or, worse than crime, the blunder of pursuing illusions of grandeur, which seem to have been realized in fact by the little corporal from nowhere. Yet while he seems to justify the illusions of the young by his own early performance, he then shows them as doomed, by his own fate. He turns away from that which created him, the French Revolution, only to show that its three illusions have led him into others equally certain to be lost. So loss of the Napoleonic, followed loss of the democratic illusion. The humblest lad failed to see the difference between what Napoleon had done and what might be possible for him. The more fantastic the exploits and the greater the distance covered in so short a time, the more certain were the young that comparable achievements were possible. Then Napoleon's failure prevented fulfillment of the ambitions that his success had invited, and his example, once inspiring and assuring, in the end had to take its place among the human illusions certain to be lost. The lives of thousands were ruined, as the personnel of his vast machine had nothing left but their *souvenirs* in place of the *avenir* once so promising, and the army of young provincials storming the gates of Paris found themselves engaged in a battle for success that could be won only at the price of happiness.

Now Balzac himself has thought mainly about the "plus fatales illusions de cette époque . . . celles que les familles se font sur les enfants," children who may possess the gifts of genius but who are lacking in strength of will or principle. He hopes fondly that his book will prevent only one young poet from leaving behind his beloved provincial family "de venir augmenter le nombre des damnés de l'enfer Parisien qui se battent à coups d'encrier. . . ." He cannot express so fond a hope without adopting his favored symbol of hell and damnation. Nor can he accept the truth in other terms than the abyss that lies in wait throughout the *Comédie*. Youth has against itself its own nature; provincial talent is unable to endure the monotony that makes every man of imagination long for the dangers of Paris: "Les Lucien sont comme les fumeurs, qui, dans une mine à mofettes, allument leur pipe malgré les défenses. Les abîmes ont leur magnétisme."

2

Strategies

M. André Bellessort did well to remind us long ago, "combien Balzac est nuancé . . . ," and more recently M. Béguin asks that Balzac be judged by the numberless hidden analogies and subtleties "dont le réseau, courant sous le drame et l'intrigue, forme la véritable trame de chacun de ses romans."

But the reader may take some time before he is aware of any network, of Proust's "des dessous de l'œuvre de Balzac" or Mr. Levin's "dense underbrush of metaphor . . . beneath the literal surface" of narrative. More immediately he will realize that Balzac is constantly reaching out from his text to include as much of the whole of life as the work in hand will sustain. He is a highly didactic writer, more of a satirist too than he knows, and *Illusions perdues* is charged with lessons for all mankind. Its subject, like that of *Le Père Goriot*, being the education of a young man in the ways of the world, the hero is being constantly taught or at least given a chance to learn, while Balzac as creator and narrator never ceases to deliver the essential lessons. This enlargement of meaning is ingeniously varied. A key chapter like "La Fatale Semaine" in *Illusions* may begin with a generalization that explains the ensuing action, which then illustrates the larger idea. There is enlargement by the offering of general ideas, by summaries of a given human quality, by wise analysis called for in the story itself, as when Daniel d'Arthez writes to Ève about Lucien at her request and delivers a kind of moral essay on the world and its values, serving the narrative both as résumé and prophecy, enlarging Balzac's meaning from the individual to the general rule. Such generalization, which is part of the action, following from the story itself, is more satisfactory than the numerous intrusive essays that Balzac thinks necessary to add. Those who enjoy exposing his glaring faults as a writer never cease to deplore these tedious interruptions for the sake of a discourse on society, on some abstract idea, on some special aspect of life, some activity or profession, as in the seventy odd pages describing Lucien's literary life or the chapter "Les Galeries de bois." Balzac is least effective when he seems obliged only to record the facts, not to imagine a fiction.

Most frequent, indeed perpetual, is the habit of seeking larger meanings through similes and other comparisons with metaphorical force. We read constantly that Lucien is "comme tous les nouveaux venus," "comme toutes les jeunes personnes," "comme tous les enfants de l'amour," "comme tout jeune homme," "comme la plupart des jeunes gens." Another behaves "comme beaucoup de pères" or "comme les hommes qui," or possesses "une de ces natures pudiques et tendres." A given woman in turn may be described "comme toutes les femmes"; she may suffer from "cette inquiétude . . . que les femmes éprouvent," or illustrate that "il existe chez certaines femmes une horreur. . . ." Such comparisons join with numerous sententiae or brief statements to convey the lessons taught by every phase of the action. The cumulative effect of these devices makes Balzac seem very wise; we believe that he knows a great deal, with a profound insight into human experience on a vast scale, so that his wisdom is equal to any complexity.

Balzac's wisdom or lack of it has been variously assessed. Henry James, who considered him a very bad but a very great writer, sees the narrative in Balzac groaning beneath a "weight of metaphysical and scientific digression." While not even Aristotle was ready to deliver himself on so many subjects, "it is probable that no equally vigorous mind was ever at pains to concoct such elaborate messes of folly." Frank O'Connor remarks that "no other novelist ever claimed to know so much as Honoré de Balzac," and Willa Cather quotes Flaubert's disdainful opinion that Balzac was "ignorant as a pot and bourgeois to the marrow." Raymond Mortimer is impressed by Balzac's breadth of interest, yet finds his abundant views often silly, and, worst of all, he charges that "Balzac believed in his own nonsense." To others he has appeared vulgar, pretentious, vain and a snob, his solemn attempts at moralizing, tasteless or absurd, his intelligence limited, as Martin Turnell says, "and his sensibility crude." Nonetheless he seems to *know* more than Dickens, for example, who, Orwell complains, does not seem to *know* much of anything. In the *Comédie humaine* the enlarging observations and comparisons descend ceaselessly upon the page, a still powerful fallout radiating inexhaustible energy and wisdom.

Balzac makes highly skilled use, at intervals, of speeches that are made to Lucien by important characters acting as *Bildungsmächte*, just as in *Der Zauberberg*, where Hans Castorp listens intently to what is said. At various times Lucien is warned or advised by David, Louise, Châtelet, Daniel d'Arthez, Lousteau, and eventually by Vautrin himself. Lousteau's prolonged account is important in its placement and function; it summarizes past action in the life of Lucien and restates the theme of lost illusions by recounting experiences like his own; it looks to the future in predicting Lucien's own course, as it reviews the life and sordid career of Lousteau, soon to be repeated by Lucien himself, unless he can learn from the experience of other men before him. His capacity to learn is continually strained as so much of life pours in upon him for the first time: he is naïvely astonished when, "pour la première fois de sa vie," he goes with Louise in a post-chaise. Here Balzac is repeating this phrase for new experience so often seen before in *Les Chouans*, *Sarrasine*, and most pitiably in *Eugénie*

Grandet, for whom the visit of her cousin Charles begins and ends her new world. The effect of sudden terror or dismay in turn will take the form it does at the disastrous reading of poetry in Angoulême, where Lucien is aware "qu'une sueur froide mouilla sa chemise," recalling *La Duchesse de Langeais*, when Antoinette sees Montriveau at a ball, and "une sueur froide sortit soudain de tous les pores de cette femme."

Let us not pretend that Balzac has the skill and subtlety of Joyce in creating echoes to the last syllable hundreds of pages apart; yet the repetitions and correspondences are so frequent and striking that we cannot dismiss them as accidents bound to occur in a work conceived on so vast a scale. When Lucien waits two hours for attention from a bookseller, and he overhears a desperate author cry out "Vous m'égorgez," we must think of David's anguished reply to his father's monstrous proposal, "Mon père, vous m'égorgez!" After his failure as poetic lion at the Bargeton soirée, Lucien makes his way back to his other world of Ève and David in a transition most skillfully executed; bitterly he tells himself, "Voilà donc le monde." Later, after his cruel abandonment at the opera in Paris, having been cut dead by those whom he has just met, he summarizes again bitterly: "Voilà donc mon royaume . . . voilà le monde que je dois dompter," telling us that he will fail, once again. The tight lines of construction and union will emerge also in the entrance or exit of characters at certain moments, in the heavily symbolic use of Lucien's recurring obsession with the change in his name, and, plainly, when the theme of his future death establishes itself as Lucien reads the somber elegy of Chénier on suicide to his terrifying audience, "Tes vers sont doux, j'aime à les répéter."

With renewed confidence now in Balzac as an artist who knows what he is doing, we may look out for the means he employs not only to control a given work but to make us feel intimate within the whole of the *Comédie* itself. This recalls the "structural approach" discussed by David Lodge, the tracing of certain terms through a long novel in search of unity. If we have such confidence also in ourselves and in our responses, we shall add immensely to our pleasure while avoiding the self-conscious, heavy solemnity that too often afflicts literary enterprises. The suggested lines that follow do not exhaust the possibilities of *Illusions;* but let us see what Balzac's text will yield if we explore vehicles and their numerous journeys; the role of clothing as it touches Lucien in particular; the many epithets or synonymous terms applied to Lucien throughout; the manner of presenting Paris and its meaning; the use of single terms such as *abîme, avenir,* with many related words, and especially, throughout, *sourire;* the recurring use of scenes of temptation, related to biblical language and situation; with at last a theme embracing all others—Balzac's pervasive dualism.

"LA VOITURE"

As the *Comédie* itself employs closely related terms and images, so the physical scene is joined; Paris and the provinces become one by means of travel to and fro in one of Balzac's main symbols of movement and union, the carriage with its many variations of form and use, befitting, too, the social mobility created by the French Revolution. *La voiture* is one of many objects common in ordinary life which, as Mr. Sayce points out, Balzac has carried to new and greatly intensified meanings. The carriage is a means of conveyance throughout, but it may itself be the scene of action, as Balzac frequently presents important meetings or conversations as taking place in the relative privacy of a carriage. Like Dickens, he dwells much on arrival and departure, on the boarding of vehicles, the creation of an atmosphere of going and coming, of separation and farewell on one hand, of welcome and reunion on the other. But the "coach" in Dickens is part of his protest against the railway, which is never mentioned by Balzac. The arrival of a *voiture* becomes a great event in such a provincial town as Guérande, in *Béatrix,* providing the only link between feudal times and the modern world. Balzac opens *L'Illustre Gaudissart* by

comparing the French traveling salesman to a carriage; he is to
ideas "ce que nos diligences sont aux choses et aux hommes,"
being neither Parisian nor provincial but only the means of joining
village and capital.

The carriage then, making movement to and fro possible, is
essential to Balzac's themes of illusion, the search for enlarged
experience, the pursuit by impatient young men of hopes to be
fulfilled elsewhere in place and time. "The desired object is situated across the distances," writes M. Poulet, so the young come
and go incessantly, eager, discontented, vain, unable to wait any
longer for slow ascent. They seem to have Balzac's sympathy as
he gives them their chance to pursue hopes, however doomed.
The carriage is the literal means of movement called for by the
story. It is a status symbol of worldly success. It is a factor in
democracy when it is public, a common carrier. How else might
Oscar Husson have made a fool of himself among the variegated
company in the coach that begins the action of *Un Début dans la
Vie?* When open to anyone able to pay its fare, the carriage stands
for the changes taking place in Balzac's world. It is, then, a metaphor of the journey that every hero's *Bildung* demands, standing for
whatever means are taken or experiences encountered for him to
pass from his obscure origin to his destiny in failure, ambiguity, or
triumph.

For Lucien, indeed, the carriage that sets him forth on the way
to his lost illusions becomes a proof that his hopes are indeed illusions certain to be lost. Louise takes him from Angoulême to
Paris in an old vehicle, which is in effect the same one taken
eighteen months later on the way back. Lucien is on foot now,
miserable in the agonies of defeat; he steals a ride on a passing
carriage, one that contains Louise and her new husband Châtelet.
Lucien and Louise ride together again, but now away from
doomed illusions, as they rode before toward and into them.
When Balzac decides to continue the Rubempré cycle, he sends
Lucien back to Paris, once more not alone. But the vehicle that

carries him back to Paris is a symbol both of desired wealth and success, and of the certain defeat awaiting him. Lucien has gone first to Paris in the carriage of the tempter Louise, and now, rescued from suicide, he returns with the tempter Vautrin. Seeing him for the second time en route to Paris in a carriage, do we not know that he is again doomed to failure because it is a carriage that bears him on?

In the first work bearing his own name, *Les Chouans*, Balzac places most of the early middle action in or near the carriage. A coach is the means of the beautiful Marie's arrival in the Chouan country; here she first meets and falls in love with Montauran, they alight from the coach and walk together, the vehicle is attacked and is the scene of danger as of awakening love, developing a silent character and atmosphere of its own, like any essential part of the Balzacian scene. In the scattered action of *Histoire des Treize*, the *voiture* lends itself to intrigue, to secret rendezvous, to murder, to the quarrels of lovers and other bizarre scenes as elegant coupés return from the ball in early morning. In *Béatrix*, two carriages depart after the wedding of Calyste and Sabine, one with the bridal pair transporting Sabine with ironic haste into the miseries of her early married life. Unhappy love expresses itself too in *La Duchesse de Langeais*, when Antoinette uses her *voiture* and livery to show contempt for the world's conventions, allowing her carriage and footmen to wait for all to see at Montriveau's door. Thus, even when empty, Balzac's carriages have their meaning. The funeral of Père Goriot is attended by one full, and two empty carriages, each revealing the nature of its owner. As the pitiable convoy arrives at Père-Lachaise, must we not remember the five hundred carriages that discharge the elite of the high world coming to attend the last ball in the mansion of Madame la Vicomtesse de Beauséant? Here Balzac joins powerfully two of his chief symbols, *la voiture* and *le sourire*. The high world has come, elegantly attired, expecting to witness the humiliation of this woman, once a proud queen on the summit, to gain access to whose salon

Delphine would have licked up the filthy mud that lines the streets of Paris, from the Rue Saint-Lazare to the Rue de Grenelle. The surface smiles behind which they glide at ease in the great salon conceal their malice, the cruel hope that one, for so long greater than themselves, may betray by a single tear or outward sign the anguish that has destroyed her as a human being. But their smiles of hypocrisy, concealing malicious hope, are matched by Madame's own smile of disdainful control: a weakness that disgraces human nature takes the form of smiles, only to be frustrated by a strength that supports impregnably the grandeur of a character too proud to yield. And just as five hundred carriages have delivered them to display their *sourires*, now at last a single *berline* waits to carry into exile the woman whose lonely greatness proved itself in a single smile, for her flight into exile begins at dawn. So at the funeral of old Goriot, once again, do not the carriages make their own statement of how important it is to possess them, how heartless is a world in which they betray the difference between one man's fate and another's, as one lonely *voiture de deuil* containing the priest, choir boy, Eugène, and Christophe, is joined finally by two carriages, empty but bearing the arms of de Restaud and de Nucingen, standing high in a false and merciless world?

But not everyone can afford a carriage, and it becomes, for our typical youth avid of success, a symbol of what he longs for, as the need to continue on foot shows his continued inferior position. Unlike the gloomy, romantic Obermann, who is bored in carriages and prefers going alone on foot, the ambitious youth soon recalls Napoleon's cynical remark: "On est considéré, à Paris, à cause de sa voiture et non à cause de sa vertu." If Napoleon's example has brought the young man to Paris, so may his wisdom guide him there. About the same time in England the sardonic Carlyle was attacking "respectability," whose sign was the keeping of a gig; so, in the *Comédie*, a *voiture* showed the measure of one's success and marked, as soon as it could be acquired, any improvement in one's worldly position. Balzac never fails to mention the *voitures* of those attending a ball, one of his principal stage settings for the drama of Paris, and attended mainly by those able to afford a carriage. In turn, going on foot meant the humiliation of being passed by others—evidently superior in position—in a carriage, especially galling to Lousteau for example, who sees his former mistress Dinah de la Baudraye in prosperity after their separation, "bien posée au fond d'une jolie voiture . . . ," as her husband, newly advanced in the world, looks out from his *voiture* upon the old Duc de Chaulieu, a former creditor, "à pied, un parapluie à la main. . . ." Going on foot involves a youth in another of Balzac's symbols, the underlying dirt or mud of Paris, which may cling to his boots unavoidably and so betray his condition wherever he goes, or which, more humiliating still, may be splashed upon him by the indifferent wheels of a passing carriage. Only by exercising the greatest care does the young Sébastien de la Roche of *Les Employés* arrive at the house of Célestine Rabourdin "sans avoir attrapé la moindre éclaboussure," and the muddy boots of young Rastignac are an early reminder of what he must do to avoid them.

Lucien himself comes to Paris in a carriage, it is true, unlike many another young hopeful too poor for one. Yet we shall find Lucien making his way toward his *avenir* largely on foot, using, that is, the slowest, most painful means, the one certain to prolong the distance between the point of his beginning and the final goal. We see him on the road, at home, walking back and forth between the two worlds of his origin and of his hopes; in Paris, on the Tuileries esplanade and elsewhere, until at last he departs on foot as a sign of ignominious failure.

CLOTHES

Those who succeed in Balzac's created world, invariably obey its "laws," the *lois du monde*, requirements of the world as it is. Of these, none is more fatal to disobedience than the Law of Appearance: the world judges by appearance, and one must conform to what people expect or wish to see. The avid youth learns that his

costume is important, especially if he wishes to seem to have what
he does not. Thus Balzac's young people express by their clothes
less what they are than what they wish to be or seem to be. Of the
2,050 people in the *Comédie*, there are 376 whose clothes are described in detail; many of these, as in Dickens, are given a costume
expressive of their nature, which never changes. Micawber's manner and appearance continue the same for years, and Joe Gargery
shows by his pitiful Sunday best during his visit to Pip in London
that any change in clothing is fatal to his peace and to the integrity
of his character. Balzac's minor clerks, landladies, and especially
his misers tend to maintain the same appearance, and the cruel
meanness of David Séchard's father is maintained without altera-
tion, like his provincial costume and bloated face. But young men
like Rastignac and Lucien must change their clothes with the
course of their lives. At any point their costumes will reflect the
stage to which their *Bildung* has arrived, the social plane to which
their ambitions have risen. They learn to dress well only after they
have learned obedience to the laws of the world; after the coming
of easy success, their perfection in dress will show that they are as
cold and corrupt as the world demands.

For Lucien, his own body is a form of "clothes" in its irresistible
yet fatal beauty. The striking effect of his appearance seems to
dress, to cover what lies beneath, concealing the truth, making
him seem more impressive than nature intended. His beauty is
one of the means whereby illusions are inspired both in himself
and others, until at last his body is lent as a masque to Vautrin, the
devil himself. Balzac discovers a kind of "conspiracy of hope" on
all sides to make Lucien vain and confident. Everyone serves the
purposes of "un jeune homme beau, plein d'avenir," for it is easier
to believe in the quality of a beautiful youth rather than a plain
one, easier in turn for the youth himself to be vain of his beauty,
which is genuine, than of other qualities, which are not. Like all
appearances, all clothes, beauty misleads, persuading to false
hopes. Lucien's beauty, in provoking illusion, is allied to his

avenir, the term used to remind us that Lucien and all who love him are mistaken by the mere appearance of things.

The clothing of his beauty having given him strong initial aid toward success, Lucien quickly sees that it is not enough, that he must find the means to decorate his handsome façade to its full advantage. As he waits with M. de Bargeton before his poems are to be read, he begins to doubt the propriety of his costume, despite the loving aid of his family. And on his arrival with Louise in Paris, she is the first to compare him with the dandified Châtelet, to see that "il était beau, mais ridiculement mis." Having come so far on his appearance, he now begins to make the telling comparisons that show him the beauty and color of Paris against the gray dullness of Angoulême. Walking in the Tuileries he sees elegant young couples arm in arm. No one wears a coat like his, which now seems ugly. He sees that different costumes are worn for morning and evening, that he now looks ridiculous in outmoded styles, in a vest grotesquely provincial and a white cravat worn here by a grocer's boy with a basket on his head, a white cravat with the same kind of embroidery that was attached to his own by Ève. Later when he thinks of having to face an evening with Mme d'Espard in these clothes, he again breaks into a cold sweat, as by now we expect. With unconscious prophecy he says bitterly to himself the sentence that Mme d'Espard will deliver as she departs from her box at the Opera: "J'ai l'air du fils d'un apothicaire, d'un vrai courtaud de boutique." His natural gifts are lost in this crude outfit, the aristocratic arch of his foot obscured by provincial boots. He feels like a stranger as yet ignorant of his way.

EPITHETS FOR LUCIEN

As the *Comédie* is bound together by recurring terms and epithets, so are characters developed in such a way that, as Peter Lock says, "certain . . . images, motifs, and recurring linguistic patterns are invariably connected with specific types of characters." Balzac orders Lucien's career also by the skillful use of various words and phrases that act as synonyms for his name and convey some trait of character that is uppermost when the term is used. Such related words attract Balzac sometimes for their sound or, as with the derivatives from ancient myth, for their associations: witness the use of *herculéenne*, *Jupitérienne*, *icarienne*, and for Vautrin *cyclopéenne*. With Lucien, the epithet varies with the action, and Balzac handles the synonyms throughout in such a way that Lucien's career may be summarized by a selection that would form a guiding line. Like the various attempts to change Lucien's own name, the line of epithets is used not only to trace the variations in the story itself, but to play on our judgments and sympathies, Balzac seeming to guide our thoughts and responses while also summarizing them. This recalls another device of Balzac to arouse curiosity about a character or to develop a certain attitude toward him before we know who he is: the device of postponing as long as possible an individual's name. Balzac's epithets and appositives for a given character are ingeniously varied, and their cumulative effect is to bring out the idea that informs the individual, all of Balzac's main characters having been, as M. Fernandez says, ideas "before being living individuals." Terms other than a person's name, qualities of his character, an activity of his, his father's occupation, an aspect of his psychic nature: these are made to stand in place of his name until the name itself comes to be a summary of these qualities. Balzac may use an appositive also to bring out tones of his social meaning, as M. Mayer shows in his useful study of Balzac's language: " 'Louise alla jusqu'à permettre au fils de l'apothicaire' " he quotes, to bestow a kiss from his burning lips upon her brow. In place of calling Lucien by his name, Balzac "choisit en lui la qualité qui donne tout son prix au baiser accordé par la grande dame." When Lucien inspires our pity, he is *le pauvre garçon*, *le pauvre inconnu*, *le pauvre enfant*, or *l'innocent*, sometimes *le néophyte*, and rarely *l'écolier*. Other single words are established to imply the same thing whenever used, and Lucien as *l'ambitieux* is always a man of *avenir*, and as *journaliste* he is always a man corrupted by the lure of quick success. More telling and pervasive is the phrase *le grand homme de province* becoming the title for Part II of *Illusions* and the means whereby Balzac rings a series of magnificently ironic changes throughout. The irony is carefully prepared by showing how mean, narrow, and crude was French provincial life so that *un grand homme de province* cannot in fact be great anywhere else and must be shown as the victim of an absurdly ironic illusion. Lucien as a great man from Angoulême, then, is great only if he remains there, is great only in the eyes of people who simply do not know any better. His *Bildung* would have completed itself, had he at last known that this was so.

More frequent than any other synonym for Lucien, however, is the title of *poète*. Balzac seems to rely on this word to explain all that was responsible for Lucien's failure—his deluded vanity, selfishness, futility, and incompetence to make his way in a hostile world. At least in describing the career of Lucien, Balzac does not see the poet in Victor Hugo's terms as prophet, protector, seer, civilizer of mankind. Mr. Lukacs sees Balzac creating a new bourgeois kind of poet, "a rootless, aimlessly drifting, oversensitive bundle of nerves," and d'Arthez himself, the ideal poet, in writing to Ève, sees Lucien as "un homme de poésie et non un poète," meaning that he will dream and maneuver rather than overcome his problems by hard work. M. Mayer also cites Petit-Claud's opinion of Lucien's chimera, that he was not a poet but "un roman continuel." The *poète* as seen in Lucien's behavior is a kind of ludicrous irrelevance, a laughingstock to the world, with whose work no sensible man would have any dealings. When his poems are mentioned to Porchon, the publisher angrily demands of Lucien, "Et pour qui me prenez-vous?" Lousteau's cool revelation that the quality of Lucien's poems is irrelevant has later echoes in the *Comédie* when the career of Lousteau himself ends in failure. Lazy, weak, and a coward, Lousteau fails to sustain the devotion of Dinah de la Baudraye, who explains his behavior by simply observing that he was a poet. The term continues throughout Balzac's portrait of Lucien, often the only synonym employed when Lucien is about to commit some irretrievable blunder. The weaknesses that lead to his failure and at last cost him our sympathy are given no other explanation. When his friends of the Cénacle remark on Lucien's vanity, d'Arthez replies, "il est poète." In Lucien too is an element of Peter the Apostle, the kind of man who professes a set of principles but renounces them in action when danger or the need for sacrifice arises. At the restaurant Flicoteaux, Lucien abandons d'Arthez to join the tempter Lousteau; d'Arthez gives him a look that falls "vivement dans le cœur du poète."

PARIS

Balzac's Paris, in its cruelty and materialism, draws upon the myth of the city, the possibilities of corruption found in any mass of human beings from the Bible through Juvenal's Rome and Johnson's London. The historian Carl Schorske sees the city as a concentration of vice and iniquity now replacing the eighteenth-century "enlightened" view of the city as a union of talent, energy, wealth, and civilization. In *La Poésie de Paris*, M. Citron distinguishes some seventy-five images employed to define the qualities of Paris as Balzac himself sees them. In addition, the *Comédie* uses over fifty images already at hand in the poetical counter of the day, standard clichés for Paris, its atmosphere and appearance. Paris is likened to a world in itself, to an abyss, to a sea dangerous for a novice who lacks *le pied marin*, to a teeming hive, to a woman waiting to be conquered, to an insatiable monster luring all to itself, devouring the rest of France, draining off its talent and money, leaving only a helpless jealousy behind. More often, especially from *Le Père Goriot* through the Rubempré cycle, Paris is like a field of battle, and finally like hell itself, a dark inferno in which he who enters must abandon all hope indeed. The circles of this hell take their damned from the various social categories, for again the physical and moral qualities of Paris are inseparable, and the infernal poetry of Balzac's mythical city dominates his created universe.

To this hellish field of battle the young ambitious come, most often for the first time, to be splashed in the sordid reality of Parisian mud, to learn that "tout cela se fait à Paris; on méprise un homme, on n'en méprise pas l'argent," to know at last that, even if conquered, Paris will somehow ruin the victor's joy. Mr. Affron points out that Balzac's only experiments in social reform are placed in far-off mountain villages. There are no utopian schemes in Paris, save perhaps in the unobtrusive altruism of *L'Envers de l'histoire contemporaine*. So Paris ruins the hopes of the ambitious young, as its fearful rhythm has destroyed Père Goriot, who, at last, dies of Paris. Lucien too will die of Paris, but as he comes to the city with Louise, it appears a promised land where alone the artist and thinker has access to the resources that will free and nourish his imaginative talent by comparison and instruction. But after seeing Louise herself with new eyes, Lucien must give up the illusion of Paris as a haven for gifted youth. Not by accident does Balzac fill the last temptation by Louise with glowing talk of Paris; so also Lucien's last thoughts that make possible his betrayal of Ève and David are all of Paris. He is about to sell his soul, not for the fulfillment of cherished dreams from the past, but for the painful realities about to unfold in *Un Grand homme de province à Paris*. The last words of Part I, in carrying us to the title of Part II and its ensuing ironies, form an ideal transition. Lucien has gone, and poor David turns back sadly, for in his heart were terrible misgivings about "les destinées de Lucien à Paris." Use of *destinées* here, or any one of its synonyms already familiar to us from Part I, shows that everything to come will expose the hollow illusion of great expectations, that Lucien's journey to Paris is a passage to defeat and failure, and that Paris, which at once contains and destroys all illusions, will compel in its pitiless realism, this new victim to see the world as it is.

"L'Abîme"

Paris readily likens itself to an abyss, a pit of hell, a yawning expanse that separates, entices, or finally engulfs the unwary. The words *abîme* and the related *gouffre* soon establish for themselves a wide range of meanings of danger and mystery. Men suffer in the "abîme de travail," "abîme de chagrins," "abîmes de misères" or are lost "dans un abîme de pensées amères." Men constantly walk on a path skirting the edges of an abyss; or their aims are made futile by an abyss of impossible separation; or, more powerfully still, as in *Le Père Goriot*, *Béatrix*, and elsewhere, an *abîme* is a condition of moral ruin into which they are about to place one foot only to draw back just in time like Rastignac, or to go on with fearful consequences, like Lucien himself. Balzac so places the word in the *Comédie* as to increase our sense of the narrow margins of a life ever more precarious, with human beings moving on or toward the edge of nameless disasters, to which a single false, unwary step must lead. The word also cries out that human desires are unattainable, separated from fulfillment as they are by an abyss never to be fathomed or transgressed. Such a term develops great tension and energy, inviting us to imagine a meeting with Thomas Mann's Joseph, from the calm beauty of that opening line, "Tief ist der Brunnen der Vergangenheit," to the stony pit into which the vanity of Joseph has thrown him, only to emerge exhausted and befouled, but with a smile soon to play ever so faintly about his lips.

"LE SOURIRE"

Balzac will emerge a master of the single word for myriad purposes, and of no one term does he ask to convey human sentiment more than of *sourire* in its versatile forms of noun, verb, and adjective. Balzac's dualism compels use of the opposite, *larmes*, and we often meet "deux grosses larmes," expressive of bitterness, anger, or silent grief. Although Balzac's range of meaning here is far less than for *sourire*, he shows Rastignac, for example, weeping only so often, each time in sympathetic grief on seeing a new evidence of corruption in others. The last tear of his youth recalls the mourning of Charles Grandet—so touching to Eugénie, but here, too, a last sign of decent human feeling from his youth.

We soon are aware that Lucien weeps a great deal, that tears seem to lie always just beneath the surface, from the first emotion on reading poetry with David to the tears of his suffering love for Louise, tears of his fear and loneliness in Paris, on many occasions of shame, gratitude, or relief, and more often a child's selfish tears of wounded pride or frustrated desire. We may now and then recall M. Wurmser's exclamation, "Que d'eau, que d'eau!"

But in its nature a *sourire* is far more adaptable; as Mr. Levin reminds us, a French smile "is a sub-laugh." Balzac seizes upon it immediately to convey inner conditions, going finally to a narrator's means of commenting on the action through a given character's response to it. A smile seems to play almost constantly over the surface of *Les Chouans*, with Marie herself smiling at every turn, no matter what the emotion inspired by events. The smile of grace, of concealment, of triumph, of calculation, of endurance, malice, or pity is ever at her lips, until her smile as the decisive maneuver in love "ressemblait à un baiser" and confirms the hope of Montauran. So often the smile is one that cannot be avoided; that a person "ne put s'empêcher de sourire" or the like becomes a recurring formula. A given smile may pass from one to another and be shared by a whole company as in *Sarrasine*, but rarely are we to suppose that a smile is one of simple pleasure or joy, made just for the fun of it. Gaudissart is one of the few who smiles out of enjoyment, befitting one at ease in a harmonious world. Balzac, then, does not waste a maneuver so full of subtle possibilities as a smile on anything so obvious as mere joy. The Duchesse de Langeais conducts the whole of her intrigue with Montriveau by management of the "sourire nuancé," and she looks about of an evening with an air natural to a woman "qui connait toute la valeur de ses sourires." The career of Lousteau ends in *La Muse du département*, as he drifts about the streets, "un faux sourire sur les lèvres," to conceal his failure.

Early in Lucien's ascent to Louise's favor, he becomes aware of the all-purpose smile of her husband, M. de Bargeton—his only language. The man smiles whether happy or unhappy and on every occasion. The smile is adjusted, modified, or increased, greeting a new arrival or speeding the adieux of one departing, so that a word is employed only as a final extreme. The omnibus smile thus becomes a substitute for speech of any kind, a smile of concealment to hide stupidity, and of transition to the next remark or question, to which, in turn, M. de Bargeton will have no answer but this identical smile. But Lucien himself is an early victim, not of the harmless and vacant smile, but of the world's mockery and cruelty. En route to Paris, Lucien fails to take proper notice of "certains sourires" from Louise during the voyage. Balzac says nothing of the nature of these smiles, but as M. Mayer writes, "nous les devinons moqueurs, dédaigneux, sarcastiques." In Paris, Châtelet and Louise herself, who will betray him "par un sourire," smile at his crudities. Attendants at the Opera exchange "un imperceptible sourire" as Lucien appears, and elegant women on seeing him bestow "sourires féminins" on the young neophyte, as if the adjective *féminin* meant only *malicious*. And the cruel disdain of de Marsay as he examines Louise and Lucien with his lorgnon and a smile makes unmistakable the irony of Part II and its title. "Ce sourire fut un coup de poignard pour le grand homme de province," now less than ever a great man of any kind.

"L'AVENIR"

Lucien as *poète* has clung to certain weaknesses of spirit, including an obstinate unwillingness or inability to see things as they are. At the end of a humiliating interview with the publisher Doguereau, Lucien hears simply, "Vous avez une tête de poète." Another function of his poetic nature prevents his seeing the difference between his own prospects and those of the young "viveurs" who pretend to be his friends. Blondet's easy axioms should warn rather than encourage Lucien, when he hears that "un homme d'esprit qui a pied dans le monde fait fortune quand il veut." The right *pied* for assured advance into the future is missing, so that we see with Balzac how illusory must be Lucien's *avenir*.

M. Poulet remarks that a Balzacian being starts with a rush into the infinity of the future, and his young men look with boldness and confidence into the future. But *avenir* soon becomes a synonym of "illusion," quite unlike the outlook of Mann's Joseph at the start of his Egyptian career when the future is benevolent and means hope, with time a gift enabling men to live in expectation. Is reality in Balzac always a thing of the present, told in the present tense, and illusion always an event still to come, predicted only in the future tense? Certainly when Lucien himself speaks in the present, he sees the truth, but let him adopt the future tense, and all is colored, disguised. His letter to Ève soon after arrival in Paris, describes the dreadful present against a glowing future, with Balzac balancing three adjectives precisely to the syllable: "Si le présent est froid, nu, mesquin, l'avenir est bleu, riche, et splendide." Like other great writers of the past, he will overcome his trials, and "je serai riche." We are soon made aware of the many synonyms that illustrate, in *Illusions*, Montriveau's bitter remark to la Duchesse de Langeais that "l'espérance est un mensonge appuyé sur l'avenir." Balzac achieves a powerful cumulative effect in establishing the same meaning for a set of terms interchangeable with *avenir:* whenever we hear of *rêves, espoirs, espérances, ambitions, promesses, chimères, croyances, mirages,* or *illusions,* of *gloire* or *une destinée à accomplir,* we know that these are only Bacon's "imaginations as one would," that they look to a future never to be fulfilled across a huge distance of space and time never to be joined. A sad pathos attaches itself then to the phrases and expressions endlessly repeated in the text, as we see no hope for "ces rêves d'or," "les espérances lointaines," or any of "les belles illusions de la jeunesse." Our hearts sink to hear Lucien being told, "vous avez de l'avenir," or to see his own references to himself as a man with a future, who is entitled thereby to accept the sacrifices of others. Yet how little these are justified by Lucien's true possibilities we see in the contrast between Ève's use of *avenir* and Lucien's foolish belief in the tempter Louise, when she assures

him that "les gens d'avenir ne sont pas compris par leurs familles."
Hearing David's proposal at last, Ève replies with moving simplicity that she had never dared to hope for so high a destiny as
the love of this great human being, she "pauvre ouvrière sans
avenir." Her use of the two words *destinée* and *avenir* shows her
nature precisely as Lucien's use of them will betray his own. Three
essential contrasts between them emerge. Ève confesses her poverty, but Lucien is ashamed of his own as of so much else and is
bent on escaping it. Then, too, Ève works and is willing to work,
whereas David has already seen that Lucien wishes to reap the
harvest without the work, for he is ashamed, likewise, of the need
for that work. Finally Ève has no future, that is, no illusions concerning herself, no false estimate of worth to which she would sacrifice one who loves her. But Lucien, in naming himself among the
gens d'avenir, shows once and for all that his coming eminence is an
illusion. It is not only false, it is evil, like accepting the family's
sacrifice and then despising a goodness too simple for the "understanding" of greatness. Lucien thus places himself in the company
of the fatally vain and selfish, partaking—to his certain detriment—of the unfeeling baseness of their obsessions.

TEMPTATION

The quality of the young protagonist on his way to the summit or
to defeat shows in his response to the temptation that is certain to
present itself at some point of his mythical journey. Balzac is careful to reveal enough of Lucien's inner nature so that we can predict
the issue of each struggle between good and evil in his soul. Lucien
is offered many cruel choices, but the most extended and dramatic
of the actual temptation scenes are those in Louise's house at
Angoulême, in the company of Lousteau in Paris, when Lucien
declares for journalism, and finally beside the river Charente,
when Vautrin himself prevents Lucien's suicide and offers him, in
so many words, a Satanic pact. The *Bildungsroman* hero tradition-
ally meets both the guide and the tempter, and he is supposed to

trust the guide and reject the tempter except when, as in Rastignac's case, they both tell him the same thing. But Lucien rejects the guidance of his family and d'Arthez and trusts himself to Louise, to journalism and Lousteau, and finally to Vautrin. His passion for going to confession and repenting supports an almost medieval reading of his temptations and their success. Temptation, then, lies at the heart of human experience, and the "world" meaning here and now, as well as a moral term, offers the lusts or the flesh and the eyes, and the pride of life, as tempting allurements to sin. Balzac's *le monde* is also both a place and a moral term, the goal toward which temptation leads. If Eugène and Lucien give way, they will win *le monde*, and the temptations of its offerings only correspond to, and are anticipated by, desires already within themselves.

Balzac relies strongly, therefore, on the biblical or traditional religious associations of the devil, hell, sin, confession, repentance, angelic influence, salvation, or doom. Along with re-creating the Old Testament loss of Paradise through Satan's tempting of Eve, Balzac raises at least two of the great New Testament questions: What must I do to gain the world? and, by implication, its opposite: What must I do to save my soul? Beginning with Louise in the role of Satan the tempter, the first of these questions torments Lucien, for Louise's proposal seems only a first move toward Vautrin's advances, offering the same reward for the same price.

This second appearance of Vautrin as the devil invites comparison between his defeat in *Le Père Goriot* at the hands of Eugène de Rastignac, and his now quick success with Lucien. Agreements with the devil were a commonly used theme, with which Balzac did some experimenting, as in *La Peau de chagrin* and *Melmoth réconcilié*. . . . A version of the Faustian legend governs *La Recherche de l'absolu* (1834), wherein Balthazar is led into a mad search for the philosopher's stone—simply another gifted man trying to transcend the limits of the human condition. This and the Melmoth theme of Maturin, which invites a man to change places with another to escape unbearable misery, seems to be set aside with *Le Père Goriot* to expose evil in the universe. To be sure, Eugène and Lucien desire to change their condition into something better, but their temptations are only in terms of rising in the world here and now, terms wholly earthly and human. Events take place, then, within the understandable qualities of human character, and the Satanic figure, while clothed in biblical language, employs no supernatural means. Balzac's young men stay within life here and now; his devil is still the Prince of this world only.

While remarking that Vautrin seems to fail against Eugène, we should recall the different circumstances in which he finds Eugène and Lucien in turn. The garden and the boardinghouse table give Vautrin several chances over a long period of time to explain the world as it is, his temptation of Eugène being a series of lessons in the nature of reality. He first attacks a life of goodness, showing that virtue does not pay. The devil cites figures to show how ruinous for Eugène a life of continued study of the law would be, and then by contrast what the possible returns might be if he should yield, how little, in fact, he must give to possess the world. For Lucien, on the other hand, such doctrines are needless beside the river and in the fatal carriage. He has already discarded virtue, and despite his failure, is still certain that success is only at Satan's disposal. Vautrin's arguments to Eugène are also supported in at least two ways: by the similar views of a virtuous woman, Mme de Beauséant, and by experience of the world, forcing Eugène to repeat to himself, "Vautrin is right." Although he first rejects with horror Vautrin's enticements, his resistance fails gradually, each rejection of the devil being less impassioned, until, just before Vautrin's betrayal and arrest, Eugène is seen intimately beside poor little Victorine, performing with odious hypocrisy his part in a crime that will insure his fortune.

It is therefore not quite true that Eugène resists a temptation to which the weakling Lucien easily succumbs. Eugène shows the success of Vautrin by the life he leads, guided by cynical exploitation of others for his own benefit. He had, in fact, decided to accept Vautrin's offer and was making advances to Victorine, knowing toward what end, finally going so far that only a miracle could save him. Eugène escapes the penalty of his crime, not in having the strength to resist temptation but by a miraculous intervention totally unforeseen. He is saved by the benevolence this time, not the malice, of fortune, which has its way with Lucien. His end shows that, for Balzac, chance must not be allowed to obstruct the fatal aims of human passion, but that sooner or later Lucien must encounter on his way the individual or the circumstances that will encourage his fatal illusions. Eugène seems destined to obtain all that he seeks, while Lucien is doomed as he proceeds, after Vautrin's offer, in a trance-like state to do the devil's bidding. He has no Satanic agility of his own to avoid the blows of fate or the enticements of the easy way.

DUALISM

Balzac's double vision displays men and institutions with two sides, like a coin. His recent biographer André Maurois sees a pervasive dualism in Balzac's life and character: he lives always on two planes, actual and imagined; he is by nature "un farceur et un poète," he views the world as material and spiritual, is at once monarchist and revolutionary. M. Bernard Guyon notes the frequency of Balzac's "dédoublement autobiographique," joining two characters who are aspects of himself, like David and Lucien, Rastignac and Bianchon, or again Lucien and d'Arthez. The *Comédie* itself is largely divided between Paris and the provinces, while its particular areas fall into pairs, clashing or harmonious. Families often are in twos, or in units of one, which combine to make two, as there are two Grandet brothers with one child each to create the meeting of Eugénie and Charles. Père Goriot has two daughters, and M. Taillefer two children, a son and a daughter—Victorine. Agathe Bridau has two sons, Mme Charlotte de Rubempré Chardon a son and a daughter, and there are four de Granville children, two sons and two daughters.

At times Balzac seems to persist in such arrangements from force of habit serving no essential use, but when he is most successful in creating his physical environment or showing life as a field of battle with opposing forces, his dualism is one source of his greatest power. He likes to create two factions or two groups contending for a certain prize, as in *Le Contrat de mariage*, where the lawyers Mathias and Solinet battle for control of Paul de Manerville's fortune or in *Eugénie Grandet* and *Pierrette*, for example, where the des Grassins oppose the Cruchots, and the parties of Vinet and Tiphaine maneuver for position respectively. *Le Contrat de mariage* even concludes with two exchanges of two letters each. And as the laws of nature have a double effect, in the moral order goodness simply invites the operation of evil, as stupidity invites knavery: "la sottise attire toujours un homme d'esprit de l'espèce des renards." The constant division into two camps seems at once both the cause and the effect of the military language that appears everywhere in the *Comédie*. If there is a single controlling image in Balzac, it is one of life as a battle, expressed in military terms. Lucien is warned of the horrible combat before him, "une guerre à toutes armes" between "les gloires naissantes et les gloires déchues." Balzac's own mode of narration in turn seems like an exercise in military tactics. After preparation, long and slow, the action suddenly accelerates into speedy, densely packed pages rushing to climactic moments, as in war, wherein attack is prepared over long periods, when vast stores of material and men are suddenly released in a discharge of overwhelming violence. But, as Mr. Affron shows, the military dualism is uneven. In order to have victory there must be defeat and vice versa, but the *Comédie* gives a much greater impression of defeat and failure than of victory or success. The battle figure presents a dualism of conflict, which ought to divide success and failure into equal parts, but this is not the impression derived from the *Comédie*—the military dualism is not consistent, since more seem to fail than succeed.

A scarcely less obvious product of Balzac's dualism lies everywhere in the physical settings of his creation. Even where it seems obvious machinery, in the opening scenes of *Sarrasine*, for example, it is striking and effective. This tale opens at a ball, the narrator seeing a dual image in the animated dance of the living within and the snow-covered garden without, a "danse des morts" against "la danse des vivants." Life and death appear again beside each other when a young woman of stunning beauty and grace is seen beside an old man whose hideous emaciation and bony form suggest the coming of death. *Le Père Goriot* moves back and forth between two worlds whose physical properties betray their moral and human meaning, from the stinking boardinghouse with its contrasts of extreme old age and youth, to the grace and style of the Hôtel de Beauséant, its owner desolate amid hypocritical friendship and betrayed love. As in other novels of provincial life, Balzac divides Part I of *Illusions* into high and low, old and new, noble and bourgeois. Angoulême is so presented as to define sharply the enormous physical, moral, social, and economic differences that separate the obstinate nobility on their high rock from the vigorous industrial life below. Everything about the old town to which Lucien aspires is built to deny access, once physically, now socially. Placed on a high rock protected by ramparts, it has the remains of a fortress on the summit, and a steep, rapid slope downward. Here the noble or old bourgeois families live in jealous isolation. Strangers are never received: "Moqueuses, dénigrantes, jalouses, avares, ces maisons se marient entre elles, se forment en bataillon serré pour ne laisser ni sortir ni entrer personne." Balzac cannot avoid his customary military language here in presenting one side of a war. It is a long way up for Lucien, as he makes his way on foot over the distance that separates David and Ève, from the elegant salon of Louise de Bargeton. The barriers are more than physical, set up by people who themselves would never send a youth to Paris, for whom the reception of a pharmacist's son from l'Houmeau is a sign of revolution itself.

Power resides on high, then, but wealth, energy, and the future are in the world below, where Lucien's fortune might better have been gained. The high rock from the past remains as always, but the river below moves on, not only picturesque but useful for communication. L'Houmeau is situated beside the river, the source of industrial energy, and along the "grande route de Paris à Bordeaux," the means of receiving raw materials and delivering finished products. This is the world of money and energy, but Lucien's illusion seeks his *avenir* in the actual past, deceived by appearances that will not endure. After Lucien departs for his great opportunity to read his poems, Ève suggests to the bashful David an evening walk by the river Charente. Balzac's title for the next section presents the contrasting of two worlds between which Lucien must choose: "La Soirée dans un salon: La Soirée au bord de l'eau."

Balzac is merciless as he compels Lucien to choose, a youth who is himself in constant dualism, even to possessing two names, who seems so evenly balanced between good and evil that he might turn with equal facility from one to the other. But the glory that he seeks will yield only to the twin forces of talent and will. Balzac's elite are more proud of a strong will than of great talent, for "le vouloir," he remarks concerning the drifting Lousteau in *La Muse du département*, "est une conquête faite à tout moment sur les instincts . . . sur les difficultés de tout genre héroïquement surmontées." Lucien has talent, as we hear on all sides, but his dreams of glory are futile when he betrays a failure in will. And so another characteristic division into two controls the very center of *Illusions*—this scene of battle ending in victory or defeat. By his universal dualism, Balzac achieves a powerful simplicity and dramatic clearness leading to his typical "exaggeration," while developing throughout the range of his imagined universe the gigantic metaphors that carry his bitter reading of human affairs.

3

Lineage

The new century of individualism, ambition, liberty, and energy released a generation of men who inspired a series of works that remain among the masterpieces of French literature. A typical protagonist emerges: from one end of France to the other he comes in great numbers to throw himself upon Paris, guided by Napoleon's memory or example. He is about twenty-one years of age, handsome, vain, serious, ardent, and sensitive, conscious of some inner force demanding an outlet, often of aristocratic birth but poor in money, the darling and only hope of an adoring family, coming in search of power, fortune, glory. His possibilities are limited, if he is like Oscar Husson of *Un Début dans la vie*, to a career in commerce, administration, the professions or military service. For the first time in his life he will make the comparisons between the life he has known at home and the Parisian scene, that inferno and field of battle. The lessons he will learn amid his "éducation parisienne" will call forth many a tear, and many a smile of bitterness or cynical realism, when, like the youth in Musset's *Confessions d'un enfant du siècle*, he sees everywhere the violation of professed ideals. A cold sweat will be his response as he contemplates the abyss that lies ready to engulf him, and more than once he will think of suicide.

Suicide will come to his mind especially after he gambles and loses, for like all men bent on quick success, he must take dis-

astrous chances. Gambling is an appeal to fate to accomplish at
once the wealth that the hero is either unable or too impatient to
acquire through work and slow merit. Gambling promises the goal
without the effort, and is in turn a diabolic pact, playing ruin
against the wild chance of sudden fortune, wherein the alternatives are dramatic, entire opposites: complete failure or great
riches. Yet the ruin may be final and the riches only temporary,
the hero learning that wealth so obtained will show itself as passing, like the capricious chance to which it owes everything. These
experiences lead finally to disillusion, already shown as inseparable from provincial life in the magnificent *Eugénie Grandet*, and
many times over in the careers of the young who leave home and
family for the world. If at last the avid youth "arrives," he may
well suffer like the inhabitants of Balzac's third circle of hell in *La
Fille aux yeux d'or*, "qui, s'ils arrivent à leur but, y arrivent tués."
So powerful is the fiction of this young man's adventures, that
M. Carrère denounces Balzac for having created the "innumer-
able and mischievous type" in French life of "the *parvenu*, the
careerist." Stendhal is similarly guilty in presenting heroes who
are "unscrupulous egoists," who are pernicious like Julien Sorel in
being wicked yet attractive. If we confine ourselves to the post-
Napoleonic French novel, we may begin with *Le Rouge et Le Noir*,
the first masterpiece of the "éducation" genre. In Balzac himself,
we shall not take up examples from his own early years before *Les
Chouans*, although such a work as *Argow le Pirate* (1824) presents a
youth bent on the conquest of society. The more remote anteced-
ents in France of the ambitious provincial youth may be studied
in Mme Suzanne Jean Bérard's admirable work *La Genèse d'un
roman de Balzac: Illusions perdues, 1837*. It is also of interest to take
note, in passing, of some features of a work appearing a century
before *Illusions perdues* in 1735—Marivaux' somewhat picaresque
story *Le Paysan parvenu*. The hero, Jacob, tells his own story, of a
poor provincial youth, low in social origin but handsome and intelligent, attractive to women who help him on his way as he

comes to Paris. A bright future is predicted for Jacob; he is greatly
pleased and excited by his new clothes, his vanity increases, and he
suffers a severe temptation to do something dishonorable, rejecting
the love of a simple, devoted girl as will Raphaël de Valentin first,
Benassis and Rastignac later. He savors the delight of riding in
carriages instead of walking, as his life improves, and before the
story ends, he is embarrassed, like Lucien, by his manners and
appearance amid the assured and fashionable young of Paris. An
evident mythical framework has clearly established itself, and our
further examples will show that Balzac has little need to invent a
fiction in detail when he arrives at the crossroads of the *Comédie
humaine*. Mr. Albert George has also shown that Balzac used his
shorter pieces to develop his characteristic fictional mode and
moral opinion. Apart from his own trial efforts before *Illusions*,
Balzac had Stendhal's great creation of Julien Sorel. Julien is not
only the first, but the greatest of his kind, as he shows the way
toward Rastignac and Lucien de Rubempré. For him the romantic sufferings of hopeless love, leading to Wertherism and despair,
give way to ambition; love is here a means toward conquest and
power; passive melancholy is lost amid the drive of individual
energy, and Julien's favorite reading is Napoleon's *Mémorial de
Sainte-Hélène*.

Julien Sorel

Although Julien will command our attention mainly as a pre-
cursor of Rastignac and Lucien, with whom he is often compared,
we shall find him in outline greater, even better than his Balzacian
followers. Our first glimpse of Julien shows him reading, but soon
weeping at the loss of his book, the *Mémorial* of Napoleon, which
fell into a stream after Julien suffered a blow on the head from his
brutal and loutish father. His appearance now at the age of about
nineteen is delicate and almost feminine. His glowing black eyes,
dark chestnut hair, slender figure, and pale countenance conceal
a fearful energy of will. He is determined to *faire fortune* at any cost,
to escape from his home in Verrières, to leave behind his father

and two brothers, whom he detests, and who in turn despise him for the seeming weakness of his nature. Julien early adopts a pose of sly hypocrisy in dealing with a hostile world, while thinking constantly of Napoleon and speaking to himself in military terms. We should note at the outset Julien's ability to lead a double life: one in the company of others when he conforms to the demands of a society he wishes to succeed in, the other concealed at all times save when he is alone and utters the Iago-like soliloquies analyzing himself and the world he bitterly resents yet wishes to command. We shall find Lucien incapable both of Julien's hatred and of his fearful cynicism or hypocrisy. Julien also develops, as Lucien does not. He goes from one experience to another and learns how to use his self-control for purposes of disguise and adaptation. This drama of inner experience, this awareness of developing change, as his life goes on, places Julien beyond the picaresque hero after a certain point. As Mr. Alter has shown, he undergoes the early picaresque rituals in learning "the ways of the world," but changes taking place within him become more important than his external adventures.

When Mme de Rênal first sees the children's tutor, she cannot believe that this exquisite youth, drying his tears as best he can, is a learned teacher of Latin. But a new outfit of clothes quickly changes Julien's manner, and the brilliance of his demonstration that he has committed to memory the entire New Testament in Latin earns universal respect. But Julien is early the center of intense hatred, although his little pupils love him dearly. He hates his father and brothers, who beat him savagely one day from their own envious hatred of him. He is hated by the jealous valet and by M. Valenod for his beauty and the favor of Mme de Rênal, while Julien, on his part, despises the new social milieu and its people. He is ignorant of the world, but Mme de Rênal notices, despite his silence and air of humility, that Julien is proud, even disdainful in seeing his enormous superiority to everyone around him. But he weeps again when, for the first time in his life, he realizes that someone loves him. Still he rejects the love of a simple girl, Eliza, relying on his hypocrisy to say that he has heard evil of Eliza's conduct, a protective lie. As his character develops, Julien becomes ever more ardent, irascible and contemptuous, and when he begins his campaign to seduce Mme de Rênal, he actively despises her, as he continues to resent her husband's treatment of him. Professor Friedrich observes that Julien begins by hating both of the principal women in his life. Meanwhile, on the way to visit his friend Fouqué, Julien dreams of his future life in Paris, where he will love and be loved by a beautiful and gifted woman. But Fouqué makes him a lucrative business offer, a kind of "temptation." Like Eliza's offer of marriage and attendant security, Fouqué's proposal does not tempt Julien to do something dishonorable to further his destiny, but only to turn aside from it, to be prudent rather than heroic, in Julien's own view. He has a plan for the seduction of Mme de Rênal which is to proceed by stages to its fulfillment, and he must continue until his plan succeeds. When at last Julien has prevailed, his usual self-analysis turns on satisfied ambition rather than love, on the joy of possessing this noble and beautiful woman when he is only a humble peasant. Yet he can still ask himself, "comment ai-je pu inspirer un tel amour, moi, si pauvre, si mal élevé, si ignorant, quelquefois si grossier dans mes façons?"

Julien becomes very much à la mode at dinners and soirées, unlike Lucien, who is humiliated in the salon of Louise de Bargeton. Julien's command of the Latin New Testament gives him an advantage as he performs what is in effect a vaudeville stunt, with huge success. But the time for departure to the Seminary comes, and Julien refuses money from both Mme de Rênal and her husband. It is hard to believe that Rastignac or Lucien would be similarly scrupulous. On entering the Seminary Julien is overcome by terror and depression. Surrounded once again by hatred and envy, he is miserable, disgusted and lonely amid his obvious superiority to the wretched peasants who attend the Seminary for

its food and clothing. He is nonetheless singled out for notice and
favor by the Director, the Abbé Pirard. Despite the jealousy and
calumny he must always suffer, Julien is befriended by men at
important stages of his career. The Abbé Chélan has passed him
on to Pirard, who in turn hands Julien up to the Marquis de la
Mole. In the Seminary he now makes a step upward to the post of
Biblical Tutor, and is moved again to tears, as he so often is before
any sign of love for him. He has made a step upward, solely on his
personal merits, a rare example indeed among his fictional peers.
In private he still calls himself a fool and a child, as he does openly
to the examiner who traps him into revealing his command of
Horace: Julien sees that he was indeed a fool, not because he knew
Horace so well, but because he had not seen the trap and avoided
it.

And so his knowledge of men and the world expands, aided by
the Jansenist Pirard, whose principle it is to find out whether
Julien has any talent by putting obstacles in his way and seeing
how he overcomes them. Rastignac and Lucien will try to overcome obstacles, but in less creditable ways than Julien's brilliance
and sober work. His performance stuns the Bishop, who gives him
an eight volume set of Tacitus, but Julien's tears continue to flow
when his friend Pirard faces dismissal through the obscene machi-
nations of the Grand-Vicaire, when it seems that Mme de Rênal
no longer loves him, and when, en route to Paris, he is moved at
the sight of Napoleon's Malmaison.

Julien comes now to the last scene in Paris, prepared, at various
stages, by *Bildungsmächte:* influences while he is still at home, including the Abbé Chélan; the house of Mme de Rênal and first
love; the Seminary and Pirard, leading to the Hôtel de la Mole
and the beauteous Mathilde. Transitional instruction comes to
Julien in a carriage bearing him to an immense doorway, as the
Abbé Pirard offers a long analysis of the dangers facing Julien in a
world that will despise him while offering the most exaggerated
compliments. He is deeply moved by this surrogate father, and

here we must note that Julien has an advantage over the pupils of Vautrin. Julien is often confronted by the devil, but in odious rather than tempting form. The Abbé Pirard warns him thus: "You and I are honorable men in a world of conniving scoundrels. Take care not to let yourself be tempted into corruption." Vautrin, however, counsels Rastignac and Lucien: "since the world is a scene of infernal maneuver controlled by knaves, there is no point in being anything else if you desire to succeed."

Although stunned by the magnificence of his new surroundings, Julien displays his excellent natural qualities. Through sensibility and ignorance he commits numerous blunders and often reaches the end of day at the point of tears, unlike the great Joseph, who begins a long rise from the inferior status of a foreigner sold into slavery, yet always makes the right move, seeming to have just the manner and procedure needed for success at any given moment. Julien holds his ground, the identity and occupation of his father always in the background as a reason for his humiliating position. Yet this does not change his convictions. Despite his former arriviste longing for Paris, he is not lost in admiration. When alone, Julien continues to analyze himself, calls himself dreadful names, praises or blames his conduct, forcing every experience to yield its lessons. His hypocrisy does not seem so hateful to him as in his Seminary days, when he was contaminated amid the society of three hundred wicked and filthy hypocrites. Now he does not lower his pride or lose personal dignity as Mathilde begins to invade his life, although it is the "paysan parvenu" who says, "moi, pauvre paysan, j'ai donc une déclaration d'amour d'une grande dame!" Twenty years before, he would have fought the world in red; now fighting in black, the son of a carpenter has beaten the world when the queenly Mathilde declares her love, choosing the lowborn peasant over the wealthy and curled darlings of the nation, indeed, for the proudest names in France contend openly for her hand. Julien's ambition then overcomes the young scruples of decency and honor in his soul, warning him

against a calculating seduction of Mathilde. But he, too, justifies
all with a doctrine worthy of Vautrin: "Chacun pour soi dans ce
désert d'égoïsme qu'on appelle la vie." Not for nothing has Julien
also memorized the role of Tartuffe, now returning to his mind as
the letter from Mathilde throws him into such a frenzy of exulta-
tion and triumph that Stendhal is distressed at having to record it.
The military language of challenge and defiant battle, like that of
Rastignac, is now unavoidable, and Julien cries, "Aux armes!" as
he has a copy of Mathilde's letter made, and again, on returning
to his room: "A nous! maintenant. . . ." It is more out of ambition
than out of love that Julien finds himself ascending to Mathilde's
room by a new ladder, past one o'clock in the morning. As befits
his quality of one low in the world bent on rising, Julien habitually
"climbs" to his great moments, unlike the noble Fabrice, who
achieves his freedom by descending.

Julien's misery, as Mathilde torments him by her seeming with-
drawal, grows beyond his endurance. He is alone with no one to
help or guide him; he is too unhappy, too ill equipped with knowledge of life as yet to understand so complicated a maneuver as
Mathilde is conducting. He fears that if someone were to ask about
his feelings, he could only respond by a flood of tears. In a similar
case, Lucien will long ago have bathed himself in tears, for his
weeping is a function of his weak inability to solve the problems of
life. The idea of suicide comes to Julien's mind, for now more than
ever seems it rich to die; death would be a delicious repose, a cool
glass of water to one dying of heat and thirst, as the desert image
recurs. But he sees that suicide would only cause Mathilde to
despise him the more, again unlike Lucien, who never considers
the effect of his suicide on others. Julien has no trouble refusing
the proposal made by his acquaintance Korasoff that he marry
one of his cousins, a rich heiress from Moscow. If this is another
form of "temptation" to turn aside from his vocation, it shows the
relative unimportance of temptation in Stendhal as compared
with Balzac. During his absurd intrigue with Mme de Fervaques,

Julien again thinks of suicide, of putting an end, with his pistols, to this "exécrable vie," but when love is restored to him, he can forget even the *avenir* of his dreams. His pride and courage enable him to face the Marquis' insulting fury when Mathilde is pregnant, and he suggests a form of suicide in letting himself be killed. His pride also accepts the change in his name. Unlike Lucien, he does not omit his father's name, merely accepting euphonious additions before and after. Then, too, why not change his name when the story of the man who bore it is over? "Mon roman est fini, et à moi seul tout le mérite."

When finally he tries to kill his first love, Julien accepts with calm assurance the ensuing penalty. The lines of his character are now formed, he knows himself and the world, alas, beyond the need of further instruction. Although the *sourire* prevails less in Julien's career than later on, he cannot help replying to a judge who seems bent on incriminating him, "en souriant, que je me fais aussi coupable que vous pouvez me désirer?" Julien's condition before his attempted murder resembles that of Lucien before his own suicide: a trance-like state of concentration on the deed to be done. It is, in effect, Julien's suicide as well, and after the deed he falls into a deep therapeutic sleep, showing the end of his abnormal condition and his recovery from it. Lucien, however, proceeds to his own death while in this condition, he who would never think of killing anyone else, only himself by his own hand. A short delay would have brought each of them to his full ambition, but they seem meant for death, since each brings it upon himself, unable to wait. After deciding against an outright suicide, Julien discusses the *avenir* so recently glowing with promise for him and his son to be. He rejects Mathilde's frantic efforts and urges her to be happy in the usual terms of the world, enjoying riches, high rank, and esteem; yet he is ashamed of his coldness and seeming ingratitude.

At his trial, everyone is struck by his continued youthful beauty. He seems hardly twenty even now, but is too proud to weep before his enemies. He declares himself a peasant in revolt against the lowness of his fortune; he has no illusions, death awaits and justly so. Yet the men before him would consider his ambitious audacity in rising from below them a crime equally to be punished with attempted murder. In prison again, he reflects on the pervasiveness of clerical hypocrisy and charlatanism, "avec le sourire amer du plus extrême mépris." During the series of painful interviews to which he is subjected, Julien is often moved to tears, but a growing sentiment at once of humility and of pride ascends in him, a disdain for the world, to continue in which he would neither raise his voice nor lift a finger. His magnificent self-analysis before death contrasts with Lucien's collapse into lachrymose self-pity. Lucien dies afflicted only for himself, not for love of anyone, whereas Julien suffers most from the absence of his first and only love. He must die, at last, consistent with his chosen role of ambitious youth. He cannot risk despising himself for some unworthy cowardice, and begs his friend Fouqué to bury him in the mountain grotto where once he dreamed alone, and where ambition had inflamed his soul. So the inherent bravery of his nature enables Julien to walk in manly peace to his doom.

The procession of young Balzacian heroes will often remind us of Julien. He resembled all of these and yet he was totally himself. Stendhal is less inventive of synonymous terms for Julien, who is variously the "jeune ambitieux," "jeune précepteur," "jeune paysan," "notre provincial," or "notre plébéien révolté." Most often he is simply "notre héros," a term never used by Balzac, who seldom has only one "hero" for our attention. But neither Stendhal nor Balzac ever calls Julien or Lucien by anything but his first name, as befitting those who will always be young, who die still in the boyhood of their first appearance. Rastignac is never exclusively "Eugène"; we may be sure that his boyhood has died with his old friend Goriot, and that Balzac will never again call him simply by his first name.

Although Julien grows up amid hatred, unlike Lucien and

Rastignac who are swathed in love at home, like them he inspires great love and sacrifice in women; Mme de Rênal gives up her honor in his cause and cannot live in the world without him. Mathilde even more dramatically sacrifices the pride and dignity of her family on the very summit of French high society. For good or ill, women's sacrifices will mark the journeys of Raphaël, Benassis, Rastignac, Victurnien, and many times over, Lucien himself. Most of these youths will not be greatly troubled by this thought, certainly less than Julien, who is more realistic, relentlessly self-analytical, taught largely by himself from work and experience. He watches his own behavior, and the terms of his self-condemnation recur as he considers how foolish, young, awkward, or ridiculous he must have seemed. He asks different questions of himself and of his advisers than do Balzac's men, who ask about money, power, and success. Julien requires self-respect and the esteem of others, wishing to know what he must do to be loved, and how to avoid selfish, cowardly, or venal actions.

Although Julien, too, sees that Napoleonic qualities are now required for the leadership of young France, he turns away from the future and his own success already gained. Lucien goes back to Angoulême only because he is defeated in Paris, whereas Julien seeks again a greater happiness in the past. He gives up willingly what Lucien was never able to achieve, because it seems inferior to a former happiness and so is no longer worth the price demanded of him to sustain it. He is most conscious of his low origin and menial state, whereas Lucien longs to be only an extension of what he already is, a half-aristocrat belonging to a world that now requires only money and influence to grant him the fondest dreams of his *avenir*. Julien is different in kind from the world in which he would make his fortune, beginning as a lowly peasant, while Rastignac comes of the minor nobility and Lucien is the well-educated son of gifted parents. Balzac's young men seem natural in the world as it is; they belong where Balzac finds them. They often seem more simply human than Julien, perhaps because more

weak. Julien is too remarkable as a single person to remain a type.
Though one of a certain kind, he is too much a man apart. He is
right: the world he has learned to know so well is no place for such
a one as he. He is too good for the scene that Rastignac succeeds
in, and so, like Socrates, Julien shows his superiority to the world
by letting it destroy him. While the great work that contains him
might also have been called "Illusions perdues," Julien is greater
and better than his Balzacian followers. None of them would have
made Julien's choice, because none is above or deserves better
than the worldly success for which he longs. Perhaps this is why
the name of Julien Sorel is never mentioned by the creator of
Rastignac.

RAPHAËL DE VALENTIN

Balzac was proud of his device of recurring characters, who move
in and out of the *Comédie*, now major, now minor figures. Such
appearances are repeated, however, not only in name but in kind.
Thus individuals appear over again as particular persons with
their special names and identities, and in the form of types and
situations. Rastignac himself appears by name more than twenty
times in the *Comédie*, but aspects of his character are repeated in
other young Balzacian heroes. On the other hand, Charles Grandet does not reappear prominently by name, but we see him as
present in the character of Lucien. Charles also strove for a
change in his name at the price of marrying a highborn, unloved
girl, and was similarly groomed for an ambassadorship. Charles
has sold out to the devil only in another form.

Now Raphaël de Valentin recurs doubly, as himself, and as an
aspect of Lucien, who repeats some of his qualities and experiences. In *La Peau de chagrin* (1831) Balzac employs the narrative
device of a story within the main fiction, as again in *Le Médecin de
campagne* and *L'Envers de l'histoire contemporaine*. In despair at his
losses, the young Raphaël leaves the gambling house, determined
to kill himself. The narrator is moved to say that "chaque suicide
est un poème sublime de mélancolie," as Raphaël contemplates

the Seine from the Pont Royal. Embittered at the indifferent world, he will kill himself at night, "afin de livrer un cadavre indéchiffrable à cette société qui méconnaissait la grandeur de sa vie." We learn by what experiences Raphaël had come to such despair in a chapter called "La Femme sans Cœur." Here the story of his preceding life is told to others, Balzac quickly establishing a number of his mythical terms. Raphaël began as a law student like Rastignac and was kept under rigid paternal discipline. From seventeen to twenty he was poor and bereft of the pleasures natural to his youth. He dreams of enjoying fine clothes, the inevitable *voiture*, and a beautiful young woman. At a ball he is so ashamed of his worn suit, bad shoes, cravat, and gloves that he stands alone in a corner. His first attempt at gambling brings out beads of sweat on his brow. Soon his father is ruined financially by the Restoration, and Raphaël, inspired by the noble sentiments of a young man's sense of honor and duty, works desperately to save the dignity of his father's name. After his father's death, like Lucien after the break with Louise, Raphaël at age twenty-two is alone in Paris "sans avenir, sans fortune," deprived now "de mes premières illusions, les plus chères de toutes." Timid, awkward, and bashful despite his talents, he is yet ambitious and full of longing for the love of a beautiful, highborn woman. Believing in his "destinée," he decides to work on a book that will make him rich and famous, for like Daniel d'Arthez he will rise solely on his merits. He shuts himself into a voluntary prison, an attic room under the roof, and for three years works on a play to gain money, and on a serious book presenting a theory of the will. As he slaves away, dreaming often of his beautiful woman and the soft cushions of a brilliant equipage, the world as it is presents him with nothing more glamorous than the landlady's daughter, the tender and exquisite Pauline. Raphaël's "romanesques fantaisies" blind him to the noble qualities of this devoted woman, especially when he meets Rastignac, here shown ten years after the events of *Le Père Goriot*, not yet recorded by Balzac.

Raphaël is now instructed in the ways of the world, made so vivid to Rastignac himself by Vautrin and Mme de Beauséant. The life of "un dissipateur" unfolds as Raphaël learns how to maneuver the world for his own profit, how, that is, to live without work. Rastignac will now present Raphaël to a mansion where he may behold the Paris of riches, fame, and beauty, including the celebrated Countess Foedora herself.

Now begins the punishment of the wish fulfilled. Foedora is indeed the incarnation of Raphaël's dreams as he becomes infatuated with her, abandoning the genuine love of Pauline. Like Rastignac he spends the little he has on this caprice, at the expense of his true needs. He is in a state of intoxication now, suffering from the inevitable dualism—the comparison between his impoverished room and Foedora's luxury. He thinks of the distance separating these two worlds, of the cost demanded by his hopes. He compares his crude appearance with the advantages enjoyed in the Parisian struggle by elegant young men, "riches, armés de tilburys et vêtus d'impertinence." Now Foedora tortures him as well, listening to his advances with a smile worn upon her face like a garment, showing Raphaël clearly "un abîme entre cette femme et moi," responding to his good night only with "son sourire banal, le détestable sourire d'une statue de marbre." Raphaël's poverty is made the more dramatic as he walks home in the snow and rain, unable to afford the carriage of his dreams. But like Lucien to come, Raphaël sells out to the journalistic bookseller Finot, and hard work yields to quick and easy profit. A cheap, shady transaction insures money, so that Raphaël may stop at Rastignac's hat shop and tailor to obtain the weapons he needs to fight the other dandies. He returns to his room, living now in the *avenir*, counting his joys. As he quits the studious life to pursue Foedora, he tries to penetrate to the truth of her character but is made aware "des abîmes entre nous," abysses not only of hopeless distance but of dangerous voids and unknown disaster. He weeps at her cruel insults, but persists in his folly. Like Rastignac, he must extinguish the voice of his conscience, and ends, after squandering his resources and contemplating suicide, by adopting another form of certain death in the talisman, *La Peau de chagrin*, which will satisfy every desire but at the cost of life itself. Thus both Raphaël and Lucien do, in fact, commit suicide at the first attempt, Raphaël by his pact with the talisman, Lucien by his pact with Vautrin, whereby he ceases to be a separate human being, as Vautrin's soul enters and controls his beautiful body.

Other anticipations of Lucien come to mind in Raphaël's Parisian career: his starting out in a cheap room, falling in love with a highborn woman, enduring, on foot, the agonies of impoverished youth, deciding between meritorious hard work and facile journalism, and finally selling himself to the devil. Félicien Marceau sees in Pauline a symbol of what the young Balzacian hero knows to be his right course: she is the hard study of law for Rastignac, the serious literary vocation of Lucien. The orgy in *La Peau de chagrin* becomes the lavish suppers at Coralie's, and Foedora, as the society to be overcome by the young arriviste, becomes the ball at Mme de Beauséant's and the hand in marriage of Clothilde de Grandlieu. These anticipations find their expression, too, in the familiar language of military struggle, of pursuing an illusory future rich in fine clothes and carriages, haunted by a cold woman with a fatal smile, while all around lie distances, separations, precipices, and fathomless depths.

BENASSIS

The hero as failure in Paris continues into the unhappy life of Dr. Benassis, whose confession comes in chapter 4, toward the end of *Le Médecin de campagne*, after the doctor's medical career and service have been narrated. His account merely explains to Genestas how he came to be where and what he is. He is sent from a small town in Languedoc to study medicine in Paris, under the care of an old friend of his father's. Like Rastignac, he is installed in a boardinghouse, and at first works diligently. He is soon led astray by his passion for the theater, and begins to procrastinate, reducing his work to the minimum requirements. Paris itself he finds alluring for a youth between the ages of twenty and twenty-five, for it satisfies appetite and encourages vice. As Lucien will show, temptation likewise appeals to desires already present, so Benassis becomes a Parisian as he permits the corruption of his youthful ideals and sentiments. His grand hopes, plans, and dreams of glory fade, as he, too, longs for the flowers of life without the labor to bring them forth. He begins to drift, and wanders for whole days about the streets, quais, and public gardens. Work and study are too slow a means toward pleasure, and Paris itself aids in his corruption by showing the happiness of evil and the misery of virtue. He, too, longs for an important woman of the high world to show him the way to success, to introduce him into circles where he may find the relations "utiles à mon avenir." But of the two kinds of men who face the world as it is—the cool realists, who learn fast, and the poor sensitive "poètes," who blunder—he is of the latter kind.

At this point Benassis sacrifices a young girl, Agathe, whom he does not love but who serves him well by reorganizing his life toward some end, reawakening his hopes and dreams. But his father dies, and Benassis, now rich and free, decides to abandon the girl in the hope of making "une belle alliance." He gradually breaks with his devoted love, and tries to overcome his remorse in Parisian gaiety and dissipation. When he is finally ruined, the girl calls to him just before her death, leaving their child to his care. As she lies dying, Benassis weeps tears of bitter repentance, but in time, as his son grows up, the doctor falls in love with Evelina, a girl of religious upbringing from a Jansenist family. Here at last is the concentration of every hope for a young provincial, and we again see the parallel with Lucien, dreaming of *avenir* and glory. Evelina is beautiful, of high birth, rich and cultivated, ideally placed in the world to satisfy the most ardent dreams. But her family discovers the lurid past, the love affair and the illegitimate child. Their religious scruples will not tolerate such a past, just as Lucien's low birth, plebeian name, and liaison with Esther will exclude him from the house of his intended bride. Now Evelina can only regret the *abîmes* that separate them. The exchange of letters here by two people ending a broken love is repeated with more poignant irony, as when Eugénie Grandet answers the only letter she has ever received from the perfidious Charles.

After the death of his son, Benassis considers suicide, which he tries to justify both in Epicurus and the Christian Gospels. He sees that only a life of service in the world can atone for his sins, and he now devotes his life, with a kind of Schweitzer-like resignation, to improving the lot of men in a neglected part of the world. Unlike Lucien, who only weeps, confesses, and sins again, Benassis makes of his remaining life an act of contrition and sincere repentance.

RASTIGNAC

The indispensable M. Bardèche urges us to be familiar with young Henri de Marsay, prominent in *La Fille aux yeux d'or* and *Le Contrat de mariage*, near the time of *Le Père Goriot*. De Marsay is the model on which Rastignac is formed, and he already is what Rastignac and Lucien are tempted to become. All that he represents, "le succès sans effort, la vie facile et glorieuse, la richesse et l'amour," is certainly uppermost in Vautrin's mind, de Marsay having been prepared for the world by the "devil in purple," the mundane Abbé de Maronis, who dies a bishop in 1812. At the age of sixteen, de Marsay is launched in full battle array upon a world which he understands perfectly, wherein he owes nothing, finally, to a single human being. Handsome, cynical, assured, believing in nothing, equipped with valuable connections in high society, de Marsay seems to begin at the point to which Rastignac and Lucien must painfully struggle. The irony cannot be accidental, then, during the fearful scene at the Opera, when de Marsay visits upon Lucien a cruelly disdainful smile, showing him his place in the world. This elegant monster is all that Lucien wishes to be, indeed has to be, his knowledge of life as it is and of how to profit from it having been recorded in his superb letter to Paul de Manerville.

Young Eugène de Rastignac begins far away from such a goal. At great sacrifice to his family, who center all their "espérances" in him, he has come to Paris for the study of law, to prepare for "une belle destinée," Balzac early repeating his mythical terms. Pale, dark, blue-eyed, and handsome, Eugène is shabbily dressed but has nonetheless an air of grace and elegance at times, as befits the son of a noble family carefully reared. As Mr. Affron says, *Le Père Goriot* is organized like a lesson: "Rastignac is the schoolboy, and life the curriculum." If we concentrate now on Eugène's *Bildung* as the important theme of *Le Père Goriot*, we may in some measure correct Martin Turnell's grotesque misreading of this masterpiece.

In a year's time Eugène has learned a great deal. He sees that society has carefully arranged strata, and the symbolic carriage is quickly important to him when he watches the handsome procession, on a sunny day, on the Champs Élysées. He sees the terrible sacrifices imposed on his devoted family, and compares his poor sisters with the beauties of Paris. His provincial illusions give way, and he is determined to "arrive" but only on his merits. Learning quickly, he sees the vast influence of women on social life and now has the good luck to secure an introduction to the Vicomtesse de Beauséant, a woman on the very summit of the beau monde, and a distant relative, too.

It is November, 1819, when Eugène attends a ball at Mme de Beauséant's, which gives him an immense advantage in the Parisian battle. He enjoys, in fact, two great advantages over Lucien: he is not weakened by any division, his identity is one and noble. He is under the patronage of a powerful figure, in whose house he now beholds the ravishing Anastasie de Restaud. Eugène begins to dream of his *avenir* and studies how to make his declaration to Anastasie. But Paris is *un bourbier*, as he tells Vautrin, so that on arriving at Hôtel de Restaud, he has mud on his shoes and trousers. If he were rich, he thinks, he would have come in a carriage, for only by such means does one avoid the mud of Paris, that is, everything undesirable beginning with the street itself. In the court stands a beautiful cabriolet with a fine horse, and a servant looks coldly at Eugène, on foot, as if the *voiture* lessons were not explicit. Cooly received and forced to wait, he overhears Père Goriot and sees the old man leaving the courtyard on foot. When Eugène at last meets Anastasie and her lover Maxime de Trailles, he compares Maxime's appearance to that of a cool, snobbish Parisian dandy. Eugène has an admirable tenacity, a staying power that Lucien will lack, as he now stands his ground. On the entrance of Anastasie's husband, Eugène's family background is made clear, and even the odious Maxime loses his impertinent air. Lucien, later, has quite a different experience, suffering when his own origins are made clear by, alas, this same Rastignac. Eugène's luck suddenly changes, however, when he remarks that he has just seen a man leave who has a room next door to his own—Père Goriot. A mere name has changed the atmosphere again, especially the Père. Determined now to escape from the *abîme* into which he has fallen, Eugène, learning fast and deriving, like Julien, a lesson from every experience, gets into a public cab. He will go to Mme de Beauséant, explain what has happened, and so discover the background of his error.

Eugène sees now for the first time the luxury, the expensive magnificence of the upper world. He is made to wait, he is coldly received at first, but he learns. When the Duchesse de Langeais enters, he sees the cruelty and malice beneath her mask of devoted friendship. Now he has a chance to make his "confession," as he calls it, of the sins just committed, and soon, in one of the turning points of his career, he learns the identity of Anastasie, and the inhuman perfidy of Delphine as well. On hearing that Père Goriot has been banished from the houses of his children, "quelques larmes roulèrent dans les yeux d'Eugène." These tears are the first in a series of eight occasions when Eugène, still tender and devoted, still believing and young, responds with a still human emotion to the corruption of the world. Balzac is movingly sympathetic toward this youth, for, after all, this is only his first day "sur le champ de bataille de la civilisation parisienne."

When her "friend" is gone, Mme de Beauséant promises to help Eugène make his way in the wicked and infamous *bourbier* that is the world. Her lecture now anticipates the sinister teachings of the great Vautrin. M. Bory has shown that the doctrines expounded to his pupils by Vautrin, presenting the world and its ways in a "code de la route pour arrivistes astucieux," have appeared in four different novels, through two virtuous women and two Satanic men. That the world is "une école de mensonge et d'hypocrisie," Rastignac learns from Mme de Beauséant and Vautrin; Félix de Vandenesse, from Mme de Mortsauf in *Le Lys dans la vallée;* Paul de Manerville, from de Marsay in *Le Contrat de mariage,* and Lucien de Rubempré, again from Vautrin, in *Illusions.* Now Rastignac hears that he must treat the world without pity as it deserves. Women are corrupt, men are vain, to be used like post-horses and left exhausted at every stage. Find a rich and influential woman and make use of her, but conceal all genuine sentiment and guard the secret of any true love. Mme de Beauséant reveals the useful fact of Anastasie's social superiority over her sister Delphine, who would gladly lap up "toute la boue qu'il y a entre la rue Saint-Lazare et la rue de Grenelle pour entrer dans mon salon." Out of the shameful truth that the two sisters hate each other in their social rivalry, Eugène may then make capital. He may introduce Delphine at Mme de Beauséant's house, she will favor him, other women will be attracted, and he will be a huge success, although Anastasie will exclude him from her house because he has mentioned her father there. After pledges of mutual aid with the Vicomtesse, Eugène departs: "Il se frappa le cœur, sourit au sourire de sa cousine, et sortit. Il était cinq heures." This is the most knowing and mature smile of Eugène's career, for in one afternoon he has learned more of the world as it is than the whole of his young life had imagined.

When he returns to the loathsome boardinghouse, his ambition is kindled anew by the sudden contrast between these obscenities and the luxurious beauty of an hour ago. Balzac lets the stinking premises of Mme Vauquer serve many purposes, among them a reason or excuse for Eugène's behavior, which is that of any young man of his kind amid surroundings as repulsive and contrasts as sudden and dramatic. Mme de Beauséant's advice now seems all the more compelling, as Eugène wonders how to obtain the new clothes demanded for entry to the high world. He forces himself at last to write home to his mother and sisters for money, and the fatal terms of their *espérances* and his *avenir* recur. He feels ashamed when he thinks of their love and sacrifice, of the anguish his mother will endure if she cannot find the money, Balzac here showing himself the master of tender love as later of dramatic hatred. And for what is Eugène committing this shameful deed? As he sees that the answer to this question is getting access to Delphine, the second occasion of his tears unfolds, as "quelques larmes, derniers grains d'encens jetés sur l'autel sacré de la famille, lui sortirent des yeux." When, after agonies of hesitation, the letters are mailed, Eugène cries out in the terrible future tense, "Je réussirai." He decides to give up study entirely for the sake of his Parisian campaign; the *étudiant* gives way to the calculating *ambitieux*. When his letters are answered and the money is assured, Eugène in shame and remorse sheds tears for the third time, seeing that his conduct for the sake of the *avenir* is fully as shameful as Anastasie's exploitation of her father's love. But with money in his pocket, Eugène changes completely in manner and attitude. He is brisk, gay, confident, his very walk and glance transformed as he orders the inevitable new outfit of clothes.

As Freud has remarked, "Temptations do but increase under constant privation," and Eugène feels deprived as he moves between two contrasted worlds. Balzac prepares for the onset of temptation by showing the compelling energy of Vautrin, the devil, and by dwelling on Eugène's youth, his quickness of reaction, his vivacity and readiness. In a long speech covering some

nine pages, Vautrin displays not only his own character and principles, but the boy's necessities and how to meet them, that is,
with money. He offers money before saying what must be done to
obtain it. The temptation begins most attractively and is greatly
advanced before Eugène has any reason to resist it. It is a masterly
display of diabolism, beginning with an offer of the essential "million," and Vautrin has so well succeeded that Eugène is eager to
know what he must do to get the money so alluringly offered and
so desperately needed. "What must I do?" is the question; what
I must do to gain the world, the devil alone can tell.

The answer is simple: "Presque rien." Marry a girl now poor
but certain to become rich, who will gladly share her millions.
Eugène is not repulsed on learning that the candidate is the
pitiable Victorine Taillefer living at Mme Vauquer's, in exile
from her father's house. His only objection is her poverty, which,
however, Vautrin will remove with horrifying ingenuity by having
her brother killed in a duel. Victorine then becomes her father's
sole heir, whose millions Eugène may possess by marrying her.
What must he do at last? Consent to murder and robbery, "almost nothing." Vautrin accepts the ensuing fury and disgust as
reactions natural in the young and innocent. He carries the temptation forward by predicting that Rastignac will do far worse than
this one day, only shedding less blood in his crime. Then with the
devil's foreknowledge, as Eugène assures Vautrin that his secret
will not be betrayed, he seems to foretell his own eventual betrayal
at the hands of Lucien: "Un autre . . . sera moins scrupuleux."

Eugène virtuously decides to return to work, to rise after all by
honor and merit alone. As Mr. Adamson has remarked, the early
advances of Vautrin do not fully engage the youth's integrity. But
temptation assumes another form, ironically assisted by Père
Goriot himself, who aids his young friend in the sale of his soul.
For Eugène's pious resolutions are interrupted by the tailor. In his
new clothes he appears a handsome gentleman, and the old man
enters to tell him that he should go to a ball the following Monday

where both his daughters will be present. Later, walking in the Tuileries, Eugène sees himself, young, elegant, and greatly admired on all sides. Clothes are fatal to his resolutions, and he forgets his loving family, forgets the sacrificial price exacted by his appearance, his own baseness in accepting it. Everything in his life now conspires to force him into the Parisian battle where he must kill and betray in self-defense, and use men without pity for his own ends. After dinner at Mme de Beauséant's he escorts her to the theater where he is introduced to Delphine. His campaign to win her begins with lies and shameless flatteries, leading to a declaration of love. On his way home he makes grandiose plans for future wealth, without dwelling on the morality of the necessary means.

Although Vautrin's proposal recurs to his mind when he sees that Victorine is in love with him, Eugène continues to resist, until one night, while dining at the boardinghouse, brooding over his penniless state, he begins to think of Vautrin's proposal and casts tenderly expressive glances at Victorine. Their conversation becomes more intimate and the poor girl is clearly moved, when they are interrupted by the fearful voice of the tempter prophesying in the form of a question, a promise of marriage between "monsieur le chevalier Eugène de Rastignac et mademoiselle Victorine Taillefer," as if publishing banns in church.

Victorine retires, and Vautrin begins the second of his principal temptations. He offers Eugène some money, but Eugène, unlike Lucien, refuses, since he knows that Vautrin is a criminal. This does not dismay the tempter, who makes his diabolic identity explicit by complimenting Eugène: "Vous seriez une belle proie pour le diable." If the youth will come over to Vautrin's side, his every wish will come true in the possession of honor, fortune, women. He will like Vautrin well enough despite his criminal nature, which contains "d'immenses abîmes" but nothing cowardly or ungrateful. Eugène manages to keep free of the offered role as Vautrin's accomplice, but soon draws intimately close to Victorine, who now believes herself truly loved. An ominous passage makes a powerful use of the abyss figure: "Il fallait un miracle pour le tirer de l'abîme ou il avait déjà mis le pied depuis une heure." Despite the torments of his conscience, and knowing that he is committing evil, Eugène has so yielded to temptation that nothing earthly can save him. The miracle does occur, when, despite the murder of Victorine's brother as planned, Vautrin's betrayal and arrest come to Eugène's rescue at last.

This fearful episode, so powerfully realized, uncovers new dimensions in Balzac's treatment of temptation and now betrayal. For temptation in *Le Père Goriot* is directed also at Poiret and Mlle Michonneau. The others had never liked Mlle Michonneau, and now her treachery confirms their mistrust and justifies their revenge upon her. The Balzacian lesson then emerges with accustomed force: betrayal is odious and always costs the betrayer his soul, no matter who the object of treachery may be. Faith is faith, and betrayal is betrayal no matter to what or to whom directed. Throughout the *Comédie* Balzac repeats the theme of love for an unworthy object; but it is nonetheless love, for Vautrin's criminality does not make betraying him any the less odious or contemptible. Treachery may succeed and vice emerge triumphant in Balzac, as many have objected, yet they are never less than detestable. The *Comédie* becomes, then, an indictment, an exposure rather than a history or a mere play. It is a lament, an elegy, an ironic satire, a moral judgment against a corrupt world, in the tradition of Swift and Juvenal.

The removal of Vautrin does not end Eugène's moral problems, however.

His continued goodness shows when, after overhearing the dreadful scene in which Goriot's daughters betray their continuing exploitation of their father and their hatred for each other, Eugène shows the old man a tender pity. The climactic ball at Mme de Beauséant's now forces a dramatic clash between the fidelity due to the old father—now clearly dying—and the frantic social ambitions of his children. With death only hours away, Eugène goes sadly to Delphine, assuming that the ball is out of the question. She is furious, however, and orders him to change his clothes. As he dresses in elegant fashion, Eugène reflects bitterly on the meaning of this new turning point in his life, the last chance to preserve the decency and virtue in his soul. He thinks of Vautrin's view of society, of his family and their love for him, of their pure lives amid domestic happiness. But these noble images cannot prevail against Delphine. He sees her for what she is, knowing that she would walk over her father's body to attend this ball, but he lacks the force to reason with her, the courage to displease her, the virtue to abandon her. He tries to excuse her behavior and in so doing sees also that she has altered his life for the worse. But the joys of love will remove all else, save that now in the symbolic carriage, on the way to Mme de Beauséant, Eugène hears in imagination the death rattle of Delphine's father.

At the ball, Eugène's *éducation* completes itself. Here, on the occasion of what her enemies hoped would be a humiliating defeat, Mme de Beauséant shows her dominance with a superb command of the *sourire* symbol. The most beautiful women in Paris are here animating the salon by their *toilettes* and their smiles. Dressed in white like a statue of Niobe, the Vicomtesse herself smiles in mockery at her most intimate friends. The most insensible wondered at her "comme les jeunes Romains applaudissaient le gladiateur qui savait sourire en expirant," Balzac here keeping to his general Parisian image of combat and deriving a threefold value from the word *sourire:* social life and gaiety, strength of character in defeat, ironic disdain in the face of death. The reader of *La Femme abandonnée* will recall this terrible smile when Gaston de Nueil presents himself to Mme de Beauséant in her exile.

At last the guests have departed, and Eugène sees Mme de Beauséant to her berline, he in turn returning on foot to the boardinghouse in the morning air, now cold and damp. "Son éducation s'achevait," Balzac simply tells us. Eugène now knows himself and the world, and reveals this knowledge in a bitter speech to Bianchon: anything evil that one says of the world is true, and he inhabits an inferno where he must always remain. Later, when the dying old man is left in his care and Eugène sees that he is no longer recognized, his eyes begin to moisten in the fifth of his series of weepings. His youthful goodness lingers in the horror, indignation, and pity that let him forget himself sufficiently to bring some peace to Goriot's final moments. To get money, he has Bianchon pawn the watch given him by Delphine. He makes futile efforts to bring the children to their father's side, and out of the watch manages at least a change of linen for the dying man. When a medallion with the names of his daughters on either side is replaced, Goriot rejoices with his last strength. Eugène for the sixth time weeps hot tears, now in company with Bianchon at the heartrending spectacle. Anastasie finally arrives in a dreadful state, deserted by an unfaithful lover, despised by a ruthless husband. In agonies of shame and remorse she can only cry "J'ai perdu toutes mes illusions" as if to give this inevitable title to the masterpiece now moving to its end.

Eugène's efforts to get help with the funeral expenses and to see the dead man's children are in vain, and about three in the afternoon he returns to the Maison Vauquer, where for the seventh time he must shed a tear, seeing the coffin of his old friend at the door, barely covered by black cloth, resting on two chairs in the empty street. The pitiful funeral of twenty minutes is over at five thirty, and at six o'clock in the humid dusk the body descends into its grave. Looking down, Eugène sheds a tear for the eighth time, token of his young goodness, as Balzac so movingly tells us, "sa dernière larme de jeune homme." When next we see this man at Père Lachaise, it will be for the funeral of Lucien, who has remembered him in his will by the gift of a gold-plated toilet set. But now we are sure that this is the last tear of Eugène's life, for he has wept only from unselfish sympathy for others, from emotions that he cannot afford, since the battle between him and the world is joined once and for all. Eugène is dead with his last tear, and Rastignac will now stride across the pages of the *Comédie* in ruthless pursuit of his destiny. Never again does Balzac call him by his first name, as he always does with Lucien, for he ceases to be young for us, an unfulfilled beginner who inspires a measure of anxiety and affection.

Although M. Jean Pommier distinguishes Rastignacs I, II, and III, for purposes of Lucien's lineage in the *Comédie* we will assume that the Rastignac emerging from *Le Père Goriot* is the essential one. Comparisons generally show the superior strength of Rastignac, who is said to triumph as Lucien fails. Like all of Balzac's arrivistes, these two begin in the Latin Quarter and are changed by Paris, which challenges and strengthens Rastignac but seduces and destroys Lucien in his more feminine weakness. Rastignac learns from his errors, and Lucien fails to do so. Both begin with virtue in their hearts, and Rastignac's dual nature allies him to both the good and the evil forces in *Le Père Goriot*. As the *Comédie* is composed of harmonies and opposites, Rastignac explains Lucien as success explains failure: opposites explain each other.

Rastignac's eventual fate permits us to wonder at the human price paid for his vast success. He begins with secure high birth, a note carried by his first name, Eugène—the "well-born." His defiance of the world after he has buried Goriot grimly suggests that he will in fact prevail against anything to be done against him, as Balzac enlarges him into a metaphor to include every youth of the century, the aspiration of this and every age. By comparison, Lucien's defiance after the Bargeton soirée seems like that of a small boy bent on getting even with adults who have overwhelmed his meager equipment to hold his own with them. The physical relation to the world is important in each case, Rastignac standing high above the Paris he defies, and Lucien walking far below the unattainable citadel of his humiliation, in no position to look down upon it or anything else, and so foretelling his final inadequacy. The role of their tears is even more revealing of strength and weakness. Eugène never weeps over himself as Lucien does more or less continuously. Eugène weeps only when seeing a new dimension of human corruption. His tears come of growing knowledge of the world, and present him as a tragic figure when the last tear falls in silence on the grave of his friend. Understanding the world now, he will compel it to do his bidding. The human price of his triumph is the innocence of his youth, the tenderness and pity that make him the last mourner at the grave of a foolish old man, that call forth a lonely tear, perhaps for the death of what he once was. Lucien's constant weeping is rarely because of anyone else, and so detracts from, rather than increases, his dignity. He rarely weeps because of a lesson learned, since he cannot turn experience to his own profit.

The careers of our two arrivistes are more explicitly joined by Vautrin, whose temptation Eugène is supposed to have had the strength to resist, whereas Lucien succumbs. Although Vautrin's diabolism is often to the fore, and at his arrest he is a "poème infernal," the devil is less a supernatural force than a summary of the world as it is; so Vautrin is constantly teaching his two pupils to see men and things as they are. In Dickens the angels are said to be inferior to the devils, and Balzac is accused of letting Vautrin's power and that of evil in general grow to the point of deserving the title "la Diabolique comédie. . . ." But if the devil assumes his more proper literary and metaphorical role, Vautrin is seen to embody a range of human qualities that help to make the world as it is. The advice he gives to his young pupils is at one level the same as that of a saintly woman, if we recall the counsel given by Mme de Mortsauf to young Félix de Vandenesse in *Le Lys dans la vallée*. She can do no better than tell anyone who wishes to succeed that hardness, dissimulation, and contempt of men will serve better than an open heart. Vautrin's teaching that women are a means, not an end, that sincere love is an obstacle to ambition, is scarcely less odious than Mme de Beauséant's own form of tempting Eugène. She offers to help him on by using the influence of women, by exploiting the envy and hatred of Goriot's shameful children, making capital out of crime—crime that is worse than open theft, cruelly unfeeling to the love of a helpless father, perverted, unnatural in its violation of human ties which Eugène himself still respects. As Lucien will discover, the "devil" appears in many forms.

If we leave Vautrin's homosexuality aside as more relevant to *Splendeurs et misères des courtisanes*, we may ask again how far Eugène resists the temptation to which Lucien yields. The temptation as a lesson persuades Eugène to accept the truth of something that has to be believed if the action is to follow. With Eugène the lesson is that only corruption will succeed in such a world as this, whose injustice compels a cynical selfishness. For Lucien the lesson is to confirm his vanity and hopes of *avenir*, which were justified by Louise's flattery. Now Vautrin appeals to vanity and to revenge, sentiments very strong in Lucien after humiliation both in Angoulême and Paris. Eugène's dual nature in turn accounts for his response to the tempter. On one side he gives in to Vautrin's hideous proposals, but at the last moment would retreat and warn the Taillefers, overcome by the enormity of his behavior. Eugène has always found Vautrin repulsive, the embodiment of what he has been taught to consider loathsome. This response to Vautrin is instinctive, a sign of the youth's basic decency, which continues in his tender pity for Père Goriot. Lucien, however, does not seem to find Vautrin repulsive. As one who in the end cares little for the means taken toward his illusory *avenir*, he considers Vautrin only from without.

M. Marceau argues that Eugène resists Vautrin more from prudence than virtue, that apart from other advantages of birth and family, he is plainly luckier than Lucien. He is not tempted under such painful conditions as Lucien, who is about to kill himself after failure that seems absolute. Eugène has reason for despair only in his desire to realize his ambitions more quickly. He is tempted at a much earlier stage, when all of his future is still pos-

sible. That he avoids crime is, we are assured by the narrator, a
miracle. When Vautrin is prevented from carrying out the whole
of his plan, Eugène foils the devil more by luck than by strength
of will.

And yet deep within Eugène's behavior lurks a shameful element that may account for the somber implications in his future
life. Vautrin tempts both young men, and Nucingen pays money
to both Eugène and Lucien, to the first as being Delphine's lover,
and to Lucien through Esther. Both men have a woman in common with Nucingen, the woman in each case being a means toward ambition. Lucien does live more than once from a prostitute's earnings, but is not Eugène being kept by something far
more discreditable to him, by the heroic sacrifice of Père Goriot
himself? He mourns the death of his friend, but profits from it at
Delphine's hands, knowing the hideous cost of her aid. The hero
as failure and as success both indict the world that ruins the one
and rewards the other. It is not always to Lucien's discredit that
he cannot perform as the world demands. The man who succeeds,
therefore, may be worse than the man who fails. Returning to
Vautrin, we see that the one who succeeds repudiates Vautrin but
in fact lives by his principles, whereas the one who gives in to
Vautrin is a failure who lacks the strength to live as the devil
teaches. Thus Rastignac is what we see him to be in Eugène's
later career, because he has taken Vautrin's advice, and he becomes a far less sympathetic figure than during his days of early
struggle. A form of cruelty, of cynicism and unscrupulous acceptance of the world, replaces the lad who shed his first tear in the
salon of Mme de Beauséant and his last at the grave of Père
Goriot. It is worth recalling, too, that while Lucien fails by the
standards both of the world and of the great Cénacle, Rastignac,
for all his success in the world, also fails by Cénacle requirements.
In *Les Secrets de la Princesse de Cadignan* he is shown as clearly inferior
to Daniel d'Arthez.

Were the lessons of Eugène's education ultimately those drawn by Rastignac? They might have been the opposite indeed, and thus better for a happy future: the lessons that no end is better than the means taken to achieve it, that if success in the world is to be had at such a moral and human price, it is not worth the cost. The *éducation* completed at the ball should have taught the falsity of the *avenir* Eugène longs for, as clearly as it has shown how to obtain it. But the modest and tender youth becomes "cet arriviste sans scrupule, ce prototype d'un impitoyable profiteur parisien, ce blagueur féroce qui . . . incarne magistralement la morale d'une société corrompue." We meet him everywhere in the *Comédie*, a familiar phantom making his way to riches and the summits of power in France, but his life itself ruined, devoid of love or joy as he finally marries Delphine's daughter, success insured by the loss of all that he cherished, the only happy days long behind him when he was young and poor, dreaming of escape from the Maison Vauquer into the glittering future.

VICTURNIEN AND LITTLE OSCAR

Le Cabinet des antiques began to appear in March 1836, just before the conception of *Illusions* at Saché in June, so that the figure of Victurnien d'Esgrignon blends readily into the development of Lucien, quite apart from the similarity of their names. Victurnien's story proceeds equally from illusion: his father and Aunt Armande have based the family's entire hope on this "enfant gâté." There is similarly someone who sees the painful truth, the devoted notary Chesnel, who is punished like Cassandra as the family accepts his devotion and rejects his shrewd advice. Chapter 2, "Une Mauvaise éducation," shows in advance the errors made by a scheme of things that ignores a world now bitterly changed. Victurnien is endowed with extraordinary physical beauty; he is an aristocrat with all the grace and style of one to the manner born. He has excellent natural ability as well, a quick, retentive mind that is cultivated much beyond a mere noble *politesse*. But along with the family's confidence in one so clearly gifted, Victurnien himself becomes, like Lucien, enormously vain but bold and impetuous as well, natural in one whose desires had never been opposed. It might have been wholesome for him to fight against poverty and hardship, but he has been indulged in his weakness for the gay, voluptuous life, for "les jouissances," as Chesnel realizes, "qui mènent aux abîmes les gens habiles seulement pour les voluptés," the word "abysses" here preparing us for the inevitable. Victurnien is further spoiled by the Chevalier de Valois, who teaches him the morality of a French nobleman in the mid-eighteenth century, for whom elegance conceals and justifies all corruption. He is seen as a kind of victim, who, like Lucien, is vain and confident of the future, but for different reasons. His illusion is to believe in the continuing value and force of an order now over and done with. The past that is supposed to insure his future is dead; his upbringing prevents him from seeing this, so that his illusions are less about himself than Lucien's are. But his nature mingles the same good and evil, leading Balzac to find excuses for the conduct of such young men. His view of wayward youth might almost seem Wordsworthian, if Mme de Beauséant's remark to Gaston de Nueil is the narrator's own: "Vous êtes trop jeune pour être tout à fait dénué de bonté," as if to say, only in youth may one cherish noble, ideal sentiments; too soon shades of the prison house close in, and all is cynicism, bitter disillusion.

At age eighteen, however, Victurnien's behavior is offensive. He makes the error containing all others: he is misled by appearances, and only Chesnel's kindness saves him from the consequences of various arrogant, foolish escapades. He supposes that he can always escape from trouble caused by his misbehavior, for between the ages of eighteen and twenty-one he costs Chesnel about eighty thousand francs without the family's knowledge. Expenses are high; his clothing is ordered from Paris, and we are sure that Victurnien must have his fine English horse, together with the fatal carriage and a groom in livery. Like Lucien, he accepts the sacrifice and devotion of others, as Chesnel plays the role of Ève and David, gradually losing his illusions while the father and aunt go on as always. On the day of his departure for Paris, Victurnien knows nothing of money or its value, even less of Paris itself. His character is reviewed with emphasis on his complacent arrogance at the moment when he begins to suffer for this and other faults. In the provinces he has been isolated from reality, and his character is such that if left to himself he must end in the mud. Now, like Lucien, he quickly forgets his devoted family, leaving them behind without the least regret while his mind entertains "ses plus beaux rêves."

But Victurnien begins to learn, first from the smile of an old man, one of the most expressive of all the mythical *sourires* of the *Comédie*. His father has written a letter to the Duc de Lenoncourt, in whose response Victurnien has his first lesson in the difference between what he has come from and "cette encyclopédie babylonienne" that is Paris. Despite his impeccable manners, the Duke cannot suppress a smile, showing again the basic disillusion of knowing the "distance" between objects: "Ce sourire avait dit à Victurnien qu'il y avait plus de soixante lieues entre le Cabinet des Antiques et les Tuileries: il y avait une distance de plusieurs siècles." For Victurnien differs from the usual arriviste in the means he will use to succeed in Paris. He would rise because of his family's past, not by seizing the opportunities created by Napoleon and the Revolution. Indeed, he behaves as if the changes in French political and social history had never taken place. The Duke's smile, then, contains decades of French history. Victurnien soon knows that his kind of nobility no longer pays at court; he must make a show of wealth and luxury, must again have "de belles voitures," as he falls in with the now established crowd of Parisian dandies, including, alas, Rastignac. His great name and apparent fortune open all doors, but he sees that the welcome is cordial only so long as he does not ask for anything. He could have made a good marriage but he is too vain to declare his true condition, and continues "sous les armes de sa fausse opulence." His debts mount, he loses at cards, and he is so soon in fashion that Rastignac is amazed "de sa prompte initiation aux belles manières du moment." But it is not long before Rastignac and de Marsay, seeing Victurnien fall before the beauteous Diane de Maufrigneuse —herself soon to fall in love with Lucien—exchange "un sourire." Later, as he faces ruin, Victurnien sees in advance the cold and mocking glance, "le sourire par lequel ses compagnons accueilleraient le récit de son désastre." What remains of his talent or probity is lost, he increases his debts to the villainous du Croisier, he, too, falls into the *abîmes* lying in wait on all sides, and learns too late the essential lesson of Paris: how much it costs. His debts continue to mount, and his friends observe him sad and preoccupied. "Ce petit d'Esgrignon" they say, "n'a pas le pied parisien." They predict that he will commit suicide, but he resolves on its alternative—a crime. He makes use of du Croisier's signature at the end of a letter to draw the sum of three hundred thousand francs from the Keller bank. He plans to flee the country with Diane, who, eventually, refuses in a scene of angry violence. Facing arrest, Victurnien is rescued by his aunt, who takes his burning head to her breast, and "elle baisait ce front en sueur malgré le froid." Diane herself says adieu when all danger is passed, advising him to avoid Paris, for "l'air de Paris ne vous vaut rien." She goes out of his life in her carriage, and Victurnien hears, in the crack of its coachman's whip, the end of his first passion.

As Victurnien drifts back into the shadows of Balzac's world, he anticipates the hero as failure. Unlike Lucien, he leaves Alençon in the light of day, all by himself, goes to Paris, fails, and returns home. He has had no one to guide his way, and we can only guess, somewhat gloomily, what might have come if Victurnien had known Vautrin and his counsels. Although his aunt Armande does not die of her sacrifice as does Chesnel, Victurnien accepts the gift of her life as Lucien does that of Coralie—sacrifices for nothing. Unselfish virtue given in the service of illusion is not only futile but harmful, since the foolish indulgence of his aunt, the devotion of Chesnel, and the father's proud fidelity to an order from the past all fail to produce the thing demanded by the nineteenth century: money in its many forms. Like Lucien, Victurnien has been spoiled by love at home, is weak and half-woman, falling into crime and prison as Paris declares its will, and equally prompt to shed tears, followed by ephemeral repentance.

If Victurnien seems a form of preliminary review for Lucien, the parallels are less striking in the case of Calyste de Guénic in *Béatrix*, one of the last of Balzac's young provincial noblemen coming to Paris and created over the same years as *Illusions*. Calyste is also extraordinarily handsome, but of much stronger character and sounder moral resources. For a time he is easily misled and capable of some base hypocrisies while he is getting a Parisian education in "la politesse des passions," which permits a man to lie to his wife and tell the truth to his mistress. We tremble for Calyste when he sees himself as one of the poor young nobles who come to Paris, there to win a great fortune by force of will and intelligence: "Je puis faire ce qu'il a fait le baron de Rastignac, au ministère aujourd'hui." But Calyste's prudence saves him for the peace of a conventional marriage, a fate also reserved for the poor and humble Oscar Husson, whose career forms the center of *Un Début dans la vie*. Since the date of 1842 comes within the years of Lucien's creation, a glance at Oscar's adventures will be of interest in showing the pervasiveness of Balzac's theme in these middle years, and providing a contrast to Lucien's failure to learn.

Oscar's narrative begins with a historical discussion of carriages and other means of transport, leading to a review of two vehicles that now, in the year 1822, carry mail and passengers between Paris and l'Isle-Adam. At the age of nineteen, Oscar is about to make his first journey alone. His mother accompanies him to the coach, saying to M. Pierrotin, the driver, that Oscar will visit a M. Moreau and that "son avenir exige impérieusement ce voyage." The public *voiture* soon becomes one of the important

Bildungsmächte in Oscar's life, and his mother warns against his foolish habit, born of bravado, of talking too much and too confidently, particularly dangerous in public vehicles where people of sense remain quiet. Balzac's eye gathers in the cruelty and tenderness of life, for Oscar is the object of two *sourires*. The first is one showing that disdain against which the young apprentice to life is too ignorant and timid for any defense. When Oscar gets into the cabriolet, his crude attire and awkward movements show how green he still is. His vanity suffers a new wound when he sees a knowing smile on the faces of two young men nearby. Meanwhile the poor mother, whose shabby appearance her son is already ashamed of, calls out a last admonition while looking tenderly at him, "lui souriant avec amour." Oscar begins to make those comparisons so revealing of good or ill to the beginning youth, comparing his own appearance with that of another traveler, and seeing that his mother's toilette was an important element in the *sourire* of the two young observers. He is greatly impressed by the elegance of his companion in the carriage, and now, in order to seem more mature, he falls into a series of lies and pretenses. When cigars are passed, he chokes, sneezes, and feels sick. After this humiliation Oscar tries to project himself as someone at least of future importance, and his reply to a question about the career planned for him by his family is: "la diplomatie." The Comte de Sérisy, incognito, "ne put s'empêcher de sourire" from his place in the diligence. If now Oscar had taken his mother's advice to be quiet in public vehicles, his worst failings might have escaped notice. But when it is observed that his mother is hardly in a social position suitable "pour une ambassadrice," Oscar commits "le crime odieux" of denying that the woman was his mother, just as the sisters Goriot deny their father, and Lucien in another sense will deny his father.

After failing in the law through his own stupidity and folly, Oscar joins the army under command of the Comte de Sérisy's son. Here at last a measure of discretion and self-control enables him to advance quickly, and he wins the favor of the Count when he rescues the Count's son in battle, losing his left arm in the fray. Now Oscar returns at age thirty-four, full of honors and dignity, and Balzac is careful to present him for the second time in Pierrotin's diligence, a magnificent new vehicle drawn by four horses. As if in deliberate contrast to the ignominious return of Lucien, we now see Oscar bronzed and manly in the carriage, in which everything is the opposite of the circumstances of his first voyage. The old tormenter Georges Marest is on hand, looking fat and debauched, in poor, neglected clothing, the contrast from his former bearing incredible to Oscar. The transformation on all sides is so great that Georges does not even recognize Oscar and his mother. And now it is Oscar who, in the midst of a discussion about Moreau, breaks in with the advice that started him on his career: You people should have learned, he says, to be quiet in public vehicles. Oscar prudently marries the daughter of Pierrotin, and becomes a model for other young men in the Balzacian universe. He ends a happy man, wise and capable, modest, devoid of pretense, holding to a middle course. "Il n'excite ni l'envie ni le dédain," and so, from a most unlikely "début dans la vie," he "arrives" in the manner suited to the other vain, ambitious youths who, in their folly, extend illusions of grandeur beyond a possible reality.

4

Illusions perdues
Part I

SETTING

We come now to this title that embraces all others, the longest work in the *Comédie* save for its sequel, which simply continues until Vautrin is disposed of. Taken together, "ces deux vastes romans," M. Béguin says, give a complete image of the Balzacian universe. Of the 265 characters who appear in the Rubempré cycle, over half, 147, appear elsewhere in the *Comédie*, showing how the Cycle is indeed a "plaque tournante" of the *Comédie* as a whole. In *Illusions* alone a much larger view of the world is taken than in *Le Père Goriot*, but as M. Guyon points out, its physical length is not determined by the time covered in the action, nor by the sheer quantity of events. We have noticed that Balzac cannot resist the temptation to write intrusive essays or to favor us with outside commentary, but these elements are less in bulk than one might suppose in a work ranging over so wide an area of French society.

Balzac has assigned himself an enormous task, which increases in difficulty, partly because *Illusions* overlaps other works in progress. Although we shall read the Rubempré cycle through from beginning to end as if its present sequence had always been the same, a reader contemporary with Balzac met with an entirely different sequence, in which a distorted chronology of composition presented events before they could have happened. Lucien's career then begins with *Les Deux poètes*, which is followed by *La Torpille*, in which he meets Esther at the opera and already seems rich and secure. Then the present Part II of *Illusions* appears, *Un Grand homme de province à Paris*, followed by Part III, entitled *David Séchard*, in which Lucien is totally defeated. The next installment is called *Esther*, with Lucien again apparently successful, and finally *Où mènent les mauvais chemins*, leading to death in prison. The tormented remains of proof and manuscript showing Balzac at work suggest that he was at greater pains than ever to produce a version that would satisfy his conscience. His laborious and costly changes have fascinated biographers; he assumed that any reading would be better than the first, any change an improvement. He was also worried about the seeming inferiority of Part III, presenting as it did the less dramatic and glamorous life of David and Ève at home, in no way equal to the powerful tableau of Paris. Nineteen times, M. Adam reports, did Balzac correct the proofs of Part III, as usual making lengthy additions.

For all of its special problems and the anguish of its creation, *Illusions* will show Balzac at the summit of his genius. More than a picture of French society, of the evils of journalism, of the dominance of money, *Illusions* is more symbolic than the familiar search for models and sources has allowed. Balzac does not discuss money because he is more interested in this than anything else. Every age may have such an all-powerful element; whatever its name it plays the same role as "money" in the *Comédie*. Similarly, the role of journalism does not require us to identify the chief journalists then living or to know in detail Balzac's own struggles against a venal press. Balzac will disclose the evil in the world by showing how evil had its way in his created universe. Journalism simply provided him with the most effective examples. We can believe, therefore, that if what is ugly and detestable in life were to show itself at any time most vividly in journalism, this is how it would do so. Thus the fate of Lucien is not only that of many foolish and vain young men of France who come to Paris seeking fortune; it is, as M. Bardèche says, "un destin symbolique" of a man, any man who is mistaken about his own character and energy and is unequal to the task imposed on himself. Yet Lucien never becomes the mature man his self-imposed destiny calls for; his effort is in the literal sense "premature," so that the distance between desire and fulfillment is never traversed. The action of *Illusions* takes place in a constant present, moving toward a world always in the future, a course inevitable for a tale of illusion. The hero moves toward hoped-for events to take place in some *avenir* still to come, for illusion again is a sentiment of the future where it must continue to be cherished or finally exposed and lost.

We speak of *illusion* as if the term as used in Balzac's title offered no problem, but if we allow ourselves to hover around the word in a series of groping questions, we shall better appreciate the scope of Balzac's meaning. Is an illusion a justified hope until proved otherwise? What other illusions are there, save lost ones, as Marianne Moore knows,

> hope not being hope
> until all ground for hope has
> vanished.

De Marsay's question, in his letter to Paul, seems to find illusions necessary: "Les illusions, ne sont-elles pas la fortune du cœur?" Illusion is indeed necessary to achievement, the narrator of *Les Employés* assures us. "Sans l'illusion, où irions-nous?" But then if a hope or desire is fulfilled, does it cease to be an illusion? Again, if we say with Ovid that only when fulfilled is desire seen to be an illusion, the problems mount. If there is a level, let us say Napoleon's, at which ambition and the desire for power and future glory succeed, does it all become an illusion when such a man suffers a last defeat? Does nothing show the falsity of ambition—its illusion, that is—so much as apparent success? Certainly at no point in Lucien's career do his dreams of *avenir* seem more mistaken to us than during the brief interval of good fortune, when we are especially moved by the irony of Célestine Rabourdin's invitation of Lucien to her salon because he is a "celebrity" and so part of a background through which his hostess hopes to promote the future success of her husband, likewise an illusion. While anyone may be the victim of unsound hopes, these are usually a function of youth in Balzac, especially of provincial youth with its lack of maturing experience. Illusion comes, then, of ignorance of life when young. It is any error or youthful failure to see the world as it is, and so will be inseparable from the *Bildungsroman* genre, immersed in the conflict between dream and reality. Maturity means the loss of illusions, which are inseparable from the human condition, lending it joy while they are cherished and bringing sorrow when lost. There is, in fact, as the narrator of *Sarrasine* speculates, only one hope that cannot be lost in human life here and now: the Christian belief in another world to come, making an invitation of death.

Balzac's title settles nothing by itself, but if we take "illusion" to mean any belief that turns out to be mistaken, not necessarily an ideal as in *Don Quixote* but any *idée fixe* or obsession, we shall find no one for whom we have any sympathy throughout Lucien's career who does not at some point suffer disillusion. In addition to all of these we have the disillusion of the author himself, who, assuming that the reader likewise cherishes illusions, sets out to destroy them. Some illusions are due to the generous sentiments of young and idealistic persons; often these should be lost or ought never to have been held, because they are directed to unworthy objects or based on ignorance. Most bitter of all, when lost, are the illusions based on sacrifice. Such loss is especially moving in Lucien's career when he sacrifices what is valuable in his own nature and accepts as his due the unselfish devotion of those who literally give their lives to his *avenir*. Balzac's somber view will carry us beyond mere negation or exposure, replacing illusion not only by seeing the world as common sense sees it, but sharing, as

Donald Fanger says, "the vision of a superior truth, as far above common sense, as it is above common illusion."

A work whose center describes a young provincial in Paris begins in a remote, seemingly irrelevant setting. The narrative opens with a calm review of old wooden printing presses, then still in use at Angoulême. One of these presses comes for half its value into the possession of Jérôme-Nicolas Séchard, who, though unable to read or write, is commissioned to make copies of decrees issued by the revolutionary convention. In time Séchard prospers greatly, but develops a strain of avarice. After the death of his wife he decides to educate their only son, to insure a successor in the business. When the succession is to pass from father to son, Balzac pauses, "dire un mot de l'établissement," which will serve, in all its crudity, as a setting for much of the coming action, and, like the unspeakable boardinghouse in *Le Père Goriot*, will at once reflect and influence coming events.

The press is nearly two hundred years old, and situated in a cavernous workshop so full of dangers that no visitor ever escapes without some injury to head or body. The court walls are covered with vines, befitting the habits of the drunken owner. A lean-to in ruins serves for wetting the paper and contains a sink—for washing the wooden forms—from which flows a mixture of ink and house slop, convincing the peasants that the devil has washed his face. On either side of the lean-to is the kitchen and a wood pile, and the working area shows not a single provision for safety, decency, or cleanliness. From this ground floor an old wooden staircase leads to three rooms above. The first of these with whitewashed walls serves as antechamber and dining room. The tile floor is never washed, the windows and door are brown with dirt, the room itself is crammed with papers, bottles, and plates still soiled from the miser's dinner. In the bedroom a leaded glass window gives light from the court. Old tapestries hang on the walls, the poster bed is decorated with curtains and a cover in red serge. Some old chairs, a desk, and a mantel clock complete the furnishings, which are somewhat more elaborate in the neighboring salon. Séchard's wife had begun the work of embellishing the salon, and traces of her labor in a sad cause were allowed to remain in the dreadful blue woodwork, the panels in tan and white decorated by paper showing oriental scenes, and the six chairs in blue sheepskin with backs representing lyres. His wife having died in the meantime, old Séchard abandons a work that shows no revenue; no curtains decorate the windows looking out on the Place Murier, the mantel has no candlestick, clock, or mirror. The exterior resembles the dingy scene within. Nothing has been repaired for thirty years, all left to the mercy of sun, rain, or storm, the result a mass of worm-eaten dilapidation, crumbling into ruin. The two young poets, soon to be met in this chaos of filth and neglect, would sometimes find the stench unbearable, escaping into the court to read and dream. The physical milieu creates the moral atmosphere as so often in the *Comédie*, and Balzac portrays a man by describing where he lives, as he does later with the journalist Lousteau's room.

Now he has once again prepared us for a sordid action by creating a scene that will contain nothing else, thereby, as Alain says, showing his power to make us foresee what will happen, yet astonishing us when it does. All is unrefined crudity, dangerous working conditions, an air of improvised expediency with nothing arranged or finished, nothing put out of sight but allowed to create an inhuman spectacle with no thought of the possible effect on others. The living quarters seem especially dehumanized, amid unfinished remnants of past efforts at color and style, the whole seemingly abandoned by anything like human concern.

FATHER AND SON

It is likewise no accident that the first character portrait is one of Balzac's "monsters" and that the first fully developed action is a typical Balzacian swindle, wherein old Séchard, with selfish cunning and hypocrisy, presents the outlines of a reality against which the manifold human illusions to come will contend in vain. The action begins with the swindle of a son by his father, and the climactic event of Part III will occur when the same gifted man is again cheated of his original work by a parcel of knaves. Such transactions are almost invariable in the great masterpieces of the *Comédie:* an honorable man falling victim to a conniving scoundrel, who cheats him of what he has. To the end of his career Balzac is moved by this spectacle, for with heartrending pathos he describes the cheating of poor old Pons and then Schmucke by the scheming landlady, the rapacious relatives, and their lawyer. Closely related is the theme of superior ability arousing the envy and hatred of mediocrity, so touchingly described by the great Desplein in *La Messe de l'Athée* and so dramatically clear in *Les Employés.* Like David, Rabourdin is vastly superior to the cheap mediocrities who ruin him; virtue in the *Comédie* is not defeated because it is stupid, but rather because it is too high-minded to have the right alertness to knavery and its capacities. David and his kind are tragic figures who lose more out of strength than of weakness, victims less of themselves than of the world and its gods.

Old Séchard displays his true nature chiefly at three points in the narrative: in the sale of a press to David, in his response to David's marriage, and in the tormented greed that seeks profit from David's invention. His nickname of L'Ours, the bear, refers to his shaggy physical presence, his drunkenness as related to the bear's habit of eating grapes, and his rapacity like that of a predatory wild animal. His avarice, then, is only one among a concentration of vices. It seems less powerful, more diffused than the kind of possession seen in Gobseck or Grandet, with whom Séchard is often compared. They have no areas of self-indulgence, and Grandet drinks none of the wine produced in such abundance on his property. Séchard certainly lacks the intellect, the philosophic grasp, and, indeed, the integrity of Gobseck. His little schemes are meager and furtive as he hunts about town for bargains, gloating over his petty transactions. He lacks the sheer size of Grandet's ambition, the foresight and calculated risks, even the joyous triumph when some cynical maneuver, like the gulling of Parisian financiers, defeats his enemies and establishes his monstrous superiority over any antagonist or obstacle. Séchard is alike incapable of Grandet's imperial accumulations and the sinister refrains of his horrible shrewdness. Typically he comes to the night in a drunken stupor, safe in the narrow confines of his villainy, whereas Grandet, at night, counts the new total of his *écus*, his mind awakening and quickening as darkness comes, like some feline jungle creature's, as he locks himself into his inner room, there in the silence of night to pore over his wealth and plan new acquisitions for the morrow. The smaller nature that is Séchard's contains only one emotion stronger than his selfish avarice: the malicious hatred of his son. The reptilian Petit-Claud will summarize the miser-father to his face: "You are jealous of your son, and have ruined him financially. You hate him because you have cheated him and because you have produced a man superior to yourself."

Late in the year 1819, when Eugène is suffering at Maison Vauquer, David returns from Paris, having learned typography through his own efforts without costing his father anything. He has no idea of his true greatness or talent, while his father is shrewdly planning to unload the aged business now that the Cointet brothers, manufacturers of paper, have bought up the other press in Angoulême. Seeing in David an enemy to be conquered, Séchard enumerates and lists every item of his wretched equipment down to the basins and wash-brushes, arriving at a figure of thirty thousand francs. With monstrous dexterity and readiness, as if having carefully rehearsed it all, the miser leaps about from one part of the machinery to the other, showing its wondrous efficiency. This old equipment and style suit the provinces, he says; they will never accept the inventions of modern Paris. He then enunciates one of the central themes of the *Comédie:* "Ha! ha! mon garçon, la province est la province, et Paris est Paris." Many illusions will be lost to show the truth of this trite yet prophetic line.

David's modest and tender nature is no match for this, and with painful irony he keeps repeating in his replies and questions, "mon père." The old man is David's father and will be treated as such, but David is not the miser's son save as one to be kept dependent and used, now cheated as a means of unloading worthless goods. The swindle can take place because the father has lost all paternal feeling, while the son cannot forget his filial duty. Séchard thus has all the advantage, for David's human decency renders him helpless, his naturally warm and faithful nature having no defense against his father's perfidy. His very intelligence and knowledge are an affliction, since they tell him clearly how worthless are the goods for which he must pay a fortune. But a part of the illusion he must now lose is that his father's intentions are good, that his father stresses the value of his machines because he is so genuinely attached to them. At last, however, he cries out, "Mon père, vous m'égorgez," and so Balzac records the first of the lost illusions of his title—David's trust in his father. Suffering and humiliation are made worse when in his lonely misery David asks after the fortune of his mother, of which there has been no accounting. The father replies that his dead wife brought only her intelligence and beauty to the marriage, the very terms David himself will use for Ève with full justification. Seeing his father now for what he is, David accepts his fate. After other negotiations and sales to the Cointets, the business is left suicidally crippled, while David's own lack of talent for administering such affairs dooms his circumstances to mediocrity.

ENTER LUCIEN

David's trials, we learn, are partly due to his negligence after he meets an old college friend. Before learning the name and age of Lucien Chardon, about twenty-one, we hear that he was "en proie à la plus profonde misère." The first statement made concerning Lucien summarizes the condition of unhappy poverty that will account for many of his later actions. Despite parents of fine human qualities, Lucien feels aggrieved. His mother, a woman of great beauty and dignity, has been reduced after her husband's death to working as a nurse to rich women in childbirth, using the name of Mme Charlotte. His sister Ève works in a linen shop, and the total income of this family of three is eight hundred francs a year. Lucien's father had been a doctor in the Republican armies, then a pharmacist in Angoulême where he had died prematurely before establishing a cure for the gout. Expecting to make a fortune, he had brought up his children at the highest level of "great expectations," consuming his resources and leaving them destitute. Lucien is therefore at odds with the world from the outset, his upbringing entirely wrong, itself based on an illusion that could not be sustained. Brought up to be rich, he is in fact so poor that in his weariness of struggling against bad luck, he is on the point of taking "un de ces partis extrêmes auxquels on se décide à vingt ans," the narrative's first hint of suicide. A further clash in Lucien's circumstances follows from another inheritance, the beauty and aristocracy of his mother. She was the last offspring of the de Rubempré family but has nothing to give her son beyond high birth and a great name. Lucien is therefore—fatally—half aristocrat, but he would have fared better without an alien presence in his blood that encourages his dreams of future greatness, his assumptions that he has a right to something denied to others, his desire to have the harvest without the labor, to possess what he has done nothing to earn. He lets himself be served, and now accepts the support of mother and sister, together with forty francs a month from David as ostensible payment for work done at the press. David's early disasters follow not only from his father's cruelty and his own goodness, but from the added burden of Lucien, who absorbs most of the income of his family, so touching in their limitless, almost religious faith in his *avenir*.

Balzac pauses in the narrative for a comparison of the two
"poètes"—one scientific, the other literary, and bound together
by a spiritual brotherhood amid their struggles against the injustice of the world. David, sharing the blind devotion of mother
and sister, draws closer to Ève herself, for whom his love grows
out of a common faith in Lucien. The portrait of David is one of
several presentations of himself offered at various times by Balzac,
especially in *Louis Lambert*, *Le Lys dans la vallée*, and *Albert Savarus*.
These, taken with the description by Théophile Gautier, give us
a clear view of Balzac's physical appearance: the powerful, thick
figure, the mane of black hair, full lips, strong nose, and magnificent black eyes of an unforgettable incandescence—obviously
a man of genius. Lucien, on the other hand, is all antique delicacy,
aristocracy, feminine grace and form. The Greek nose and fore-
head, beautiful blue-black eyes, in which M. Abraham sees an
ominous dualism of poet and arriviste, penciled brows and long
chestnut lashes, cheeks shining with a silky down in harmony with
the blond, naturally curly hair, white-gold temples of a divine
delicacy, short and noble chin—all of this seems drawn together
by the sad angelic smile, playing on coral lips enhanced by exquisite teeth. Lucien's figure is slender, of medium height, with
hands and feet to make one think him a woman in disguise,
especially in view of his feminine hips. The narrator seems to find
in this womanly contour a hint of Lucien's future unscrupulous-
ness, as if one unluckily deprived in society were justified in taking
any means to succeed. A creature half man and half woman
cannot in any case be effectively unified, and Lucien as man
becomes vain and foolish, while as woman he is passive and re-
ceptive, easily tempted, and taking without scruple whatever aid
or sacrifice comes his way. On one side Lucien is more confident,
more audacious than the melancholy David. He is more enter-
prising and changeable, his boldness clashing with his soft and
graceful appearance. Exaggerating the good and minimizing the
evil in his choices, he will not shrink from actions that seem

profitable. Balzac is careful here to show elements in Lucien's character of which the youth himself is not yet aware, restrained as he is now by "les belles illusions de la jeunesse," not yet tested in action by the world. The idolatrous devotion of his family, joined with the equally selfless love of the humble but superior David, are certain to encourage Lucien toward fatal illusions. His physical beauty is at once a striking asset and an ominous danger; it will encourage in others, as now in David, false notions of Lucien's superiority. Despite his timid and self-doubting nature, David will fight his way with heroic courage, whereas we are already made to suspect something missing in Lucien, despite his assumed superiority and David's belief in it. The lack of stamina, of principle and consistency, now only suggested, will show itself in compromise, haste, and the facile acceptance of any means toward illusory ends. As Mr. Beebe's résumé of Lucien at this time says, he is "a physically attractive, morally weak, and po-etically talented young man."

But now an interlude of work and thought helps the young poets to forget their grievances. They read enormously, think and dream, write various abortive works in the inexhaustible energy of youth, and so lay the foundations of their future renown, seemingly far removed from their favorite André Chénier and his "Elégie sur le suicide." One day when they are lost in extravagant flights of young hope, reality intrudes in the person of David's apprentice, Cérizet, capable, in the end, of a monstrous betrayal of his benefactor. We see again how closely *Illusions* is written when Cérizet is established so early as the messenger of reality— reality such as he represents indeed lying in wait to destroy the last vestige of David's youthful hopes. Cérizet introduces a man with a large manuscript, come to obtain an estimate of its printing cost. Is he now addressing Lucien Chardon himself, "un jeune poète promis à de si belles destinées," the fatal synonyms already coming forth with ironic force? When Lucien hears that the man has come from Mme de Bargeton, he so blushes and stammers as to reveal that he is hopelessly in love with a highborn woman inaccessibly removed from his own lowly world. David reminds him of distance, and is answered in terms of Lucien's illusion of love, more creditable to him than his illusion of social ambition: "La volonté de deux amants triomphe de tout."

LOUISE

As Lucien draws near to the woman whose influence will determine his destiny, he still seems the noble youth capable of loving friendship. He tells David that he has refused an invitation to read his poems before an aristocratic gathering unless David, "mon frère, mon ami," and his superior in talent, is also invited. He awaits a reply, and if it is negative, Lucien will never set foot in Mme de Bargeton's house. This is a noble sacrifice by a friend willing to be faithful, to live by his declared principles. Yet Lucien has fixed the terms of his sacrifice with dramatic eloquence, making David realize to the full how much is surrendered on his behalf. He offers a sacrifice that David would never have asked, one that David never would have mentioned if he had been making it for Lucien. This open declaration makes Lucien's failure to live up to it the more ironic, showing how at the very moment of the sacrifice, he is in fact insuring that it can never be sustained. If he had said nothing, his yielding to temptation would not seem so great a betrayal when it comes. But he is too vain and melodramatic for silence, with a kind of humorless Chattertonism on this side of his character. Nothing is so important to him as *his* suffering, *his* sacrifice, the injustice that *he* suffers. The *Bildungsroman* hero, in striving toward maturity, must learn to forget himself, as Lucien never does. Typically, Balzac now pauses to analyze Mme de Bargeton and her past, so that we will understand her fully and will accept the fantastic accident of her permitting Lucien to enter her house. Mr. Bart has commented on the dynamic presentation of Louise's early life, which comes powerfully alive through Balzac's language. She was Marie-Louise

Anaïs de Nègrepelisse, Louise as Lucien is allowed to call her, of an ancient noble family, related to the Marquise d'Espard, an important fact later on. By chance during the Revolution she learns to enjoy music and literature from an Abbé hiding out with her family, who in gratitude oversees her education in humane and scientific learning. Thus Louise early developed qualities of mind and culture, of judgment and perception totally unsuited to the life she has to lead. Set apart from others she becomes vain, cynical, and disdainful. Like Mathilde de la Mole, she is superior to those about her, which has the bad effect of increasing her arrogance and diminishing the graceful if perfidious politeness of the true grande dame. In marriage she preferred someone greatly inferior, whom she could dominate, and this need to command helps explain Lucien's attraction for her in his helplessness. She marries a man over twenty years her senior, with whom she has no problems, who will leave her free, when her father dies and her money comes, for adventure in Paris. Meanwhile in the narrow life of the provinces she has no outlet for her mind and accomplishments, and so indulges in fanciful flights, adoring Byron and Rousseau until she idealizes men of genius. The first eighteen years of her marriage pass with no access to what she so admires from afar. A brief passion for a young officer ends when he is killed in battle, and she retires into a pensive, half monastic seclusion.

Such is the woman to whom Lucien is introduced by the Baron Sixte du Châtelet, the man sent with a manuscript to David's press. He has come to Angoulême as director of excise taxes, and poses as a man of the world, an experienced diplomat and soldier, who knows nothing of music and the arts but is careful to seem informed. He quickly realizes that Louise is the most considerable figure locally; he gains access to her through a supposed common interest in music, and lays plans at long range to marry her when her aging husband is no more. Châtelet's calculation, shrewdness, and balance of everything toward his own ends is an almost comic exaggeration of the means required to rise in the world. He now cultivates Louise assiduously, bringing her books, reading to her, and arousing interest in the new generation of young poets. Indeed, he assures her, there is here, in Angoulême itself, a fine young poet, truly "un grand homme futur," whose poems have been shown him by the headmaster of the college. Louise is overjoyed and would be happy to see the gifted youth. Châtelet, thinking to increase his own favor, arranges for Lucien's presentation.

Balzac has prepared us for this moment in some twenty pages of careful background. We must be made to appreciate the stunning impact on Lucien's mind and heart when he receives the fantastic news that the doors of the Hôtel de Bargeton are about to swing open before him. He first confides his secret to Ève, who in her devotion provides a new outfit of clothes and shoes, decorating Lucien's best shirt with a new frill herself, overjoyed and proud when at last she sees her brother in the new finery. So clothes also establish themselves early as inseparable from Lucien's illusions of future glory. As in *Eugénie Grandet*, Balzac is here deeply moving with the simple phrase "la pauvre fille" as Ève walks with her brother to his meeting and finally sees him go from a distance. We think of Eugène when Balzac again makes his theme explicit: "La sainte créature, elle ignorait que là où l'ambition commence, les naïfs sentiments cessent." The effect on both Lucien and Louise of their first meeting, however, is all that they had hoped for. Balzac fixes this in our minds in contrast to the first sight they have of each other in Paris, clearly identifying the illusion eventually to be lost. Louise is enchanted with Lucien's beauty, his appealing voice and shy manners. To him in turn Louise is ravishingly beautiful, glamorous, and feminine, everything about her distinguished as she keeps her seat with a royal air. Three hours pass in a dream that he longs to make eternal as her soul speaks eloquently to his own. As he is gradually drawn into this new society, Lucien foolishly supposes that

Louise's friends are gracious until he sees that they despise a pharmacist's son as of no consequence, and that, like Julien Sorel before him, he must see politeness from above as a sign only of contempt. But Louise herself flatters him and pushes him forward, for her own feelings hover between reserve and tenderness. After two months their intimacy increases, they grow more familiar, until she confesses an unhappy love for the young man lost in war whose portrait he admires. The narrative here falls into familiar military language; Louise seems to review the usual female deceptions and sets up fortified positions which the young lover is then to overcome by assault. When she permits herself the chaste pleasure of giving him a kiss on the brow, he loses a golden chance for progress. He should now have fallen into impassioned discourse to sweep the beloved object into his arms, but he has too little knowledge of women or of the world to seize his advantage, foolishly giving in to her apparent reserve.

Meanwhile the wily Châtelet grows jealous, and thinks to get rid of Lucien by revealing the fact that his mother is the Mme Charlotte who works as a confinement nurse. But Louise is adamant and forces her circle to accept Lucien's presence; she plans a great evening, at which Lucien is to read a work of his own creation before an audience containing the flower of provincial aristocracy.

TEMPTATION

We come now to the first in the series of temptations that will beset Lucien in his quest for glory. Louise assumes the role of Satan the tempter, and Balzac refers directly to the Bible and *Paradise Lost*. When Louise holds out high society to Lucien as his proper sphere, "Lucien mordit à la pomme de luxe aristocratique et de la gloire." What must he do to gain the world? He must repudiate his father, ignore the outcry that will arise against him, and allow Louise's powerful relative, Mme d'Espard, to persuade the king to make legitimate the change to his mother's name.

Lucien must also discard his liberal sentiments in favor of royalism; he must step back in history and quit the fanciful equality of 1793, to thirst once more after social distinctions. If we remember throughout this scene David's modest resignation and genuineness, the full measure of Lucien's danger will emerge. David would never fall so low to obtain rewards so specious: elevation in the world, disappearance of social barriers, a sudden bound upward into the empyrean.

Louise's method is to attack Lucien's prejudices and inhibitions. She offers him the romantic concept of a poet genius who owes nothing to his family: a gifted man is above the ordinary demands of law and nature, and the lives of others should give way before his needs. Louise cites the behavior of great men like Caesar and Napoleon who seemed bad sons, fathers, or brothers but who became the pride of their families and the world. Lucien fails to see the absurdity in this portrait of himself as a superman to whom all is permitted. Louise anticipates and so helps to destroy the remnants of decent human feeling in her victim. To her reasonings he responds without pausing to consider the price being demanded for success, that he become a bad son and brother. Louise seems to think that success is worth this or any price, but Lucien does not so much as notice that a price is being asked that lies outside the permitted bounds of natural feeling. This first great temptation reaches down to the most elemental of human relationships. Louise points out the troubles besetting one who faces the world; men of genius must face great dangers that are insurmountable to mediocrity. In Lucien's case he must audaciously repudiate his father and take his mother's name. Lucien is therefore tempted to do far worse than Vautrin's proposal to Eugène: he must kill his own father, or act as if he had never existed. Lucien is ashamed of his father for no proper human reason: he was a gifted, superior man of whom any son might be proud. Balzac presents the emotion of this scene with such power that we ask whether he is not in error. We can never be surprised by any future act of Lucien's, however degrading, cowardly, or selfish. If he does this, then he is already corrupted and capable of anything, so that his eventual failure as a human being seems clearly marked too soon.

But Lucien has enough remnants of youthful honor to make a fight for his moral dignity, and his suffering is the measure of a soul worth saving. He writes Louise a long letter full of noble sentiments, idealizing his family and David, for whom he asks a reception like his own. He would renounce all rather than betray David, who must share in his success. This is, to be sure, a foolish, impetuous letter, but it shows Lucien aware of the feelings he ought to cherish. He does have a soul to lose, and Balzac thereby makes him more of a tragic figure than simply a failure. He now sways between good and evil, as thoughts of his family suggest that he should rise by his own powerful effort to fulfill their hopes so tenderly concentrated in him. The military language adopted is appropriate to struggle, to Lucien's being assailed, to an object of aggression hard to oppose. He is beset, then, by doubts and fears, taking the form of questions. Will Louise be angry at his letter? Will she receive David into her house? Will the ambitious one himself be cast out, to fall back into the plain below? Lucien sees the distance between a queen and her favorite, and certainly David cannot undo in a moment his own labor of five months. Balzac continues to excuse or at least to explain the course of Lucien's behavior, and now shows the change into worldly calculation. This follows in part from Lucien's born aristocratic instinct, which makes difficulties, for noble sentiments do not create noble manners. The way of the world, if one is not born to it, commits one to an education that chance must second by a certain elegance of figure, a certain distinction of tone. Lucien himself has all of this, which is sadly missing in David. He has the highly arched foot of a gentleman, while David has flat feet and the general cast of countenance of his appalling father. Lucien can even hear the raillery that might descend on David from high Angoulême, and see the smile on the face of Louise.

Although Balzac is careful to shield Lucien from the charge of being ashamed of David, the emotion of shame enters, the shame that Dickens understands so powerfully in *Great Expectations*. Shame comes certainly to the *Bildungsroman* hero, who is rising in the world to become socially above his past and the people who were once good enough for him. He puts these aside when they no longer serve his purposes or even obstruct them, and despite Johnson's facile defense of men who drop their early associates by the way, Balzac and Dickens reveal with sorrow the wounds so inflicted on family and friends. Lucien begins to see that introducing David as planned will not do, and we again have the sense that he is undergoing one of a series of experiences that affect all like himself. He is representative youth, being acted on in ways not always part of his own character, presenting obstacles that he must face as they are made to appear by the recurring forces of life. Thus after the hours of poetry and devotion, "l'heure de la politique et des calculs sonnait pour Lucien." The time simply has come for other sentiments to declare themselves as Lucien arrives at a new stage in his *Bildung*. So he repents of having sent the letter and wishes that he could recover it, for he suddenly catches a glimpse, through an opening, of the pitiless laws of the world.

His agony is the greater as he sees his father's name displayed at the pharmacist shop over which he lives in a humble room. Lucien undergoes shame of his father, of his father's house, and indeed of his own behavior. There for all to see in yellow letters on a green panel are the words, "Pharmacie de POSTEL, successeur de Chardon." Anyone who passes by in a carriage can see this, and will therefore know who his father was. No concealment is possible of the thing that must be concealed if Lucien is to rise in his *avenir*. We see that Lucien is suffering, and that Balzac will allow some sympathy for him. He cannot bear the disharmony between his coming good fortune and this house; he who loves and may soon possess Mme de Bargeton must now return and live in this rat's nest. Shame clearly allies itself to fear and deception, and discloses ever new dimensions as Balzac looks more deeply into this young soul. If the father's name will do him harm, then it must be hidden or done away with like the body of someone Lucien has murdered. But the constant chance of its being discovered engenders, in turn, the fear of discovery and its consequences. The shame of his father compels Lucien to a kind of patricide, and just as he must conceal his father's identity, so he must conceal his own crime in destroying it. Mingled in all these complex emotions is some bitterness against his father, who, as Lucien is reminded by Postel the chemist, was over-cautious in not confiding the secret of his discovery. Had he done so, Postel could now finish the experiments, and they could all be rich. Is the true shame, then, not of his father's name but of his poverty? If Chardon had made a fortune for his children, would Lucien now be ashamed to bear his name?

Presently Lucien receives a reply to his letter. Louise writes with an air of ambiguous caution, admitting all the reasons for receiving the worthy David, but posing some hesitations and, indeed, a restriction on her consent that contains an ominous phrase. She would like to see David first, to judge him, "savoir par moi-même, dans l'intérêt de votre avenir, si vous ne vous abusez point." The appeal is to Lucien's selfish interest, and he makes the mistake of supposing that the letter is a clear victory for his high principles, not seeing that in the high world of his aspirations, "yes" and "no" may lead to their opposites. Absorbed in reading the letter, he does not attend to Ève, who has prepared dinner. She gets his attention by saying, "Tiens, Lucien. Je t'ai eu des fraises." Thus when he returns in disgrace from Paris, the narrative will itself return to this moment, when Ève asks Marion to get Lucien some of his favorite strawberries.

David himself now solves the moral problem in a speech of the deepest pathos and resignation. He sees that he would be unacceptable in the world above, crude and humble artisan fixed low in society as he is. Lucien, however, is destined for honor and the world's applause. David does not envy his friend; on the contrary, he consecrates himself with unalterable love to his friend's glory. Amid this overflowing eloquence, David looks timidly at Ève. Her eyes are full of tears, "car elle devinait tout," the narrator simply says. She divines all? Is it Ève, then, who is the first to see what Lucien really is, to divine his coming, totally unpardonable behavior? David refers to Lucien's beauty and the handsome appearance he presents in new clothes by way of contrast to his own awkward crudity. We know that David is ironically expressing nothing more than Lucien's own thoughts, when he finally suggests that, in order to conform to the prejudice of names, Lucien can call himself Lucien de Rubempré, whereas his friend is and always will be just David Séchard: thus poor David declares his own value and exposes the folly of Lucien.

Lucien rushes to David and embraces the friend whose decent modesty has rescued him. Indeed, why should he not now be tender to a man who is expressing, out of friendship, the same thoughts inspired by his own ambition? The effect of this heroism is, alas, to increase Lucien's vanity and to devour the remains of his goodness. Three devoted people support his egotism, which in turn is soothed by Louise, who justifies his forgetting any obligation to sister, mother, and friend. So with eager confidence Lucien faces his great chance at the soirée in his honor, where he is about to absorb "sa première expérience des ignorances et des froideurs mondaines!"

Two Evenings

Balzac conveys these lessons by a device already common in French fiction, the "soirée" with a literary or musical performance. In his ignorance Lucien arrives too early, finding only M. de Bargeton himself in the salon. An amusing "conversation" follows, and the stupidity of Louise's husband is almost as great as that of Lucien's own responses, Lucien foolishly thinking the man to be impressive and substantial. Châtelet arrives, dressed in elegant Parisian style, takes out his lorgnon like de Marsay to come, and crushes the poor youth by an arrogant survey of his costume, obviously of local origin. Lucien is rescued by the entrance of Louise herself, groomed with almost theatrical effect. The guests now arrive, the clergy first, then the aristocracy including the Baron and Baronne de Rastignac, the Baronne's aunt and two daughters, and finally members of the administration. Balzac does not attempt to take his reader by surprise again, and he prepares us for the humiliation of Lucien, which becomes inevitable when we know where and before whom it will occur. In great detail the company is made to pass before us, showing how remote they are from Lucien's experience, how hopeless his desire to make way among them by means of his poetic talent. The long description has an immense cumulative effect like Balzac's other strategies. Lucien has no chance whatever in this society. The impregnable stupidity, smugness, and narrowness of these people protect them, along with their vigilance, their envious resentment of anything different from or superior to themselves. Balzac keeps Lucien waiting for a length of time covered by more than six pages, until there can be no mistaking the hostile air. A whole area of the world springs to life, with scarcely any conversation. These people need say nothing as Balzac, with deft and infallible touches, shows them for what they are.

With equal mastery Balzac exposes the consequences, unforeseen by Lucien, of a change in his name. He hopes to rise in this world under a new name, but this is only a means of confusion and terror when most of the guests call him Chardon while Louise and others use his mother's name. We remember now, as we return to Lucien's other world, that David was the last to urge a change in name, and we see in the name-change the betrayal of that world for the sake of this cruel and false one.

Lucien now faces the audience, the women ranged in a circle, the men standing behind. His heart pounds, all eyes are turned upon him, as upon an alien presence, a guilty thing about to be fatefully summoned. His malaise grows through something he should have foreseen, but something certain to terrify a youth new to the world. What is his name? A man still unsure of himself should at least know who he is. One name clearly known to be his own is a fact, an identity from which he can exert himself. But two names divide his force and make ridiculous his ambitions in this company. Interrogatory glances seem to ask, "who are you then?" making a falsehood of either reply. The change intended to gain access to this world now ironically excludes him. Lucien becomes impatient to begin reading, so as to assume a new posture, an attitude that might end his inner torment. But all around him the talk goes on of people and things he knows nothing about, the audience itself containing scarcely anyone who comprehends poetry or has any idea of what to expect.

At last, Lucien places himself at the round table near Louise and begins to read from André Chénier, of whom no one in Angoulême has ever heard. As the reading goes on, Lucien is a victim of hellish torment amid a buzz of conversation and before yawning, half-open mouths of the bored, impatient, or indifferent. Lucien is frantic, a cold sweat inevitably moistens his shirt, his heart bleeds. He forces himself to continue until an inward melody isolates him from this odious world, and he sees the onlooking faces as through a mist. When Louise asks him to read from his own work, Lucien recites A Elle, his poem to her, which reveals her secret before the other women. One of them, Amélie de Chandour, resenting Louise's pride, now summarizes the aristocratic objections to Lucien. Louise has degraded her class by introducing the son of a pharmacist and a nurse, whose sister is a shop girl, and he himself employed as a printer. The element in common here is clearly work, so that Louise has offended the company by patronizing a man who works, whose family is now working, and who is descended from a man who worked. The primacy of work is unmistakable in the *Comédie*, and the falsity of this world that despises work will return to mind when Lucien makes the fatal choice of the easy road to success.

Now, with a cruelty for which Lucien is unready, his enemies prepare for execution. The former consul, Francis de Hautoy, talks to the Bishop and pretends to share the prelate's interest in Lucien's poems. He refers to Lucien's mother and her qualities, saying that she helped her son with his compositions, he in turn adoring his mother so that he is pleased when justice is done to her. Amid these strangers Lucien continues to suffer: he cannot think what to reply to the stupidities uttered, he is called by both his names, he commits a blunder that causes Louise to blush to her ears. One by one, the guests deal with him as maliciously and disdainfully as they can, but the Bishop seems kind as he defends the poet and poetry as sacred and beloved of God, and places his hand on the handsome brow before him. Louise looks around in triumph, and Lucien is happy again as he launches into a spirited reply on the nature of a poet, his sensibility, the knowledge and experience he must have before the birth of his creation. He falls unhappily into a childbirth metaphor—saying that a mind must be pregnant for a long time—when de Hautoy interrupts to say, "Votre accouchement sera laborieux." Then comes the maliciously prepared blow: the Bishop innocently observes, "Votre excellente mère pourra vous aider . . . ," thinking to please Lucien with a reference to his mother's aid, only to insult him and her by alluding to her work. We return again to Lucien's other world, to the shameful price he is willing to pay for success amid these cruel and ignorant enemies. The scene has been managed with telling effect as a kind of drawing-room drama. The plot moves toward the humiliation of the poet as planned. He seems unable to defend himself as the blows fall one by one. This trend is seemingly halted when the Bishop defends Lucien and places his episcopal hand in a sort of sacrament of Confirmation on the poet's head. Louise's eyes flash, but the plot

suddenly gathers new force and rushes to the final blow in the
Bishop's mention of Lucien's heroic mother and her work.

We can be sure how the happiness of the cruel will now show
itself, as their eyes light up and "un sourire de satisfaction
aristocratique" appears on every mouth. Louise does her best to
console the poet when the company scatters for conversation,
cards, or dancing. Lucien himself is furious, his obsession to
triumph over this high world intensified. At first the blow sends
Lucien "au fond de l'eau," suggesting his first contemplated
suicide by water, but he stamps his foot and returns to the surface.
Louise continues her whispered flatteries, and her predictions of
future success, aided by compliments from the Bishop and Laure
de Rastignac, only deepen the bitterness of present defeat.

The contrast between two worlds of which Balzac is such a
master becomes devastating when Lucien returns to find Ève and
David beside the river. If the powerful exposure of the false world
just experienced leaves him still aspiring to succeed in it, he must
be foolish and corrupt to prefer those who have tortured him in
their stupidity and arrogance to those he now sees again in this
world below the citadel: here all is natural, genuine, tender,
and devoted. As he leaves high Angoulême and takes the long road
down, "Voilà donc le monde," he cries. Yet, knowing the world
for what it is, he does not abandon it. On the contrary, the rage
of ambition renews its force in him. Like all men arriving in a too
elevated sphere before they have the strength to maintain themselves, Lucien promises himself that he will sacrifice everything to
remain in high society. Ève and David listen in silence as he pours
out the torrent of his sorrow, declaring that he will marry Louise
when her husband dies, assured as he is of her love for him and her
belief in his future. The speech betrays a monstrous self-absorp-
tion, a vain forgetfulness, so that he is astonished when Ève and
David announce their coming marriage. Balzac's skillful use of
varied synonyms for Lucien, depending on the action of the moment, emerges again as Lucien is called "l'amant de Madame de

Bargeton," this role accounting for his response to the news. He had begun to plan a marriage for Ève into a powerful family, a marriage that would be a support to his own ambition. Now her decision looms as one more obstacle to his own success in the world, for Louise would not accept David as her brother-in-law. She is right, he decides, as similarly Eugène would tell himself that Vautrin was right, Louise being a step toward Vautrin in Lucien's life. She is right, for "les gens d'avenir" are never understood by their families. *Avenir* is steadily gathering its illusory force.

But Lucien's mobility comes to his rescue as the other side of his nature responds to David's happy predictions and Ève's caresses. Then, too, the lovely night, the river, the stars, and the mild air conspire to make him forget the bleeding crown of thorns thrust on him by society. We see that all is not finally lost of Lucien's young goodness, which, as the narrator assures us, might in other times and circumstances have prevailed. So the ambitious one presses his brother's hand and returns to peace.

TEMPTATION

Louise's response to the news of a coming marriage in Lucien's family brings another form of temptation, the second in a series of three leading to the betrayal of his family. She offers her exclusive interest in Lucien, a devotion to his future greatness, while in return he must give up his family and friend, devoting himself wholly to Louise. The price is all the more terrible since Lucien continues to accept the labor and sacrifice of those he is asked to betray. Louise's approach now is almost maternal: she seeks, through pity and sympathy, by reassuring, calming fear, to alienate Lucien from his family, and then by specious argument, half-truths, and cunningly devised questions, to overcome his remaining scruples. She passes her hands through his beautiful hair, asking, What is your family—"où tu es une exception"—to me? She withdraws him farther from an influence that combats her own, while flattering his vanity and blurring his vision. Indeed his family means nothing to her, though it should mean a great deal to him. Then comes an argument from false analogy: If Louise's father were to marry his servant, would not Lucien be upset? This seems to make David a servant, and Ève an aristocrat, like Louise's father. Here the effect is almost subliminal, degrading David and so making it less of an offense to betray him, appealing as well to the aspiring half-nobleman who is thinking of changing his name. The simple assertion, too, that lovers are a complete family to themselves alone, makes Louise seem enough for Lucien, who has no need of his family.

Meanwhile, the relationship between Louise and Lucien is much debated, although she keeps the door of her room open during his visits, to avert suspicion against a still virtuous love. Louise's life is so public that she is finally exhausted by the tyranny of scrutiny and suspicion. Châtelet spies continually on an affair that he does not consider as innocent as it is, and poses everywhere as a defender of Louise's reputation. Lucien himself, after six months, has developed the assurance to bring the affair to completion, and appears one day bent on final conquest. She repulses him, saying "ne gâtez pas l'avenir," and he now falls in tears at her feet, the tears of a half-humiliated poet, of a half-frustrated child. At this moment Stanislas de Chandour enters, sees the tableau, and withdraws to Châtelet, who is at the door. Here follows a kind of preposterous snowball comic effect, as in Cervantes. Stanislas and Châtelet spread the word, the story is enlarged and embellished, everyone in town hears of it, new details are added, conclusions and suppositions become more extreme until word of it reaches the Bishop's palace itself, the snowball ever increasing both in size and rapidity. Châtelet informs Louise of the rumors, and when she insists that her husband demand a retraction from Stanislas, the duel for which Châtelet is hoping follows. Like Iago, Châtelet manipulates evil deeds from his own posture of innocence and honor. If de Bargeton is killed, Louise as widow cannot marry Lucien, the cause of all the dishonor. "Du Châtelet fit le grave et le mystérieux," honest Iago that looks dead with grieving, indeed.

After the duel and de Bargeton's success, Lucien receives a letter from Louise asking to speak with him. The scene changes to David and Ève, making another contrast to the cheap intrigue of Louise's world and the misguided folly of Lucien's striving after an *avenir* still further contaminated by the means taken to attain it. David's house is now ready for Ève after the wedding planned for the day after tomorrow. The love and sacrifice lavished on the house have transformed it. When David shows it to Ève's mother, she murmurs, "Ève sera comme une princesse." Lucien himself is at this moment in the presence of Louise, who is announcing her coming departure for Paris and her desire that Lucien should accompany her. The narrative in typical Balzacian style gathers an astonishing rapidity and concentration, the excitement and dramatic force more effective in contrast to the measured pace of the beginning and the slow movement of provincial life. After Châtelet's conversation with Louise, less than three days pass from the challenge and the duel itself next morning through the wedding date to come. Events pause briefly while we see the house that David has prepared for Ève. Then Lucien goes to Louise, and events resume their headlong pace. She is leaving tomorrow night; he is to precede her and wait for her carriage en route. In less than forty-eight hours after the duel, they have stolen away for Paris.

Louise's third and last temptation is mainly a rhapsodic speech on Paris, and the need of all great men to go there. With intense rapidity, as if not wishing to allow time for reflection, Louise repeats her flatteries of Lucien's talent and paints a glowing picture of the capital of intellect, where Lucien will meet the great men of his time. Louise will see that he meets Mme d'Espard, in whose salon he will have access to the rich, the great, and the famous. His beauty and genius will excite their interest. Once in view, he will find a thousand opportunities, and the Bourbon kings will favor him if he comes forward as a religious, royalist poet. The price for all this does not fully emerge at once, and Satan-Louise ends: Let Lucien go where all men of genius have gone; now let him follow her. Showing the kingdoms of the world, as it were, Satan cries: All this will I give thee, if falling down thou wilt adore me. "Ne le voulez-vous pas," Lucien hears; he sheds a tear, embraces Louise, and covers her neck with violent kisses.

BETRAYAL

He suddenly expands, as if before he had employed only half of his mind. His ideas enlarge, he is obsessed by dreams of Paris and its splendors, Paris—an Eldorado to every provincial imagination —in contrast to life in exile, provincial life, which is, Henry James observes, "a tissue of sordid economies and ignoble jealousies and fatuous tittle-tattle, in cold, musty, unlovely houses." Paris wears a golden robe, its head is crowned with royal stones, its arms are open to talent. Lucien forgets that in Eldorado itself the jewels were worthless mud and pebbles. Next he dreams of the tributes in store for him where everything smiles on genius, where poetry is welcomed and repaid. Lucien is sure that when the publishers see the first pages of his novel, they will ask only how much he wants. To crown all, Louise will belong to him alone. But as he devours Louise with kisses, he utters a cry, which, like Eugène's final tear, marks the end of his youthful goodness: "Mon Dieu, ma sœur se marie après-demain." Balzac pauses again over a meaning that must not escape us. The powerful bonds that attach young hearts to their families and first friends, "à tous les sentiments primitifs," were about to receive "un terrible coup de hache." The essential ties binding him to the human relationships that still remain to him are about to be broken. If Lucien does this, we are warned, he will be capable of any iniquity. He has already betrayed his natural father and will eventually betray Vautrin, acting as his father. All of this, and for what? For Paris, the illusion that contains all others.

Louise's behavior seems astonishing at this point, unless we have understood the depth of her own feelings, or underestimated her powers as an actress, her obstinate determination to impose her own will. She is intensely female, the woman scorned, and the contemptuous aristocrat all in one when she refers bitterly to "cette noce de bourgeois et d'ouvriers," for which Lucien would give up their love and "les nobles joies." As she falls swooning to the sofa, Lucien rushes to her begging forgiveness and cursing his family, David, and Ève. He would kill himself in his despair, but Louise forgives him and so has her way. After his surrender, Lucien returns to his apartment, pursued by his "espérances" like Orestes and the Furies. But are these hopes also the torments of his own conscience, as in Aeschylus? Balzac leads us to another metaphor to explain the hero's anguish: Lucien divides his reflections between self-accusation and then self-justifying excuses, knowing full well the baseness of an action that is now unavoidable, "car il n'y a rien de jésuite comme un désir."

M. Cayrol has likened Ève to Iphigenia, "la jeune fille qui marche au sacrifice," and Balzac spares us nothing of her pitiable wound. David enters, the four people in the room "gardèrent un profond silence," a silence that will return to mind in the wordless greeting to Lucien a year hence: as silence and shame are the only responses to the fact of his betrayal, so also will they be the only possible greeting when Lucien's failure is visited once again upon his family. The need for ready money is met by Postel, whose note David consents to sign, his eyes full of tears at his friend's cruel indifference to their labor and sacrifice. After a moment of tender affection, Lucien falls back upon his trusty Jesuitism; when he should be so ashamed of himself that he would revoke his treason, he invents lofty excuses for it instead. The excuses take the form of seven questions, which, as in Louise's temptations so far, tend to blur the sin being committed and justify all on supposititious grounds of his destiny, his terrible *avenir*. Ultimately, Lucien is demanding: Must I not sooner or later do what I am doing today? Does not my whole fortune depend on entry to the salon of la Marquise d'Espard?

So once again David and Ève make the sacrifice for Lucien's ambition. The two poets go to Postel and sign his note, returning to find Ève and her mother on their knees in prayer. The prayer scene draws together the entire effect of Lucien's betrayal and its meaning for them all, and Balzac achieves a heartrending pathos, an almost Shakespearean beauty in the spectacle of so much human goodness offering itself for hollow illusion. The fact of illusion is clear from Balzac's repetition of the terms he has so carefully established as the synonyms of folly: "combien d'espérances," "le bonheur à venir," "les destinées de Lucien." Prayer, indeed, the appeal to God is the final resort, as if to say, only God can preserve such illusions any longer. Looking on now, David issues a powerful warning that is also an ominous prophecy: "Si jamais, tu oubliais cette scène . . . tu serais le dernier des hommes." Will the day truly come when Lucien falls into a sin past any forgiveness? As he goes with David to the rendezvous and they see the old coach appear, Lucien throws himself into David's arms. Does this mean that his shame has become contrition, that he would now turn back if he could? Then David prays aloud, "Dieu veuille que ce soit pour ton bien." This is at once a prayer to God and a plea to Lucien himself, equally futile in both cases. It is too late: a prayer for God's help seems as hopeless as a plea for the return of nobility to Lucien's soul, nobility that took its last breath in Lucien's cry in the midst of his impassioned kissing of Louise. Is it true, as the narrator still believes, that Lucien's shifting character could lead him as readily into good as into evil courses? The action as it unfolds suggests, rather, a weak, deluded fool, who must sooner or later behave abominably, to his ruin. Insofar as Lucien has the stature of a tragic figure, he must have possessed the best qualities as well, and this gives us the essential feeling of waste and loss. Yet he seems good only if there is no strong temptation to be otherwise. As Ève sees when she refuses, later on, to disclose David's hiding place to Lucien, he must not be enabled to commit folly, since he seems more likely to do wrong than right if he has the chance.

A year hence Lucien will be afflicted by feelings of guilt and shame when he steals back in defeat. Yet he will not accuse himself of having been foolish in his illusions and wicked in the shameful means taken to fulfill them. He will be ashamed only of failure, his only sin defeat. Now he makes a clandestine departure, starting like a guilty thing indeed, stealing away from home to go to Paris with Louise. Does he feel guilt and shame? Unless he is doing what is clearly wrong, why this concealment? If success is to be achieved only by such means, it is clearly an illusion not worth pursuing, an enterprise doomed because of its moral and human price. An illusion of success, based on his illusion that Louise loves him and will aid him unselfishly, in turn demands for its fulfillment the basest ingratitude and the betrayal of genuine love and sacrifice. The means are not only wicked, they are unsound, and so doubly worthless. Lucien's ignominy is ironic, then, for it is in vain and never to be repaid.

Mme Bérard has written perceptively of Balzac's portraits of Louise and her young lover, seeing Louise in particular as growing steadily less sympathetic. The many corrections made before Balzac rested his case all tend progressively to darken the figure of Louise, so that we are adequately prepared for her behavior in Paris by early hints of perfidy and meanness. So also Lucien displays a progressive corruption. First he seems pure, although menaced by a secret weakness. Then Balzac's view of him changes: he is seen as a corrupt being who still conserves, like a fallen angel, some regret for the paradise from which he has fallen. The changes may seem too rapid, but they are imposed on Balzac by the novel's own requirements, which cannot wait for a natural evolution. Lucien is thus made to develop qualities demanded by later parts of the work but not yet fully implied in his first innocence. Yet this very innocence makes him as ignorant of life as he is, and he cannot be blamed when he fails to see the damaging consequences of his early choices. It is often remarked that in dreams a going up means a descent, and vice versa, so that Lucien's ascent to high Angoulême marks the fall of his moral being. Once he is bent on conquering these heights, as the military metaphor demands, he must beware of a pyrrhic victory. By definition, then, the world to which he aspires is no better than the one from which he comes. Its superiority is passing, ephemeral, wholly material and of the moment, made to seem alluring by the immediate difficulty of attainment. Lucien does not see that to get what it has to offer, he must give up something priceless from within himself. Every step "upward" then, every temptation yielded to leaves its mark, like sin on the picture of Dorian Gray, like compromises on Eugène's soul.

Yet Balzac is at great pains to excuse, to make allowances for, or at least to explain Lucien's conduct, giving reasons for the "conspiracy" of elements that combine to make the hero vain and foolish, and showing why such a young man will do just such things in such a way. Lucien often seems acted upon—even a Christ-figure in the crown of thorns image. Here society is blamed, and Lucien's behavior is only the result of his age, one that awakens excessive ambition and forces the young to adopt calculating cruelty to achieve that ambition. Society deprives youth of its graces, vitiates its generous sentiments. Lucien is simply the young man as the nineteenth century has made him, and Balzac so excuses him until his actions are such that they defy any human forgiveness.

If Lucien is something of an innocent victim of the nineteenth century, he represents a type, becoming an allegorical figure, or an example of the zoological "kind" whose depiction, according to the Avant-Propos, is one aim of the *Comédie*. But if we are to see Lucien as acted upon by laws against which he was helpless to contend, Balzac ought not to have set him in such dramatic contrast to Ève and David, idealized human beings whose betrayal by Lucien is rendered the more monstrous since they and their love for him are given a lyrical glow. Unlike some predecessors in his lineage, Lucien does not reject the wholesome love of another woman as a substitute for the enticements of the perfidious Louise. Julien, Raphaël, Benassis, and Eugène all in some measure turn away from a first love that is beneath their ambitions. In Lucien's case the rejected love is that offered by Ève and David, and the finer they are the greater is Lucien's offense in abandoning them. Their special qualities also indict society, for the novelist Balzac surpasses the moralist and social historian when he shows two noble people so unjustly beaten and impoverished by the world, and he writes more vividly of them than he does in any number of interpolated "essays" on nineteenth-century corruption or venality. The nature and quality of Ève and David likewise make us doubt Balzac's stubborn and persistent belief in Lucien's innocence, as Lucien now takes his place beside Louise in the symbolic carriage, stealing away at night toward the dawn in Paris.

Illusions perdues
Part II

The ironies begin at once in the title: a man great in the provinces will be small in the capital. The title has been steadily prepared for by the narrative's long exposure of the provinces in their narrow meanness, their lack of style, interest, or variety. If Lucien is "un grand homme de province," we are to see "grand" as contradicted by "de province," which so limits and confines greatness as to have no meaning elsewhere. The title is also prophetic of the hero's fate, as if to say that Lucien's "greatness" lies all in his past, and we shall see how "great" he is when Paris has had its way, has finally rendered its pitiless judgment.

COMPARISONS

The flight in darkness, inspired by illusion, is not over before illusion itself begins to fade in the light of day. Lucien is horrified at the price of everything, as the supply of money obtained at so great a human cost begins to disappear. Louise in turn is not pleased by the spectacle of his childlike inexperience. For her, love is grafted on pride, and she cannot forgive Lucien's display of naïve ignorance; he should have more pride, keeping the upper hand over Louise by confident ability to meet problems as if he has solved them readily before. In the crude hotel of their first arrival, Lucien sleeps until four in the afternoon, is awakened and

116

hurries to dinner with Louise. She is reserved and thoughtful; clearly something has taken place during his absence from her. Châtelet has given her the benefit of his knowledge of Paris, having followed the escaping pair and presented himself in Louise's room at two o'clock. She is not to live with Lucien or to let anyone know that she has traveled with him. Mme d'Espard, in particular, must never know that Louise has been at this hotel with the son of an apothecary. In short, since last seeing Lucien, she has heard the language of the world spoken with unmistakable accent. Her speech to him now betrays her monstrous egotism, and we must sympathize with the tears of a youth, weeping in fear and disillusion over a lesson that is too much for him, genuinely hurt as he is. He fears that the separation she now decrees is the prelude to complete abandonment, leaving him helpless, for "vous êtes ma seule espérance et tout mon avenir"—terms never more synonymous with futility than now.

Alone and a stranger in Paris, Lucien feels diminished. When Châtelet takes him and Louise to dinner and the theater, Lucien sees the superiority of a man of the world and he is ashamed of his own shabby dress. Comparison is the most relentless of teachers, and Lucien for the first time looks at Louise by comparison with the fresh and elegant women of Paris. As Dinah de la Baudraye first saw herself beside a friend who had just come from Paris, with devastating effect, so Louise suffers when seen in new surroundings. Lucien seems pitiable to her; she seems to lack taste and style. All they need is a "coup de hache" to alienate them fully. Châtelet continues his pressure on Louise, exposing Lucien for what he is, a youth having no great talent or manners, in Paris "un garçon extrêmement ordinaire." His advice, "attendez et comparez," will be painfully followed, but not only by Louise. Lucien falls into despair over his appearance, and consoles himself with an elegant dinner for fifty francs, the cost of an entire month in Angoulême. The pathetic source of this money comes back to us when Lucien reflects that Ève was right: she had warned him that prices here were not the same as in Angoulême. He cannot, furthermore, appear before Mme d'Espard so dowdily attired, and he spends two hundred francs on a new outfit. Thus over ten per-cent of his little fund, so dearly bought, is already gone when he finds himself in Mme d'Espard's box at the Opera.

Here Louise falls once and for all from the pedestal of Lucien's former love. The narrator summarizes his impression in a series of ten adjectives, ending with "mal arrangée surtout." Lucien judges her as Paris and Louise have judged him, by appearance and out-ward manner. He is ashamed of having loved this dried-up old woman and resolves to quit her at the first chance provided by her cautious virtue. Seeing Mme d'Espard's indifference to Lucien, Louise tells herself, too, that he must not be as handsome as she had thought, or as *spirituel*. So each discovers the same thing: that they are both provincials, and each resolves to be rid of the other.

Now the great Henri de Marsay enters with his powerful eye and cruel smile, to be followed by Félix de Vandenesse, Général Montriveau, and the celebrated poet Canalis. Beside these great figures Lucien seems a pitiful foreigner who does not speak the language, until Mme d'Espard herself takes pity on him, and in-troduces him to Canalis. As he listens to these five men in the box, Lucien is astonished by the assurance of their talk as he is by the style of their clothes. He himself, trying to appear at ease in his new clothes, has the stiff manner of an Egyptian statue or, as de Marsay says, of a mannequin all dressed up and standing at a tailor's door. Lucien *is* then, the clothes he has on. More impor-tant is Lucien's response to Mme d'Espard herself, his mobile spirit now seeing in her what he saw long ago in Louise. He deter-mines to possess this elevated woman as the best means of attaining his Parisian aims. He succeeded in Angoulême, why not in Paris?

Lucien rushes toward another illusion no less quickly than bitter reality deprives him of it. Behind the scenes, Iago Châtelet has contrived to reveal Lucien's name and his father's occupation. The cruel jokes of the Parisians are inspired by "l'artisan de cette

trahison Carthaginoise," Balzac drawing again on his Roman
storehouse. Louise is made to see what a blunder it was to invite
Lucien to the box. Four people are involved, M. Mayer observes,
none called by name but all "désignées par un nom affectif tiré de
leurs qualités dominantes de gravité, de snobisme, de noblesse ou
de manque d'élégance." Mme d'Espard is furious, refuses to be
seen "avec le fils d'un apothicaire," and departs instantly with
Louise. She realizes the immense difficulty facing anyone wishing
to change his name to a noble one. Apart from this, Lucien himself is handsome enough, but seems to be stupid and crude: "enfin
il n'est pas *élevé*." True, but now he appears to learn rapidly, after
bitter reflections on the world.

M. Poulet has described the sudden effect of the Champs
Elysées on Balzac's hero. Lucien ventures at times into "broad
daylight, into the real," a world in which the conditions of life
have changed. He sees life offered to his desire, but things refuse to
yield. "He is in a world of resisting objects." He walks home and
recalls the men and their elegant manners at the Opera, then buys
himself new clothes for the second time, as if this alone would bring
him to the desired level. But a cold note arrives from Louise: the
Marquise is ill; the dinner for which the new outfit had been a
costly preparation is canceled. Now the symbolic carriage, without a word, tells him the full measure of this new catastrophe.
Walking toward the yet unfinished Arc de Triomphe (1821), he is
astonished by thousands of vehicles, luxurious in horses and equipment. In a handsome calèche, perhaps like the one that Père
Goriot used to watch for as he stood along the way to catch a
glimpse of his children, Lucien now sees Louise and her cousin
attended by a plumed footman in gold embroidery. De Marsay
and Rastignac are on horseback among a group accompanying
the two women to the Bois, obviously not in the least ill but well
and happy. As Lucien approaches the carriage, he is again the
victim of that executioner's instrument, the lorgnon, this time
without the smile by which de Marsay had dealt him a blow "de

poignard." The Marquise "le lorgna et ne répondit pas à son salut," but "le pauvre poète" is seized by a deadly chill "quand de Marsay le lorgna: le lion parisien laissa retomber son lorgnon si singulièrement qu'il semblait à Lucien que ce fut le couteau de la guillotine. La calèche passa."

The effect of this insult is to inspire a violent rage, to renew ambition, for Lucien sees that the need for money is the only thing that counts. He makes again his fierce predictions of future success, although now his conscience tells him that it must be sought through work, as David knew. We might be encouraged by these signs of tough determination if Lucien did not fall into the ominous future tense, already established as the signature of illusion. He will triumph, he will pass down this avenue in calèche and footman, he will possess some Marquise d'Espard. His new desire to work is blemished by his goal; for mere trappings and suits he will give up his youth to labor. Such an end is worthy only of means as shabby as itself; an end appealing only to vain selfishness is an end to be sought by equally worthless, even sinful means. If Lucien were now to work for a new form of glory, the past could be forgiven as a necessary phase toward his maturity. But we lose heart when we see that he will work only for tawdry things, because he will learn that these can be had without working, and then he is doomed.

When Lucien tries again to see Louise, he is repulsed from her door but profits from a meeting with Châtelet, who emerges about noon from a visit to Louise. Lucien asks the reason for his disgrace, and Châtelet, spokesman and instrument of the world that he is, tells him the brutal truth. The cynical Rastignac, his own compatriot, has disclosed the facts of his origin and name, leading to a summary of Lucien's offenses against the world in this order: your name is Chardon and not de Rubempré; your mother is a midwife; your father was an apothecary; your sister is a charming girl who irons shirts well but who has married a printer named Séchard. Then, Châtelet adds another of those resounding final terms that echo sonorously throughout the *Comédie:* "Voilà le monde." His advice is not unlike that of d'Arthez to come: Lucien should return to work and show his talent in the creation of masterpieces. He should give up all letters to Louise and so insure that she is not his enemy. As for Châtelet himself, we read, "j'ai une si haute opinion de votre avenir, que je vous ai partout défendu." Like Iago, again, he constantly "defends" the man he hopes to destroy. He leaves the young poet in a state of pale dejection, his countenance reminding us that the effect of life in Paris is to produce a certain kind of visage, a mask of stunned defeat, like the one over the face of poor Godefroid in *L'Envers de l'histoire contemporaine* (1843). Another of the classical young men of low birth but hopeful parents who has come to Paris "faire fortune," Godefroid realizes, in the wake of dead hopes and ambitions, that he lacks the talent to achieve his aim, and finally leans on a parapet over the Seine to contemplate Paris with the dejected eye of one who has lost.

But Lucien is by no means at this extremity. When his resolution is taken, his bills are paid, and a cheap room is found near the Sorbonne, he is left with a fraction of his original fund of two thousand francs, having been in Paris only a week—"cette fatale semaine" as he says now before writing in anger to Louise. This telling phrase will recur to remind us how Balzac keeps control over his vast portrait of the world. For all of the fourteen hundred odd pages of the Rubempré cycle with its intrusions and sometimes expendable masses of detail, if we keep to the action as it touches on or centers in Lucien, the work will often seem to have the intimacy of a sonnet cycle. Lucien's first week in Paris has indeed been "fatale," and we shall remember it during the chapter "La Fatale Semaine," in which he comes to the end of his Parisian hopes.

WORK AND THE CÉNACLE

We share Lucien's happiness, however, now that he is determined to strain toward glory on his own merit. Yet he seems almost aggrieved that he has to work, as if this were only a last resort after other means to success had failed. He should not feel abused; rather, he is lucky that he is forced into the only genuine way, the right alternative to dependence on Louise, so clearly a false hope. Men who expect to succeed only by work are not the victims of illusion, and now Lucien surrenders to his new destiny. At Flicoteaux he meets another provincial youth come to Paris, Lousteau, in search of fame and money and destined to exert a sinister influence. Lucien is astonished as Parisian life unfolds; he is shy and awkward; he is frantically sparing of his little money, remembering Ève and David and their generous hopes. His sense of obligation reasserts itself, and all his good qualities, including his natural ability, come strongly to the fore. Like Raphaël before him, Lucien is compared with Rousseau as he lives in his attic, Rousseau the prototype of provincial genius marching on Paris. Lucien works away and returns to his room near midnight without having spent anything on heat or light, using Sainte-Geneviève and a bookseller's, his mood alternating between belief and despair. The fear of exhausting his money brings on a cold sweat, so he decides to approach the booksellers and publishers, a set of merchants who buy cheap and sell dear, as if literature were another commodity, such commercialization being, according to Mr. Lukacs, the principal theme of *Illusions*.

Going for a walk, Lucien meets by chance another shy, lonesome youth whom he had seen in the library and at Flicoteaux. This is Daniel d'Arthez, who, like Ève and David, will love and sacrifice for Lucien, and who in turn will be betrayed. Now d'Arthez tells him that the library is closed, and seeing Lucien's evident distress, he hears the tale of defeat. His speech of consolation at once dismays and inspires his new friend, whose story is so much like his own, like that of the thousand young people who come to Paris annually from the provinces. But greatness can be achieved if one has the will to accept and overcome the ordeals before him. Like Hamlet's bitter review of the insolence of office,

the law's delay, and the scorn of merit, d'Arthez' price of greatness conceals none of the coming trials in calumny, injustice,
effrontery, and the harsh ways of commerce. The title once again
rings out as d'Arthez says calmly, "on ne peut pas être grand
homme à bon marché," as if to say there is only one kind of great
man, with no qualifying adjectives suggesting his origin. His words
take on a prophetic note: Lucien's talent is not enough; he must
have will, patience, dedication to the only way. After listening to
a reading of Lucien's work, d'Arthez gives a brilliant analysis of
its qualities and shows how it can be revised. Then his ominous
summary assures Lucien that after ten years of persistent work
"vous aurez gloire et fortune."

Happy to have met this generous heart in the desert of Paris,
"le grand homme de province" attaches himself like a chronic
disease to d'Arthez, the title as synonym here acting to show the
contrast between Lucien's present insignificance, his true status,
and his former position at home—an illusion. D'Arthez introduces
him to the Cénacle, a group of nine gifted young men of the greatest integrity, incapable of envy or meanness of spirit, who now see
Lucien's talent and possibilities on equal terms with their own.
They seem an extension into Lucien's Parisian life of Ève and
David, offering the same unselfish devotion, the same trust in his
genius, the same willing sacrifice of their meager resources. Lucien
has written home again in his distress, has received three hundred
francs in money with moving expressions of love and hope. Meanwhile members of the Cénacle have themselves raised two hundred francs for him, which he insists on paying back from the
money just received. They are grossly offended and proceed to
make a shrewd if brutal analysis of their young friend. To return
their money promptly seems on the surface honorable and con-
scientious. The Cénacle, however, sees in this a sign of narrow
vanity, since Lucien refuses their help in order to make a show of
honor, promptness, and reliability, virtues that he lacks. He who
will one day live from the earnings of a prostitute cannot accept

the aid of generous friends, who now warn him of the dangers posed by his character. He seems open and frank yet inclined to justify things contrary to his principles. He is in conflict with himself, vain, sophistical, inconsistent, so that they fear the consequences of his tendency "de bien penser et de se mal conduire." Lucien bows his head and admits that he has not their strength. After only a month of the kind of work that d'Arthez has said will take ten years, he is already tired. His friends offer to sustain him, but no, things are too precarious, they are all as poor as he is, and none can help him with the booksellers. Bianchon is there, and perhaps thinking of Eugène, he urges Lucien to suffer with courage and to put his trust in work. Alas, it would be his death, Lucien knows, and here the New Testament once again predicts Lucien's course, as Léon Giraud invokes the example of Peter: "Avant que le coq ait chanté trois fois . . . cet homme aura trahi la cause du Travail pour celle de la Paresse et des vices de Paris," the capital letters used for the two abstractions giving us more than ever the sense of watching a morality play. Lucien is here faced by one of the dominant questions of the Balzacian universe: Can you work, and further, will you go on after you see what can be had without working? In Balzac's morality, here, a thing is valuable only if work is required to achieve it, and if Lucien's *avenir* is attainable without work, it must be hollow and unsound. And yet work is at the center of the high world's case against Lucien—that he and his family, and his father before him all have worked—so making dramatic the worthlessness of such an estimation.

Now when Lucien speaks of journalism as a possible choice, his friends descend upon its corruption with all their power, and Balzac draws the narrative together in their use of the future tense and the terms, now so ominous, of hell and the abyss. Journalism, they say, opposes pleasure to work, and Lucien will be enchanted by its specious power, he will forget those who love him, he will not give up a witticism to spare the tears of a friend, having, as he already does, all too many journalist's qualities. Fulgence Ridal uses epithets that should warn Lucien away from the step he is about to take: "Le journalisme est un enfer, un abîme d'iniquités, de mensonges, de trahisons." But no, the man who was great in the provinces will show them, he will prove, they will see, and perhaps one day he will become the herald even of their glory.

TEMPTATION

Lucien's first reception at a newspaper leaves him frustrated, for he is unable to see the editor, Andoche Finot. He decides to seek out Lousteau for help, and one day at Flicoteaux, sitting at conversation with d'Arthez, Lucien sees Lousteau come in. Although d'Arthez has revised his friend's novel and has written a brilliant preface for it, he is now abandoned as Lucien goes to approach Lousteau. D'Arthez pierces his soul with a look "où le pardon enveloppe le reproche." Presently Lucien goes out to fetch his poems, and on returning he sees d'Arthez still there, sadly leaning on his table. The denial by Peter is now explicit as Lucien pretends not to see his friend and follows Lousteau. At the end of his "Introduction," M. Adam is at pains to give this scene the largest possible moral significance, with specific reference to *Paradise Lost* and the fall of man. Lousteau is Satan, Ève and David the guardian angels watching over the goodness of Lucien until "le malheureux enfant cède aux appels de l'enfer." Lousteau now provides the temptation to which Lucien has already decided to yield. He takes his place in the series of important *Bildungsmächte* that influence Lucien's career, beginning at home: Louise, the journey, Paris itself, Mme d'Espard and the dandies, the Cénacle, and now Lousteau. When discussing Lucien's sonnets, the journalist explains the literary war in Paris, the need to choose one's side, the hopelessness of trying to live by writing poems, and concludes with a bitter lament over the world as it is. Again Balzac brings us to the close of day, as Lousteau in the fading light shows Lucien the world below them, where consistent virtue is rare and a successful literary career means prostitution and the doom of illusion. He, too, refers to the annual inflow of ardent youth from the provinces. Every year the same things happen to them, the same descent into shame and infamy in order to succeed, the same cheap, odious shifts and devices. The more mediocre a man is the sooner he arrives, because "il peut avaler des crapauds vivants, se résigner à tout." Lousteau sees in Lucien another young arriviste as writer, who will, in a year or two, be just as he now is himself. Speaking as one of the damned he foretells his coming shame, a bitter counsel from the despair of one who is damned and no longer able to leave hell.

Lousteau paints no different a picture of journalism than that suggested by the Cénacle's charges: it is the abyss, it is hell that Lucien is about to step into. He should flee this danger, not invite disaster by curiosity about it or by foolish confidence in his ability to draw back after savoring its delights and rewards. Lousteau draws the clearest parallel between what he once was and Lucien's present state, he too having come to Paris with just these same hopes, dreams, and illusions. His words are a temptation by warning against fearful realities, against a suicidal course indeed, which is the more alluring to Lucien the more terribly it is described. With tears in his own eyes, Lousteau shows that there is still time to draw back from the corruption of his soul. He admits that in his own desperate life he has been reduced to cheap and contemptible prostitution. His portrait in the later *Muse du département* (1843–44) shows Lousteau declining into futility, old before his time, disillusioned, and marked by the stigmata of debauchery in keeping with his life in hell.

Now Lucien is silent, but suddenly breaks into a cry to the future, "Je triompherai." Nowhere is he so clearly the *poète*, the deluded weakling incapable of understanding himself or the world, as in this ironic moment of prediction. When it is clear at last that Lucien will persist in journalism, Lousteau offers to introduce him to Finot. Lucien then makes a different prediction, which carries us back to David's warning and prophecy. "Je n'oublierai jamais cette journée," he says, and we tremble for him, seeing that this prediction will—to his sorrow—come true. He will remember this day, but has he forgotten the spectacle of his mother and sister on their knees? Balzac here skillfully draws his work together, telling us just where we are, looking back and onward, explaining the meaning of this action. He outlines the clear dualism of the choice facing Lucien, the kind of mistake about to be made, the flaw in his character that accounts for it, and the deception by Lousteau to get Lucien on his side: all that we must keep in mind before proceeding.

The Abyss

Suddenly Lousteau seems like a fine comrade, jovial and helpful, inviting Lucien to a party where he can meet Finot. Lucien responds to this apparent camaraderie, and of the two ways before him, he takes the short, the quick, and the easy way. The Cénacle is not an ideal for him now—only an expensive luxury to be paid for in the world as it is. He sees no difference between the noble friendship of d'Arthez and the facile amiability of Lousteau, whose easy handshake and offers of help conceal his perfidy. As Lucien takes the fatal step, Balzac dresses him once more in the handsome clothes he had planned to wear before Mme d'Espard, reminding us of the connection between Lucien's beauty and his foolish illusions. Once again he is a magnificent sight, beautiful as a Greek god as he steps into a world in which his beauty will make it easier for him to appear to succeed. He should have been warned by the odious squalor in Lousteau's room. The narrator observes that all poor and struggling youths are reduced to impoverished surroundings, but the character of the one suffering leaves its stamp everywhere. Now the disorder around Lousteau is different from the thoughtless chaos in Esther Gobseck's room but it reveals the difference between Lousteau and d'Arthez, between the obscenities of journalism and the dignity of true literature. The room is morose and dirty, declaring a life without dignity or repose. What a difference between "ce désordre cynique et la propre, la décente

misère de d'Arthez." This effect of moral descent in Lucien's world
continues in the Galeries de Bois, where the new friends go to see
the bookseller Dauriat. The general flimsiness, cheapness, and
dirt, the various shops with their wares and manner of sale, the
pervasive side shows, quackeries, and frauds, and finally, toward
evening once more, the "infâme poésie" of prostitution, all combine to give an air of licentious corruption to the world of Lucien's
choice. Finding himself among the people seen here, Lucien asks
whether he will ever be fallen so low as this, and Balzac, in another
summary conclusion, combines the themes of prostitution, learning by an ignorant unknown, the Cénacle, the illusory future
tense, and money, with the ironies of his title, as "le grand homme
de province recevait des enseignements terribles." As he now tries
to join Dauriat's stable of writers, Lucien feels a cold sweat damp-
ening his back, always a sign that he is trying to break in where
he should stay away. Dauriat's cruel and cynical discourse unfolds
to afflict the "poète de province," doubly handicapped as shown
in the terms of this synonym—as a poet, because his work cannot
be sold, and a man from the provinces, hopelessly behind in having no Parisian experience. The poet's irrelevance consists mainly
in not being vendible: what is the point of work that cannot be
sold? Lucien is furious at the contemptuous condescension with
which his poetry is treated, and should now give way to his anger,
justified and right as it is, and so be spared his impending folly.
Here a young man's sudden anger—so often ill advised and ruinous to his chances—would be his salvation. His vanity here is part
of a sensible pride in his own dignity, but he lacks the courage to
assert himself before all this seeming power and assurance. Lucien
still has the remains of the right stuff in him, but suppresses it
fatally. He has no defense against the *sourire* that plays over the
lips of all present, the same smile of contemptuous superiority as in
the Opera box, of malicious satisfaction in another's misery. His
poems are like his pitiful new suit, crude manners, ignorance, and
ignoble name before the descending lorgnon of de Marsay.

Lucien suffers, is enraged, humiliated, and ridiculed but he goes on. He is torn between his alternatives: Lousteau is right about the power of money, but d'Arthez is right about the price of success. The narrative rightly adopts the passive voice for Lucien as new experiences pour in upon him. With Lousteau he goes backstage at the theater to witness a new world of sordid chaos, discordant clamor. When he is introduced to Florine and Nathan as a great poet of future celebrity named Lucien de Rubempré, we again see the elements of his fatal illusion about himself: he will achieve future greatness under another name. He can still be shocked by an arrangement whereby Matifat pays the cost of Florine's luxurious life while she has an affair with Lousteau, the very depth to which he is soon to fall with Coralie. He is bewildered by the contradictions in the journalistic and theatrical worlds, and terms like "étonné," "hébété," "stupéfait," "engourdi," and "abasourdi" recur to describe his response to the blows that the power of money "martelaient" on his head and heart. Sitting in the theater during the overture, Lucien thinks of David and the Cénacle, tears beginning to shine in his eyes. In answer to Lousteau's question he can only say that he weeps because "je vois la poésie dans un bourbier," and Lousteau truly concludes, "vous avez encore des illusions." Yes, indeed, for these tears are better than others soon to be shed; they are a lament for lost friends and love, tears of remorse, sympathy, and repentance, and, also like Eugène's, a response to the spectacle of the world's corruption. Lousteau now further reveals the cruelty and injustice that render young men of genius helpless before publishers, and Lucien's disgust warns him that he should die rather than fall to his knees before a sordid ignoramus like Finot. He is appalled by the crude swindle that makes Lousteau editor of a paper, the whole made possible by Florine's exploitation of Matifat. His demand to know whether Lousteau is devoid of scruples or conscience is answered by the simple question, "de quel pays êtes-vous donc, mon cher enfant?" Where are you from, indeed? Certainly not from Paris.

Satan now reemerges as Lousteau, when he brushes conscience away and outlines the reward for the coming sale of Lucien's soul. As Lousteau rises as editor, Lucien becomes drama critic with a variety of perquisites whereby he can be sure of a good four thousand francs a year. Lousteau seems not only Satan but Moloch, Belial, Mammon, and Beelzebub as he pours forth a torrent of infernal gains in money, power, luxury, privilege, sensual love, and revenge—all this will I give thee, while d'Arthez starves on in his pitiful attic room. Alone after Lousteau's departure, Lucien is lost "dans un abîme de pensées," contemplating the world as it is. He sits motionless for perhaps five minutes, an eternity as in the brief but momentous dream of Hans Castorp on the snowy mountain. His need to choose between two worlds compels him to think of the past, of the pure and exalted love once given to Louise, as so often before, the past seeming wholesome, the *avenir* corrupt. His remaining sense of decency inspires disgust as a dual temptation calls for the sale of his mind to journalism, and the surrender of his beautiful body to sensuality and luxury when the oriental beauty of Coralie reveals itself on stage. Temptation again takes the form of questions; just as Lousteau asks a series of rhetorical questions in persuading Lucien, so Lucien asks them of himself, and by the Jesuitism of passion he is led to accept what earlier disgusted him. So far he is ignorant of love and wine; should he not know life better? Why not accept the delights now so enchantingly within reach, he wonders, as he strikes down, at last, the remnants of his hesitation.

ENTER CORALIE

Lousteau now returns to Lucien in the theater, again assuming his Satanic role, assuring the vain youth that Coralie has fallen hopelessly in love with him. Her story is told briefly—her having been sold by her mother, her becoming the mistress of de Marsay, whom she hates, her tolerance of Camusot, her unhappy life, and her longing for happiness with her first and only true love, Lucien. She is stunned and helpless, unable to go on with her part unless

Lucien rescues her, and his vanity is caressed by such a tribute. The odious sharing of a woman with someone who merely pays for it all—the source of his earlier disgust—is now brushed aside, as "il tombait dans cette fosse . . . entraîné par le jésuitisme de la passion." The enticing voluptuousness of the world backstage is like "une peste qui dévore l'âme," and having agreed to attend an after-theater supper with Coralie, Lucien writes his first article for a newspaper, seated at a table in Florine's boudoir lighted by candles from Matifat, Florine's keeper. At the same time Lousteau writes an article attacking Châtelet, his temptation having assured Lucien that one of the benefits of journalism lies in the opportunity it affords to attack one's enemies. Later Lucien reads his own article aloud to the company as the room reverberates with compliments, embraces, and fulsome praise. To the last possible moment, Balzac continues to find excuses for Lucien, at least to explain why he should succumb to the success he suddenly enjoys. The narrative deftly reviews the experience of a youth from the monotonous provinces, attracted once more by "les abîmes de Paris," weary of poverty, harassed by enforced continence, worn out by his monastic life and futile labor.

At the same party, Vignon repeats at length the influence wielded by newspapers, their crimes that evade the law, the malice, insolence and ingratitude of the mediocrities who own them. Looking at Lucien, he sees certain fate awaiting this handsome, spirited youth, who, like a thousand others of his kind, will waste his talent for the profit of these merchants of poison. But it is in vain that the *Bildungsmächte* have all tried to save Lucien from the fatal step he has taken, and Balzac again carefully draws our attention to the point reached by the hero in his suicidal course. The contrast between the way of d'Arthez and the way of evil has been made dramatic; the abyss into which he must fall is clear before him.

When at last, unused to Parisian orgies, Lucien is helped up the stairs to Coralie's apartment, he suffers crudely and vomits on the stairway. With a maternal tenderness Coralie takes this infant into her bed and hears him say "Merci maman"; so begins the period of his enslavement. Lucien himself moves toward his final degradation of living on the earnings of a prostitute, as he accepts the luxury paid for by Camusot. Coralie beguiles him of the shame he feels at the lies that are told, the deceptions that cheat an old man—a man whose very bounty makes possible this betrayal.

But now Lucien has access to a carriage, the obvious sign of success. As he drives out into the Bois with Coralie, he is intoxicated by the pleasure of revenge on meeting the calèche of Louise and Mme d'Espard. The glance of disdain and satisfied vengeance that he bestows on them gives Lucien one of the most exquisite moments of his life, and may fix his destiny once and for all. It seems to mean that what he most desires—to rise above those who have wounded him—may in fact be had by the means he now employs. As at all decisive moments, Balzac adds his own comment, contrasting once again the thoughts in Lucien's mind, on the one hand of the way demanded by the Cénacle, the way of dull virtue and slow, hard work, and on the other, of the gay good cheer, the easy luxury and women of the journalist's life. Thus "Lucien sentit une irresistible envie de continuer la vie de ces deux folles journées."

As flattery pours in upon him, Lucien expands into a fatal hubris. When Coralie warns him against Finot, he cries that he feels strong enough "pour être aussi méchant et aussi fin qu'ils peuvent l'être," and he considers all too readily Hector Merlin's advice to be cruel and abusive to a world that will only love him for it. When he suffers the inevitable losses at gambling, Coralie replaces the money, which he decides to accept, though at first ashamed. On returning to his odious room from the luxury of Coralie's, the key grinds in the lock to open the door and reveal the poverty and nakedness that would continue to be his if he followed the Cénacle's way. The present is here in this stinking place, the *avenir* in Coralie's room. Seeing a note from d'Arthez along with his corrected manuscript, Lucien, like Eugène before him, again finds the dramatic contrast that makes his life an incessant problem of choice. In tears now he sees that these great human beings have transformed his work in masterly style. His volatile nature, rushing to extremes, drives him toward d'Arthez once more, although he is haunted by the shame of his behavior, knowing that d'Arthez would never accept Camusot's money if he loved Coralie, knowing also that the Cénacle despises the journalism he has adopted. So Lucien knows that the two lines of corruption to which he has already yielded—sensual and spiritual—will accuse him in the presence of superior men.

And so it is, as he comes to a meeting of his true friends. The discussion reveals how far he has retreated from their ideals, and the sad truth emerges in the prediction by Michel Chrestien, using past and future tenses at once, which ends: ". . . tu pourras être un grand écrivain, mais tu ne seras jamais qu'un petit farceur." As Lucien departs, his conscience continues its terrible repetition: "Tu seras journaliste! comme la sorcière crie à Macbeth: tu seras roi." *Macbeth* here seems to bestow tragic dimensions on Lucien's coming doom, if his illusion and its ensuing waste are comparable to Macbeth's. Now he has a presentiment, as the witches' prophecy was also a presentiment, that his true friends have pressed him for the last time to their hearts.

With nothing to stop him now, Lucien joins Lousteau's enterprise in complete surrender. He arranges to do articles, columns, reviews, which with other perquisites will insure an income of about six hundred and fifty francs a month, for the money will pile up in proportion to the falsity of what is done to obtain it. When he has sold out completely to Finot, "Lucien serra la main de Finot avec un transport de joie inouï," and we remember the pressing of David's hand when he left home, and of d'Arthez' hand at Flicoteaux.

On joining the Finot stable, Lucien is presented by Lousteau as one upon whom they may surely count, as he in turn may count on them. Coralie is to be praised and her career advanced by favorable notices, while Lucien's own novel and poems will be strongly supported. As Vernon says, "Vous verrez comment nous arrangerons les choses." Our hearts sink again at the future tense: Lucien will see, indeed. So the new slogan is "vogue la galère!" with no thought of the consequences.

Lucien seems to be winning on all sides, as success and flattery pay tribute to his growing power. Dauriat cautiously makes peace with him, agrees to pay three thousand francs for the poems, and, when all is harmony, he makes our hearts sink as he raises his glass with the toast, "à votre gloire!" Most ominous is the fact that Lucien is feared by someone. After all his sufferings, Dauriat is afraid of what Lucien may say in his sharp reviews. As predicted in the Cénacle, the sense of power so conveyed has the effect of increasing Lucien's vain illusions, since Dauriat pays his money without having read the poems, whose quality has nothing to do with the transaction. Lucien does not see that the money therefore proves no merit in himself, being only a bribe of a particularly sordid kind. He lives intoxicated in the present, as if the past and its meaning were irrelevant. He thinks with increasing rarity of his family and of David, this rarity an exact measure of his growing corruption. He does not wish to think of them, and his inner decline prevents it. Suddenly he has a vivid recollection of beautiful Ève, of David, and of his mother, a "holy family" truly, but the sole effect of this recollection is a hasty sop to his conscience in the form of a gift of five hundred francs to his mother. Coralie praises him as a model son and brother, her influence continuing to make him worse by encouraging his vanity and forgetful conscience. So also she caters to his fatal beauty, being constantly dissatisfied with his clothes, taking him to the tailor for new garments that will let him outshine de Marsay, Rastignac, and the other dandies. The rising action of his drama continues now as Lucien appears at the Opera to assume insolent airs in triumph over those who had only a few months ago presided over his humiliation.

In a state of intoxication, reveling in success, Lucien writes an article of savage cruelty against Châtelet and Louise, taking a fiendish pleasure in this revenge and aware of a growing sense of power. This too is illusory he finds, as he delivers a sharp attack on the play he has seen at the Ambigu theater, only to find it changed into a favorable review in print. Lousteau explains that a given theater has to be supported for the sake of what the paper receives in subscriptions and gifts. So Lucien is not a "grand homme" full of power and able to use it as he sees fit. He learns that the traffic in theater tickets is like that in books, with success on the stage being controlled by the claque under the formidable Braulard. He pays the claque in tickets, which they in turn resell for their wages, while they deliver the applause essential to success. Braulard agrees to give Lucien tickets for the theaters presenting plays that he is to review, and also says that he likes Coralie and will work for her success. As Lousteau and Lucien are leaving Braulard's, they see a hideous-looking crew ascending the stairway, looking like Falstaff's company of scarecrows. They are the claqueurs coming for their orders and wages, those who make the glory of actresses and dramatic authors. The scene inspires bitter reflections in Lucien. One cannot retain illusions about anything in Paris: everything here is bought and sold, everything is forged, even success itself. One thinks again of ancient Rome, the Rome of Juvenal, as Balzac takes his place in the tradition of moral satire. He says what all satirists have said and will say of the "city," that is, any concentration of humanity which, by multiplying men in one place, increases the mass and variety of evil.

Coralie announces her form of soirée, to which some thirty guests are invited, and Balzac does not forego the opportunity to review Lucien's condition amid all the outward signs of satisfied ambition. A vastly different style is now possible for Lucien as he struts about in total command of Coralie's salon, his attitude in complete contrast to the sweating terror that afflicted him at his first soirée in Angoulême. The sudden change from poverty to

opulence has the effect of a dream, of unreality, but Lucien is confident to the point of *fatuité*. He has, himself, changed in appearance, is paler, more languid in expression, more handsome indeed
than ever, as we must expect while watching him move steadily to
the abyss, his beauty being one of the chief causes of his danger and
thus bound to increase as the danger grows. He is conscious of
power and force, he contemplates the literary world and society
face to face, believing himself capable of dominating them. He
reflects only when unhappy, and now in the glowing present he is
carefree. All that he needs is at hand: a house provided for, a
mistress who is the envy of all Paris, a carriage of course, and,
above all, incalculable sums in his writing desk, incalculable, indeed, less in their size than in their uncertainty. Lucien does not
ask the source of the finery he sees all about him, for if he did, the
answer would be ominous: the basis of his prosperity is frail, only
Camusot's orders to the furnishers. Coralie is to have credit for at
least three months, and the horses and servants come as if by
enchantment. As Lucien and Coralie enter the dining room now,
Balzac gives his usual warning of impending disaster in Lucien's
use of the future tense: "J'arriverai, mon enfant . . . je te récom-
penserai de tant d'amour et de tant de dévouement."

Close to ten o'clock, three of the old Cénacle friends arrive.
D'Arthez is not with them because he is completing a book, the
very book that Lucien will be forced to attack, leading to his duel
with Michel Chrestien. Lucien greets his old friends with patronizing confidence, assuring them that he has not changed, regardless
of his situation. They can only exchange a mocking smile at such
folly, a *sourire* at his apparent success, which shows his weakness
as clearly as any defeat. When Nathan rushes up to thank Lucien
as "un grand homme" for the favorable notice of his book, the
great man lies outright in his assurances of favor. He now appears
to be in a position to promise his old friends that when d'Arthez'
book appears, he will be able to give it his support, thus merely
justifying his continuing in journalism. In answer to Michel's
question about his being free for such assistance, Lucien tells in

effect another lie, since he knows that he is not free to write as he chooses. Here Balzac returns with intense irony to the moral and religious associations of his drama, as Finot arises to announce a sacrilegious baptism. A crown of roses and champagne descend on the blond head of Lucien, and Finot's sacramental formula is heard, "je te baptise journaliste" in the name of receipt stamps, bail, and fines. Amid derision and blasphemy, Lucien's three friends take their sad departure, but after some remorse and foreboding, Lucien continues his heedless life of luxurious pleasure and easy work. Poor Coralie ruins herself to provide the elegant clothes whereby her lover is once more to rival de Marsay and the formidable Rastignac. Her passion for adorning his handsome body is part of the falsity that Coralie represents in Lucien's life. Balzac as narrator connects it with one of the first and most telling of the *Bildungsmächte*, the moment when, on first walking in the Tuileries, he saw the need for new and elegant clothing. To fulfill the wish then established, Coralie now ruins herself, as the narrative keeps to its plan of composition, repeating themes and calling in voices toward a last resolution.

TEMPTATION AND REVENGE

One evening at the theater l'Ambigu, Lucien is engaged in conversation by the Duc de Rhétoré et de Tullia, a close friend of Louise who has mentioned the distress caused by newspaper attacks against her and Châtelet. In the ensuing conversation, the Duke refers to Lucien as Chardon, which opens—now fatally— the dualism of his name, its division of reality and illusion. In a masterly display of malicious hypocrisy, the Duke plays upon Lucien's vanity with the air of a man who is sure of his victim. Clearly, he says, Lucien needs a name and a title more than mere talent. Our hearts sink at his words and the future tense: "esprit, noblesse et beauté, vous arriverez à tout." The New Testament and Satan tempting Christ are explicit when Balzac compares this offer of success in another realm to the journalists' showing of the world to Lucien, "ainsi que le démon à Jésus, le monde

littéraire et ses richesses." Images of something woven, a net to
entrap the unwary hero, again recall Agamemnon and Othello,
as Lucien's vanity ensnares him in the elaborate scheme prepared
by Louise and Mme d'Espard, of which the Duke's maneuvers are
only the preliminary stages. The Countess of Montcornet's dinner
gives Mme d'Espard her chance for the heartless and insinuating
treachery that will not surprise the reader of *L'Interdiction.* She
chides Lucien for his neglect, and says that Louise is hurt. Her
old husband now dead, she would not be averse to such a title
as the "Comtesse de Rubempré." She prefers Lucien to Châtelet
and has always intended to work for Lucien's benefit. Lucien has
learned much from the perfidies of journalism, but he is no match
for this practiced executioner, who offers to protect him from the
treachery of the world while planning to make him its victim.

In answer to Lucien's question about Louise's plans for him,
Mme d'Espard continues her magnificent speech of temptation,
which by now, alas, has no surprises for us. The appeal to his
ambition and vanity, the contrast between a man to be called
"le Comte de Rubempré" and someone named Chardon, remind
us again that successful temptation only releases what is already
there and gives form to decisions already made. The Marquise
makes powerful use of two simple questions that should stab
Lucien to the heart and bring tears to his eyes. Do you belong to
"une grande famille," she wishes to know, as the magnificent
portraits of Lucien's Angoulême days arise before us to make the
more poignant this dreadful moment: the beautiful and devoted
sister Ève; the loving mother, majestic in her patience and
resignation; the brother-friend David, willing and capable of any
sacrifice. These are a great family by the values of any genuine
world that Lucien should wish to inhabit, but his response is only
silence, just as this truly great family will one day be silent to him
as well. Then the question, "avez-vous un nom," makes us think
of Dickens' Pip and the problem of identity. Lucien is again
silent instead of saying, Yes, the name of a gifted scientist, who

died on the threshold of great discoveries, a name that his noble mother was willing to take as her own, giving up the name for which, on the contrary, Lucien is bent on selling his soul. But Lucien does not see that in this denial he betrays his mother even more deeply than his father.

The Marquise is abetted by the company, which shows Lucien clearly that he must become a royalist to further his ambitions, and now the attitude of Rastignac changes on seeing Lucien on good terms with the Marquise. He decides that he can afford to associate "avec le grand homme de sa province"—a "great" man seemingly destined to become "greater." He sees the supposed instrument of his rise later at dinner, and Louise, in mourning, is an elegant widow before whom Lucien is again undecided, remembering the beautiful, voluptuous Coralie in contrast to this haughty but cruel woman. The elegant ladies combine with infinite finesse to make Lucien feel caressed and petted as the darling of their grand society. Mlle des Touches seems impressed, and the Marquise promises to move toward a royal order permitting the change of his name. Like Victurnien he lets himself be drawn into the expensive life of the *viveurs*, where all is cleverness, waste, and dissipation. This winter he lives in a kind of drunken state, with occasional bursts of work at journalism, his time disappearing in thoughtless pleasure without concern for the morrow. His gambling increases as he loses control of his own existence, lacking, as he does, the alertness and cool head demanded of the successful parvenu. Châtelet again becomes his friend, joining with Rastignac to draw Lucien ever more deeply into wasteful dissipation. Meanwhile, debts continue to mount for the *poète*, the *poète-journaliste*, as the text ever more frequently refers to Lucien. Exact figures reenter the narrative as well, an ominous sign in the Balzacian universe that a day of reckoning is at hand. In three months Lucien earns scarcely a thousand francs. He therefore transfers to the royalist paper in the vain hope of ministerial generosity, while the *viveurs* drown all worry in champagne. The once luxurious menage of Coralie is gradually stripped, and the symbolic carriage, horses, and furniture are seized by creditors in payment of four thousand francs of debt.

Lucien's hopes now center entirely on the royalist press, although his Cénacle friends warn him that he will not only besmirch his own life but will eventually find himself on the losing side. Here the future tense holds a prediction that Lucien ignores at his peril, like the prophetic fears of David. Likewise, the prophecy now made by Coralie should give him pause, again foretelling her own death. She consoles her lover and with impassioned fervor predicts his success. He will become the Comte Lucien de Rubempré, and has she not told him that if he ever needs to mount one more step for the seizure of his prey, he may count upon "le cadavre de Coralie?" Now, at a great dinner lasting nine hours, Lucien formally enrolls with the royalists, who declare open war on the liberal press. The enemy fights back, however, making Lucien their special target as with cruel mockery and fiendish accuracy they strike him at his weakest, offering a specimen sonnet from the "futur Pétrarque français." Since his poems are as yet unpublished, the word "futur" marks the cruelest penetration into Lucien's foolish illusions. He weeps hot tears of shame and guilty recognition as the sonnet ridicules his ambitions to rise above his origin and change his name. His journalist friends, such as they were, are alienated, and he must now count his enemies on both sides of the struggle, both equally bent on his ruin. He is so enmeshed in the vanity, intrigue, and greedy selfishness of his world, that he can do nothing right to recover a measure of stable security, and the title "grand homme de province" becomes an obvious sneer amid all that now contradicts it. Hated by the journalists, who continue to find new reasons for their hatred, Lucien is equally the object of fierce jealousy among the royalists, the singleness of his ambition for a title making him an easy mark as the trap into which he is certain to fall is gradually prepared.

"LA FATALE SEMAINE"

In his fashion, Balzac proceeds to discuss the meaning of the human situation about to unfold. It seems that all men who, like the *Bildungsroman* hero, set forth on an attempt to make life yield their desired results, and are compelled to rise on personal merit and effort, must expect that they will set in motion forces that oppose them. They will arrive at *La Fatale Semaine*, and the prime example will necessarily be Napoleon and Moscow, Napoleon also having exemplified the man who comes from nowhere to attain the summit. Any special effort to force an advantage from life creates opposition, for which one must be alert and prepared. The resourceful man will not be dismayed, taken by surprise, or suddenly found wanting in the qualities needed to stand up to the opposing forces. Hardy remarks in *Tess of the D'Urbervilles* that the laws of chance are true in general but fallacious in particular; they may drive a single man toward a sudden concentration of evils, for which there seems no explanation. For Balzac, circumstances seem personified or endowed with a will of their own toward an assigned task, like Grecian Furies, in this case to test the hero's will. Circumstances are directed to rise up against the hero's effort to force them into line with his ambitions, to make them yield a result for which they have not been arranged, of which they have not been warned. They are bent on finding out whether he is really stronger than they, more determined to arrive at his goal than they are to prevent his doing so.

Now it is Lucien's turn to be tested by all that fate can do against him, the most cruel test of all coming soon through Coralie, striking him where he thought himself invulnerable. The narrator pauses to give a tender and sympathetic reading of the nature of "cette pauvre enfant," her sensitive response to an audience, the pride and genuineness that keep her above the scheming intrigue for success, all the qualities, in fact, that make it easy for Lucien's enemies to ruin her. The fatal week may be described as the visiting, in succession, of six principal blows, the effect of which, as they descend, is to deprive Lucien one after another of his principal illusions. D'Arthez' book, Coralie's ruin, losses at gambling, the revelation of Finot's enmity, exposure of the ordinance swindle, and at last the duel in turn destroy the dreams of friendship, love, riches, professional success, and social elevation.

Thinking to insure Coralie's success, Lucien goes to Braulard to arrange a great reception for his mistress. He gets promises of favorable reviews and all seems ideal when he receives an impossible assignment: he must review d'Arthez' book and condemn it, though he sees that it is a masterpiece. The royalists have chosen d'Arthez for slaughter, but Lucien at first refuses. His new leaders point out that Coralie will be ruined by the liberal journalists unless the royalist press defends her. They will not defend her unless Lucien does the article on d'Arthez as required. By his scruples he will ruin both Coralie and his own *avenir*, but this future is now worthless, if dependent on such means. So Lucien faces one of the cruelest of his many choices: he must choose between friend and mistress, she being lost "s'il n'égorgeait pas d'Arthez," like David's father, cutting his son's throat. His tears are a genuine lament over evil, as they fall on one page after another of his friend's great work. After writing a devastating review, Lucien shows that Balzac's claims for a considerable strain of virtue in his nature are not unfounded. He would vastly prefer to do right than wrong, despite the evidence of his choices, and now his good angel drives him to knock on d'Arthez' door. In tears again he tells his friend that the book is sublime, but that he is ordered to attack it. D'Arthez says that he can so change the tone of Lucien's review that it will give the effect of a serious analysis of the book's faults, a form of praise if taken seriously. In further tears, now of relief and joy, Lucien throws himself into d'Arthez' arms, but this truly great man, speaking in sacramental terms, doubts the quality of Lucien's emotion. He sees repeated repentance at intervals as hypocrisy, a kind of special reward for good actions, Lucien repenting only to obtain absolution for the next moment of weakness.

Devoured by melancholy and a sense of coming disaster, Lucien faces the second blow, Coralie's failure on stage, partly aided by the treachery of Florine. The claque master Braulard has betrayed them, and the newspaper attack on Coralie is devastating. Lucien sees her now a victim of the wicked ridicule he once heaped on others. Even the royalist papers are full of perfidious damning with faint praise, as Florine takes over Coralie's role to great applause. In his fury Lucien makes ever more vain predictions of future success, whose stupidity even Coralie must now admit. In desperation he goes out to gamble, and after seven hours of varying fortune he is left without a sou. Returning home, he sees Finot, to whom he promised several short articles and who now gives him a fearful lesson in present realities. His article on d'Arthez has caused a tremendous outcry, so that "Marat est un saint comparé à vous." Finot now asks for the promised articles, including one on a subject now going the rounds, an amusing article against the Keeper of the Seals. Finot's plot is now complete, for this article will infuriate the royalists and kill the royal ordinance for a title.

But after dressing for a party at Mlle des Touches, Lucien is assured there by Louise with a gracious *sourire* that he is to go next day to the chancellery, where he will at last find his ordinance signed by the king. Next morning, however, Lucien reads in Lousteau's paper the anecdote ridiculing the Keeper of the Seals, his wife, and the king himself—the subject of his own article commissioned by Finot. Even now Lucien can see nothing in this but an agreeable canard. On presenting himself for the ordinance, he is received with a violent outcry denouncing the article and demanding to know how he dares to come here after such an offense. Lucien walks into the street as if stunned by some bludgeon, as the narrative draws a sad portrait of his fate, "un enfant" who sacrificed all to vanity and pleasure, "un poète" like a butterfly going without reflection to one light after another, a slave of circumstances whose good thoughts became evil actions. The narrative picks up the characteristic Balzacian speed as it races toward catastrophe; Lucien is suddenly met by Michel Chrestin, who spits in his face as payment "de vos articles contre d'Arthez." This is clearly unjust, since Lucien has written only the one article edited by d'Arthez, but others have been maliciously attributed to him. The ensuing duel seems, in effect, an attempt at suicide by Lucien: he does not move, and falls at the third shot. Michel regrets that the chest wound is not fatal; Lucien repeats his words, "oui, tant pis," and bursts into tears.

As one woe treads upon another's heels, Lucien falls ill, Coralie overtaxes her own strength, neither can any longer work, the creditors take all that can be sold. Balzac now anticipates events in Part III, as Lucien, desperate for money, forges David's name to three bills of one thousand francs each. After paying his own and Coralie's debts, he has three hundred francs left, which he wisely conveys to the faithful maid Bérénice. He tries to work, but no one will buy his articles. The word is circulated that Lucien has nothing "dans le ventre," and he struggles like one accursed, his every effort in vain, Balzac's pity mingled, as elsewhere, with a measure of contempt.

SURRENDER

This is not all, for Lucien must give up the one remaining treasure from the world of his illusions. The sacrifice of Coralie, twice so touchingly foretold, is now made, but her wasted body can no longer serve as a last *marchepied* toward the upward surge of the man she has loved so well. In a scene of great lyrical beauty, Lucien watches her die in the morning light, her lips murmuring, with her last breath of life, his name and that of God. She dies transformed by the special magic of Balzac's imagined universe, the salvation that she yet believes in assured by love and devotion that wipe away her sins. In total wretchedness, Lucien thinks of begging the money to pay the funeral, and finally agrees to write ten popular songs for two hundred francs. He spends the night working in the presence of Coralie's body and at last tries to sing a bitter refrain to a current melody:

Rions! Buvons!
Et moquons-nous du reste!

He is fallen almost to the level of the "réfractaires" described by M. Vallès, "ces pauvres diables" too poor to buy their own bread. His friends Bianchon and d'Arthez enter, and he bursts into tears, sobbing out the tale of his agonies to these patient ones, who forgive him all. Yes, the priest says gravely, "heureux ceux qui trouvent l'enfer ici-bas," as the narrative keeps its language of hell and damnation. In response to a note written during his period of greatest despair, Félicité des Touches comes and slips two bills of a thousand francs into Lucien's hand, this sympathetic and beautiful woman herself destined to leave the high world after her unhappy love for Calyste in *Béatrix* (1838–44). At Père-Lachaise Coralie joins the unhappy father Goriot; it is August, 1822, as a memorial stone will say with her name and age—just nineteen. Lucien remains alone until the sun goes down, like Eugène when he had buried a friend, looking out from above over the city of Paris. Unlike the grim defiance of his predecessor, Lucien thinks of himself, "par qui serai-je aimé?" His true friends despise him, and he must wonder what the remaining three at home think of him now. The unhappy title recurs, now with an adjective, as "le pauvre grand homme de province" descends to the Rue de la Lune to abandon the empty place for a cheap hotel nearby. Mlle des Touches and the sale of furniture combine to pay remaining debts, leaving a hundred francs for the two months during which Lucien falls into a morbid prostration, unable to write or think, simply lost in his misery. He must go home on foot, he decides at last; he pawns all but the merest necessities and goes once more to the gambling house,

returning with nothing, to ask Bérénice for a shawl to hang himself with. But Bérénice promises to obtain the needed twenty
francs. He is to return at midnight and he walks the boulevards,
overcome by his misery, thinking now of home and the family
joys forgotten in the days of his ephemeral triumph. Balzac seems
willing to make excuses for this half-feminine nature to the end,
as Lucien's final act in Paris is to take money from Bérénice,
knowing how it had been earned. He has seen her in the street
talking to a man, but in answer to his question, Bérénice gives him
the essential twenty francs "qui peuvent coûter cher," indeed.
Let it be said to the credit of the *poète* that the money burned his
hand and he wished to return it. But he must keep it after all,
"comme un dernier stigmate de la vie parisienne."

   In his fall, Lucien is so abject that Balzac's tact as narrator
seems doubtful. The concentration of ill luck, of disasters from
every effort, makes Lucien too much a victim, yet Balzac has
carefully prepared these events so that nothing should be less
unexpected than Lucien's disgrace, which follows out of poetic
necessity, in Mr. Lukacs' phrase. From the beginning, others
have feared that he lacks will and character. David and old
Séchard, Châtelet, Doguereau, d'Arthez, and the Cénacle have
all remarked that Lucien's character will not support the demands of his ambition. He tends to throw himself impetuously
upon one project after another, inconstant, unreflective, and as
M. Marceau observes, "prêt à lâcher la proie pour l'ombre."
His instability resembles the cowardice of Peter's denial, for out
of fear, shame, or false pride he denies d'Arthez and the Cénacle,
denies even his father's name and is thus more culpable than
Oscar Husson, for example, who denies his mother out of an
adolescent stupidity soon overcome. Lucien changes from passion
for Louise to desire for Mme d'Espard to the embraces of Coralie,
and goes from poetry to journalism, from honorable poverty to
false prosperity and dishonor. His "jesuitism" leads him into
constant problems. His response to temptation contains a con-

fession of guilt and a purpose of amendment as he says, in effect, to journalism: "I will do what I know to be wrong. Then, after profiting from evil, I will repent and return to a life of virtue, made possible by gains from a life of sin." The ideal is always betrayed in the service of a lesser good, and Lucien shows his immaturity in thinking that he can have all things both ways, forgetting that once he has incurred the guilt of selling his soul, he has nothing left whereby to lure it back. His reasonings eventually involve his life in such a mass of contradictions that he sees no choice but to end it.

M. Citron thinks it appropriate to compare Lucien with the unspeakable Philippe Bridau, whose atrocities lend so much power to *La Rabouilleuse* (1842). They are truly "de faux grands hommes," confirmed in their egotism by adoring families. But this alone will not account for the ruin that Lucien brings on his own, since Eugène too comes of an affectionate family, to whose well being he finally contributes. Yet it might have served Lucien's career better to have been like Julien, totally without aid from home, and so obliged to share his self-reliance, his pitiless and constant self-examination toward removal of his faults. As he first walks out in Paris, Lucien does tell himself the truth, that he has a provincial air and looks like a bumpkin. But it is not long before he ceases to be self-analytical, and so fails to see himself as others in Paris are bound to see him. He quickly learns to give up his illusions about others like Louise, as indeed he should get over, once and for all, his blunders in thought and judgment, based on ignorance of himself and the world. But the deepest illusions of all, those about himself, he never entirely loses and so takes the fearful consequences.

In a perceptive study of the courtesan in Balzac, M. Van der Gun sees the influence of Coralie and her world as fatal to Lucien's "élan poétique," despite her devoted love, a means of corruption. The venal woman in Balzac emerges as essentially impure, an agent of disintegration, so that when Lucien goes behind the scenes he should be content to observe and learn. Once his own life is mingled with these surroundings, he no longer controls, but resembles them. The courtesan's nature shows in images of a shapeless and morbid danger amid humid filth and disorder, which should act to warn Lucien that if he continues here he will share the general contamination. Better still, he should leave Coralie amid the falsity and glitter of the scene, for she comes into his experience amid hallucination where he should leave her, never going backstage to know the reality behind the scene. The difference between what he sees from his box and what he sees backstage is the same difference he should be aware of between his illusions and reality, between the *avenir* he dreams of and the actual future he can attain. A hidden warning comes to him in the chilling cry of the actress Florville, who, in response to Lousteau's intimate prodding, practices a fragment of her part, "arrête, malheureux," with terrifying effect. The detached line seems addressed to Lucien by those very fates who confront him in the fatal week, warning him to turn back from the abyss into which he is now taking an irretrievable step.

Lucien's danger increases as the movement toward prostitution grows more certain in *Illusions*, the prostitution of literary talent and the bodies of women as seen in the "galeries de bois," foretelling the depth to which Lucien himself will fall in selling himself and his talent, while accepting money gotten by the sale of a woman's body. As he watches Coralie from his place in the theater, he sees her constantly taking various forms, performing movements that bring to his mind the image of a prostitute. The capacity to be anything in any form by changing one's appearance and outward behavior must be a corrupting influence on Lucien, himself already so reliant upon, and easily influenced by appearances. If we follow the many sacrifices on his behalf, we may trace a decline wherein each acceptance is less defensible until the final degradation. His mother, Ève, David, the Cénacle—whose help he should take but refuses—Coralie, Bérénice, Vautrin, and finally the beautiful Esther—sold to Nucingen for the money that will buy Lucien's title, estate, and marriage to Clothilde: each demands a greater moral price. If he has a right to count on a mother who is responsible for him, a sister who loves him, and a friend who joins his family, we see that the effect of each sacrifice is to lead to another. Filled with an ever more corrupting expectation that he may go on accepting, he will go on to the next acceptance the less resistant to its moral stigma, until he accepts the ultimate pollution, and, unable to fall to a lower depth, destroys himself. So does every sin leave its mark, like the obscenities that disfigure the portrait of Dorian Gray, who likewise can put an end to his moral decline by killing himself. The recollection makes more understandable Oscar Wilde's passion for *Illusions* and his love for Lucien himself.

While at this point, Lucien is far removed from his end in prison, yet he seems all that his *Bildung* can make of him, and Balzac has nothing to add. In the genre before us the hero changes in response to the various influences of life, which continue always the same. But Lucien will not change, and will seem to us as he does now: a figure asked to contain too much, to represent so vast an area of human folly, agony, and endurance, an area carrying such comprehensive lessons, that he is too frail a vessel for Balzac's energy, for the aim of Prometheus, indeed.

6

Illusions perdues
Part III

THE ROAD HOME

M. Cayrol finds himself in close sympathy with Lucien as he now starts on his way back, and when he leaves us in a street in Paris, he is like the little hero created by Chaplin, with a winding road before him, which is "une espérance, une issue, une aube." But Lucien is moving toward no promise in the dawn as he departs on foot, a beaten figure, having lost all thought of his appearance or dress, once uppermost in his mind. Overtaken by night, he sees a carriage and mounts behind two parcels, unknown to anyone within. In the morning he is awakened by the sun and the hum of voices. He recognizes the little town of Mansle, where eighteen months before he had waited for Louise, his heart full of love, hope, and joy. Now covered by dust amid a circle of curious people, he is about to speak when two travelers emerge from the calèche—Châtelet and his wife, Louise. Like Teufelsdroeck seeing Blumine pass in a stylish vehicle after her marriage to Towgood, Lucien sees the contrast between his defeated condition on foot and the elegant carriage that means success in the world, the very carriage that had once borne him with Louise on the way to Paris. She invites him to enter, but he responds coldly with a look at once humble and menacing. "L'auteur des Marguerites"

150

he is here as he turns back to the road, and the allusion to his worthless poems accurately reflects his place in the world.

At last, sick and exhausted, his money nearly gone, Lucien takes refuge with a miller and his wife. He falls asleep, and after fourteen hours they are not sure whether he is still alive. They speculate on his occupation or identity. His hands are white like those of a man who does nothing; for them he combines the qualities of an actor, a prince, a bishop, and a poet. Awakening and overhearing their speculation, Lucien gives the most accurate identification of himself possible, and we can only hope that his defeat will have taught him to know himself as never before. His name is Lucien de Rubempré, he is the son of the pharmacist Chardon at l'Houmeau, and his sister has married the printer, David Séchard. For the first time Lucien says who and what he is, whose son and brother he is, who they are and what work they do. All that was held against him in the Opera box of Mme d'Espard is now honestly acknowledged; all that once ruined his *avenir*, now helps him on his way in the present. The revelation of his identity prompts an account of the plight of his family, and Lucien hears the terrible result of his having forged David's name. He collapses, is overcome by his usual remorse. The priest and doctor are sent for, but references to Lucien's great personal beauty, by which the miller's wife is deeply moved, tell us again why he can behave as he does in the world: his beauty, which supports his other weaknesses, insures forgiveness. Amid hot tears Lucien performs his favorite religious exercise, the sacrament of penance, pouring out a tale of sin and woe to the priest, eagerly pursuing the line of confession, repentance, and absolution, the formula that enables him to be free of his guilt, to go and sin the more. The dramatic tale ending in vows and resolutions excites the curé's pity, and he agrees to visit Angoulême, to discover whether Lucien may in fact return now to his family. The priest does not know how often in the last eighteen months Lucien has similarly repented, each repentance, as the narrator says, "une scène parfaitement jouée et jouée encore de bonne foi."

Balzac has skillfully made the transition back to Ève and David, so that while the curé is en route, the narrative glances at life in Angoulême during Lucien's sojourn in Paris. We learn of David's steady work at the paper he has invented, the heroism and resourcefulness of Ève, the treachery of Cérizet, who is in the pay of the Cointet brothers, the brilliant handling of the Cointets by Ève, and their agreement to insure the continuity of David's researches. At this point, after hearing nothing from Lucien for six months, David gets word of the forging of his name, something he is not to reveal to Ève or to her mother. But Ève has already endured the most disquieting reports of her brother's failure. On a visit home, Rastignac gives her a full account of the Parisian disaster. Now fallen into cynical cruelty and malice, Rastignac spares Ève nothing of the consequences of Lucien's behavior, including the loss of the king's ordinance. Ève hears the tale, wounded in the most sensitive part of her nature. The most natural and justified illusions of a loving and tender heart are bitterly lost. The silent tears flow down her cheeks onto the brow of her first child, a tiny Lucien, contrasting in their genuineness with Lucien's intermittent effusions brought on by his weakness or folly.

Unwilling to believe Rastignac entirely, Ève asks d'Arthez for the unadorned truth. D'Arthez' letter of analysis serves the narrator as a typical summary and prophecy. D'Arthez does not conceal the truth: Lucien is a man of *poésie* but not a poet; he dreams but does not think, is a weakling who loves to show off. With an insight foretelling Lucien's response to Vautrin, d'Arthez says that Lucien would sign a pact with the Devil if it insured him a few years of brilliant and luxurious living. To be sure, society is quick to reward the cheap and specious façade, though it demands work and discipline from genuine talent. Society is right, Ève is told, as Balzac intrudes his favorite doctrine of work;

society is right to amuse itself and then promptly forget its mere
entertainers, while demanding "de divines magnificences" of
true greatness. Lucien's weak response to temptation, his lack of
will, his easy repentance would not, perhaps, allow him to commit crime as such, but they will let him accept its profits without
sharing the dangers.

With tender pity and lyricism again, Balzac shows us Ève and
David and their love for each other, as David tries to console his
wife in the shock of these new disclosures. She has idealized her
brother and now sees him in "la boue." Lucien is the only
individual in Ève's life about whom she has cherished mistaken
illusions. Everyone else passing before her is analyzed with infallible shrewdness, but she has never dreamed that Lucien would
write against his conscience, attack his best friend, take money
from an actress with whom he appears openly, and finally reduce
his own family to beggary. Her consolation must be that if her
brother falls, her devoted husband will rise to true greatness.

In league with the perfidious Cérizet, the Cointet brothers
obtain Lucien's three forged bills from Paris, hoping to get control of David's invention. They plan to work through the lawyer,
Petit-Claud, whose portrait now, as he plots with Boniface
Cointet, has a fine Dickensian quality, which appears in Balzac's
numerous exposures of legal treachery. As Boniface, his own first
name being an ironic comment on his own villainy, estimates
Petit-Claud, he sees in the lawyer an ideal instrument for the ruin
of David: a Uriah Heep figure, somewhat like the Gupil of
Ursule Mirouet, a hypocritical scoundrel devoured by ambition,
everything in his odious, pockmarked appearance and insinuating
manner indicating to Boniface that "Voilà mon homme." Poor
David is surely doomed against such classic monsters.

Ève herself is driven ever more bitterly into disillusionment as
her judgment of Lucien takes the only form possible. The narrator asks the simple question, "Mais à combien d'illusions ne
disait-elle pas adieu?" Many, indeed, before she can think calmly

of Lucien's terrible perfidy committed when he must have known that they could not pay his bills. The state into which Ève has fallen now is revealed in a *sourire*, that terrible smile once more that moves in sorrow over the pages of the *Comédie*, even reaching into the heart of this, one of Balzac's most idealized creations, yet one compelled by knowledge to record in a smile the end of illusion.

As Lucien shows himself at his feeblest when disaster threatens, so Ève doubles in courage and resource to support the greatness of David. She even tries to solicit help from old Séchard, but after a painful struggle of two hours must confess herself beaten. In their sorrowing despair, Ève and David are moved by the offer from Marion and Kolb of their pitiful savings. This offer reminds us, during Balzac's relentless campaign to make us see the world as it is—a world showing the miserly baseness of old Séchard, the ingratitude and treachery of Cérizet, the cynical brutality of Cointet, the scheming villainy of Petit-Claud, and the shameful failure of Lucien—that another reality, the opposite of all this, though weaker in its genuineness, is equally credible, reassuring, and steadfast amid shifting illusions.

Feeding the baby one day, Ève receives a letter from Lucien, only the third from him in the eighteen months of his absence from home. It is, alas, only a tear-stained lament for his own agonies, reporting the death of Coralie, the terrible dualism of Paris, at once the glory and infamy of France, a place where "j'y ai déjà perdu bien des illusions." More follows of his own sorrow as he tries to get money for Coralie's burial, a problem solved, he then admits in a postscript, by the kindness of Camusot. The letter serves only to deepen the unhappiness of the ones receiving it, Ève and David forgetting, in their sympathy for Lucien, their own disasters so largely caused by his folly. Meanwhile, to escape his enemies, who are plotting to throw David into prison, he hides in a room of Basine Clerget's, where he can go on to the end of his labors. As old Séchard, Cointet, and

Petit-Claud intrigue to get control of David's invention, the narrative returns to Lucien, whose return home is now imminent. His mother, who has suffered greatly, shows that as mother she knows her own children, has indeed known for some time the full meaning of Lucien's behavior. She too sees the intended irony in Louise's carriage, the carriage that once bore off her son, then seated beside her and now ignominiously stealing a ride behind.

THE PRODIGAL RETURNS

In his chapter heading, Balzac recalls the biblical tale, though Lucien, of course, returns chiefly to his brother and sister, not to his father. In the Bible we read that the father "ran" to meet his returning son, and ordered the sacrifice of the fatted calf in his honor. But as Lucien returns, Balzac is careful to dwell on his appearance and, within, on his mingled feelings of vanity, shame, and self-justification. His clothing and boots reveal the hardships of a journey made largely on foot, and Lucien dwells on the contrast between departure and return. He decides to be bold; he praises his own heroism, but his self-deception is excused because he is, after all, a poet, and his spirit struggles between shame and "la poésie de ses souvenirs." Yet, as he goes by Postel's door, his ineffaceable vanity permits him to note with pleasure the absence of his father's name. Lucien's mood lightens as he draws near, and he luckily meets no one. Marion and Kolb see him first and cry out, "Le voilà !" He sees Ève and his mother on the stairway, but no one "runs" to meet him. Embracing him, they forget for the moment their own misery when they see this image of despair, his color burned by the sun of the highway, his brow shadowed by profound melancholy, the spectacle of suffering and poverty precluding all but pity. Balzac shows first the effect on Ève in "le sourire des saintes au milieu de leur martyre," her beautiful face sublime in its grief, with a certain gravity in place of former innocence. Lucien will find that, although he is himself unchanged, Ève is no longer the tender girl, enslaved to her brother's caprice.

After the first outburst of feeling, the reaction is one of silence; each one is afraid to speak, as Lucien looks about for the missing David, a search that forces Ève to weep in her understanding, and Lucien as well. The mother remains pale, "et en apparence impassible." Suddenly Ève rises, goes out in order to spare her brother a harsh word, and cries out to Marion, "Mon enfant, Lucien aime les fraises, il faut en trouver," the strawberries she once prepared for him while he brooded over Louise's ambiguous letter.

In the prodigal's return, Balzac carries us to one of the artistic summits of the *Comédie*. The scene must bear, in our recollection, the weight of the entire mass of the two preceding volumes of *Illusions* with all that they have told of Balzac's terrible understanding of the human condition: of agony endured, folly committed, and ensuing despair. We think of Shakespeare when he calls attention to a coming moment, creating an expectation, a tension of mood that cannot be satisfied by anything less than a stroke of genius. Here Balzac's tact as narrator is infallible as he discovers the only way to avoid anticlimax. The scene brilliantly sustains all that it must bear, is equal to all that Balzac demands of it; but how? Only by silence; no one dares speak until Ève breaks the terrible wordlessness by a homely domestic order, such as may be heard any day in the house, making this day like any other, an order recalling Ève's reminder to Lucien of the strawberries she used to prepare for him. Again she thinks only of and for him, as always. Any attempt by anyone present to say one word would have been dissonant. Ève knows that to speak must be to reproach, and a reproach would be anticlimactic, an inadequate expression of the enormity of Lucien's behavior. Balzac, after Ève's exit to give her order to Marion, now wisely assigns the word that breaks this silence to the mother, in a speech that spares her son nothing. She pauses in a terrifying silence, which Lucien must accept in the impassiveness of his admitted guilt. Her speech is one of pardon to the prodigal son, rather than to the brother, since it is the mother who speaks. But before pardon, the speech indicts, stating in cold and somber tones the complete offense to be pardoned, a speech that starts with reproach, unlike that of the Bible story, and only ends with pardon. Lucien confesses that his mother might have been more severe, and this returns us ominously to his sacramental impulse. As the penitent, in confession, hears in silence the priestly admonition while forming his inward purposes of amendment, so Lucien, on his return, accepts all blame before making predictions of amendment, which, being expressed in the future tense, make us shudder in our painful recollections. Since his entry and reception he has said nothing; he makes no attempt to deny or excuse his guilt, as indeed he seldom does. The virtue of confession is the removal of guilt for such as he, so that he may confess, accept all blame, and make a firm purpose of amendment, clearly shown by d'Arthez to be worthless. Now he tells his mother that he accepts her pardon, "parce que ce sera le seul que j'aurai jamais à recevoir." We recognize this tone of lofty resolution: he will not require his mother's pardon since he will never again offend her, he says in all sincerity, yet we know this sincerity for an interlude that will pass, however copiously may flow the tears of contrition.

After pardon there is renewed affection, but Lucien sees that his sister and mother have accepted the opinions of d'Arthez and that he is no longer their hero, that "toutes ses belles espérances avaient fui sans retour," especially when they refuse to tell him where David is hiding. Lucien indulges in vain and bitter reflections on the evident change, forgetting that the atmosphere in this house was his own work, that they understand him only too well in their determination not to be mistaken again about his character or his *avenir*. He should be warned when the local newspaper gives an absurdly swollen and flattering account of his return, used by Balzac as a summary of all that is wrong with Lucien, all that makes him ready again to fall into his enemies' trap. The synonyms for Lucien's illusions recur in references to great men, dreams, glory, and poets, as the account compares him with great men of other cities, carefully concealing his Parisian disaster, referring six times to the *poète*, who is home again to rest from wearisome struggle, and who is now in the process of adopting the title and name of the illustrious de Rubempré family. Alas, we fear that the *Bildungsmächte* have done their work in vain again, when Lucien refuses to listen to Ève's warning that the newspaper tribute is a mask for jealous hatred. He seems justified when, at eleven o'clock that night, a serenade from the youth of Angoulême brings the great man to a window, where he thanks his townsmen for such an honor. The night rings out with happy cries of tribute to the author of a novel and poems, then cries of "Vive Lucien de Rubempré," using a name not yet his own, clearly a symbol of the falsity of this tribute. These signs of glory are for someone else, we say, for Lucien has not earned them; they are addressed to someone with a name not his own. The rally ends with crowns of flowers tossed to the window; in return for his Marguerite poems, he gets back these flowers, as ephemeral and worthless as the poems. Seeing Ève in tears, Lucien misinterprets them as tears of joy; he has forgotten not only his own misfortunes but those of his family as well. With her calm realism, Ève sees that the triumph must have been staged by some perfidious agent who knows everything from within; since the Marguerite poems were never published, how can anyone felicitate Lucien on their further success "à venir"?

Now we fear again that Lucien is not strong enough to contain all that Balzac demands of him. He seems something of a fool, the only explanation being that he is a *poète*. But this is far less lame and artificial, has less the appearance of being dragged in where nothing else will do, if we keep in mind the structure of meaning built upon this term throughout. The word *poète* then explains everything and is adequate to do so. Yet clearly his previous sufferings cannot have been as real to Lucien as to his family or even to us. We have been deeply moved by experiences that only touched Lucien on the surface; our hearts were rent while he escaped into vain revery and illusion. We have no remaining illusions about the realities in Balzac's universe, but Lucien still has, and the lessons of the hero as failure become not his but our own, so accounting for his defeat. As we have learned more from Lucien's agonies than he has, we have again that frequent sense that he is a creature acted upon, a vehicle through whom more of life is conveyed than he himself can understand or profit from.

The day after the serenade, all cunningly staged by Petit-Claud, this gifted scoundrel pursues his campaign to befuddle Lucien with flattering courtship. He proposes a banquet in the poet's honor, to be held ten days hence. Petit-Claud, in response to Lucien's absurd airs, maintains the posture of a humble small-town lawyer. In league with Louise and Châtelet, whose hatred of Lucien he sees and understands, he hopes to find out from Lucien where David is hidden, and if David perishes through Lucien's fault, the poet will be driven out of town in disgrace. Meanwhile, Petit-Claud poses as David's champion, the hero of an effort to secure the success of a man of genius. Ignoring Ève's further warning, and confident that he can regain his power over Louise, Lucien sets out to get a new outfit of clothes in order to appear at the banquet to his best advantage. He writes to Lousteau reminding him of the thousand francs still owed; he lists in detail what he will need by the end of the week, for "je suis le héros d'un banquet." He thinks he can employ the clothes in the good cause of repaying his obligation to David, but he only exposes the falsity of what the clothes stand for. Here Balzac chooses to make his first link between Lucien and Esther, for long before he has ever seen or heard of her, she gives him something, and he takes it, something gotten from another man, something worthless, just as he will go on taking from both of them to the end. Lousteau's reply tells how his old friends in Paris have combined to supply Lucien's outfit, friends "assez riches pour emmener la Torpille," who sends on, with the other gifts, a broken gold watch given Esther

by "un imbécile." When dressed in his new outfit, Lucien stuns
Ève by his appearance, then gives her the watch, which he says
is like himself—out of order. Is it fanciful to see, in this gift of the
gold watch that does not work, a prophecy of the money that
Esther leaves to Lucien after her death? For the recipients of this
money, too, will be Ève and her children.

These new clothes, the things said of them, and the uses Lucien
makes of them, carry rich and ominous meanings from the preceding narrative. At the outset of his career Lucien sees the need of
the right clothes, and we look at him as he then was, because
again he lacks the right clothes. But every time he changes his
clothes, he reassumes his illusions. He should therefore remain
clothed as he is, since the garments needed to succeed in the world
to which he aspires stand for the false qualities that enable one to
rise to that world. Is he here given another chance in just the
position he was in before when he made the wrong choice? A similar choice is being offered again, by similar people in the same
place with the same opposing values in question, symbolized by
the same need for clothes of a certain kind—clothes to make him
fatally handsome again, to bring out the unsound values of his
outward attraction, and so to revive the forces that have ruined
him. Then, too, the sources of Lucien's new clothes are allied to
the false value of those clothes as outward trappings to enhance
his fatal beauty, letting him repeat his former sins. He obtains the
clothes from the same cheap journalists and Parisian knaves, plus
an actress and a courtesan as before, Florine and Esther combining to make the equivalent of Coralie. We can only expect the
same blunders and stupidities as before, even though Lucien's
motive is now to undo the harm wrought by his previous use of
these same means in Paris. Is he now, by the same reliance on the
false value of his beauty and its adornment, to achieve an opposite
result? The whole weight of Balzac's painstaking metaphorical
development denies this. From these means will come what must
and did before, something equally disastrous because false and

illusory. But Lucien sees himself as owing everything to clothes, as indeed he owes his failure to them. For him they are the arms he bears into the warfare of his life, now to be waged at least once in a righteous cause.

At the banquet he is a stunning sight, the recipient of extravagant praise and absurd tributes. He finally rises and receives upon his head a laurel crown. Drunk in more ways than one, and in tears, Lucien speaks gratefully of this tribute. He modestly projects into the future—his terrible *avenir* again—the means of justifying such praise, and Balzac shows the falsity both of the tribute and what is supposed to justify it, by his use of the word *avenir*.

David, now in hiding, has received letters from Ève and Lucien. Ève has to warn her husband against Lucien; he must act as if the poet were not there. She is afraid precisely because Lucien so much wants to help, to get the debts paid, as she sees, out of pride. When Lucien thinks he is doing the right thing and is confident of his solution, Ève's fear increases although she admits that they are now living on the money that Lucien's friends sent with the clothes from Paris. Lucien's message is full of glowing confidence. David's emotion overcomes his prudence, and he goes out to meet his friend, just after the banquet, away from which Petit-Claud has accompanied Lucien at midnight. The two brothers rush weeping into each other's arms, and all seems about to end happily when the world as it is asserts the right to intrude. It again takes the form of the reptilian Cérizet, for he who once before intruded on the poetic reveries of the two friends with a message from reality is now hiding behind a nearby wall to overhear their conversation. This in turn he will convey to Petit-Claud, who has promised him money to buy David's printing business if he can deliver the inventor in person.

Petit-Claud has made progress in other lines of his ambition as well, and with the aid of Cointet has arranged to marry into the aristocracy. The signing of a marriage contract gives Lucien an opportunity to display his reestablished elegance when Petit-

Claud, ashamed of his mother, pretends that she is ill and asks Lucien to sign for him. The great man of Angoulême presents a ravishing, Apollo-like appearance and with studied assurance he adopts the air of a *grand seigneur* on a visit to common men. Modeling himself on de Marsay, Lucien astonishes Louise, to whom he speaks with cool impertinence. Seated with her on a sofa, he begins his effort to reenter her life, pretending to be moved at sight of one whom he deeply loved. The narrator refers to him as "l'élève de Coralie," a playactor who now manages to force some tears into his eyes. The allusion to Coralie is poignant and ironic in this context: for such pretentious, hypocritical effrontery as this, did she throw away her young life? But Lucien does not forget his chief aim, and mentions David's problems. When Châtelet comes up and promises to help, and when later on he says in so many words that he will arrange to free David, Lucien has every reason to believe that his acting has been successful. It is the only sort of success that he can hope for, based on clothes, manner, appearance, acting, or pretending, and so leading again to illusions in others. Poor Ève allows herself to hope at last, and goes for a late evening walk with Lucien. In his familiar dramatic structure again, Balzac has permitted a measure of hope and confidence just before irretrievable disaster. Cérizet forges a note in Lucien's hand, assuring David that he may now come out of hiding and go to Châtelet. A genuine letter from Lucien preceded this earlier in the day, assuring David of success and of the protection of Châtelet. The forged note seems a natural sequence, like a report on something accomplished in the meantime. David then comes out, only to be captured.

At home, Lucien admits to his mother that he was the cause of David's arrest. Stunned by his mother's look, which contains her malediction, he locks himself in his room. Just as after each failure Lucien writes a letter or goes to confession, so now he writes what he imagines to be a final letter to Ève. He is a fatal influence on his family because of the unresolved paradox that he brings disaster upon them from tenderness, and thus, for their devotion, he renders only evil. He condemns himself without pity, seeing that his vanity would always lead to the commission of *sottises*. His nature needs to be supplemented and enforced; he should have married a strong woman like Louise. In this passage he anticipates the coming of Vautrin: the weakness needing domination will then meet the force of character that needs to dominate. But in this last mood of despair Lucien sees his efforts coming to nothing through his lack of equilibrium, a fatal disproportion between means and ends. In sad contrast to his many boasts of future success, he can only say of his future now, "je serai plus vieux que mon âge, sans fortune et sans considération." Having resolved on suicide, he asks that no inquiry be made of him; his tomb will be in their hearts, so "encore adieu."

The farewell letter is brought down and placed on the cradle of the infant Lucien, and the self-doomed hero, in tears, places a last kiss on Ève's brow as she sleeps in exhaustion. Going, he awakens Kolb, to whom he gives a message for David, then quickly descends to the river Charente, dressed, the narrative says, as if going to a festival, though his elegant clothes, the harness of a Parisian dandy, are soon destined to become a shroud. Lucien departs, then, in darkness and silence. Just as silence was the only response possible for this house to his return from Paris, so no other response is possible to his final going but the silence of admitted guilt.

ENTER SATAN

The narrator pauses, while Lucien is on his way to the Charente, to give us a discourse on suicide in its three principal manifestations, which declare themselves when a man's self-esteem can no longer endure the clash between the realities of his life and his vain hopes. Lucien, now called only the *poète*, as if this term were intended to contain all others, hesitates like Raphaël Valentin over the manner of his death. If he dies in the open river, his suicide will excite comment and inquiry, his body will present a hideous deformed spectacle, distressing to one for whom appearance had been everything in life. He remembers having seen, on the way back from Paris, not far from the mill of those who had befriended him, a deep, quiet pool of water, into which he might fall, weighted with rocks, and so be carried deep into oblivion, final and absolute. No one could inquire, no one could see his body, which, so attractive in life, had inspired a mass of illusions. Lucien then tries to keep out of sight as he walks toward Marsac, but having picked a bouquet of yellow flowers, he attracts the attention of a traveler, a Spanish priest who has alighted from the coach en route from Bordeaux to Paris. The man is struck by the profoundly melancholy beauty of the *poète*, by the symbolic bouquet and elegant attire. This is Vautrin, we say, though now called the Abbé Carlos Herrera. It must be the Vautrin of *Le Père Goriot*, for he could not have become Herrera or any other incarnation had he not first been Vautrin, the most spectacular of all Balzacian monsters. He descends on Lucien like a hunter who has at long last found the object of his chase.

In tears, Lucien first rejects Vautrin's consolations, saying that he is bent on suicide. Vautrin assumes that he must be suffering from an incurable disease, the only irrevocable cause of suicide in Balzac's theory. Yes, Lucien replies, and the disease is poverty. For some twenty pages, now, Vautrin assumes control of the narrative with a set of instructions in the way of the world. He gives this discourse in the symbolic carriage that leads Lucien into temptation and now back again to Paris; he passes his hand under Lucien's arm and "le força littéralement à monter dans sa voiture." In his role as priest, of course, Vautrin urges Lucien to go to confession, and for the third time in the last fifteen days Lucien repeats the confession he loves to make of his life's vicissitudes, so that he may repent and sin again. As they pass the house where Rastignac's family lives (a scene much admired by Proust), Lucien remarks on the success of his townsmen, while Vautrin evades a question that would have allowed him to disclose his own role in that success. As Vautrin resumes his discourse, the effect is to return Lucien to his state before the first departure from home for

Paris, and the words *avenir, ambition, destinée* and *grands hommes* are again restored to their illusory meaning. The familiar doctrines pour out again as Lucien hears how to dominate the world: one must study and obey its laws, showing that other human beings are only instruments used to gain success.

The temptation encounters little resistance, and Vautrin finds, in this youth who needs only to be told what he wishes to hear, an attractive tabula rasa, well disposed to accept his influence. Lucien is tempted also by a man who has saved his life by preventing suicide, a man who gives another chance at the success he failed to achieve before, offering the lessons of cynical experience with confidence and the steadfast support of a parent. As he watches Lucien's growing response, Vautrin permits himself "un malicieux sourire." His temptation comes at the right time and the right place certainly, in a carriage on the way to Paris, and is effective in its summary of Lucien's previous lessons, its giving him anew the rules to follow if he gets another chance. The rules emerge in a "sermon," which tells Lucien to forget morality; to be discreet and show the world only an attractive exterior; to observe the right *forme* in his actions, a certain Chesterfieldian style that will wait until riches and a title are secure before indulging in the luxury of virtue. Vautrin is here a synthesis of many themes and types—the detached criminal observer of life; Satan tempting Christ; God or Providence taking possession of a created object; the old man in *La Peau de chagrin* offering a gift analogous to the fatal skin accepted by Raphaël; Mephistopheles, an earthly devil, offering the worldly wisdom common to all intelligent men. The "temptation," according to Mr. Lukacs, consists in the now familiar Balzacian fact that Vautrin's reading of the world is shared by the wickedest and most saintly beings of the *Comédie*. Vautrin therefore stands "in the graveyard of all illusions developed during several centuries," bearing the demonic *sourire* of satisfaction, because he is right and because the best people that there are admit it.

When the right moment has come, Vautrin offers Lucien a Satanic lure, "ce pacte d'homme à démon," "All this will I give thee," if Lucien will consent to obey him. He offers once again, in all their falsity and illusion, Lucien's *espérances*. Obey me, the devil says, and in three years you will be Marquis de Rubempré, you will marry one of the highest of noblewomen, and one day you will become a peer of France. Vautrin's language is heavily biblical, invoking the dualism of Cain and Abel, the role of God the father-creator as well as of Satan the tempter. As the carriage draws near to Paris, Vautrin appeals to the worst in Lucien, even hinting at homosexuality. What Lucien could not accomplish alone may come with the devil's own energy to aid him. Forgetting the past, Lucien sees that he has no moral problem here; he already knows that Vautrin's advice is evil, but he asks a series of brief questions: why is Vautrin interested in him; what price does he desire; why is he so generous; what is his own share going to be? Vautrin replies with a smile, and they alight from the carriage to walk and speak in the open air. Vautrin's reply is again Satanic, like his terrible smile. He refers to *Venice Preserved* and the superior love of friendship; he admits that he is himself an atheist beneath his priestly garb; that he is like the Satan of *Paradise Lost*, who shared mankind's horror of solitude and thus required companions on the way to his infernal destiny. Vautrin is equally explicit in repeating his father-creator role; he wishes to love his creature as a father loves his child, the creature made in his image, in whom he lives—"Ce beau jeune homme, c'est moi." But the final step is not taken until the offer of money itself, fifteen thousand francs to secure David's freedom. They reenter the carriage and are seated after Lucien's question, which in effect commits him, "Où sont-ils?" Vautrin reaches his enormous hand into a pouch made up of three compartments, and three times the hand emerges filled with gold. Then, "Mon père, je suis à vous."

At home, meanwhile, Ève and David are finally beaten down, and they decide to accept Petit-Claud's proposal, however costly to them. So David is free and his obligations are removed just before the arrival of Lucien's message and his fifteen thousand francs. His mother can only recall the self-accusation of the suicide letter: there is a fatality in Lucien's actions toward his family, no matter what good he tries to do. His message implies an insight into his coming destiny: instead of killing himself, he writes, he has sold his life; instead of physical death, he has undergone a spiritual one. He has become secretary to a Spanish diplomat: "Je recommence une existence terrible. Peut-être aurait-il mieux valu me noyer."

M. Bardèche is convinced that this last supposition of Lucien's is right, that he is in fact dead on meeting Vautrin, his new life only a surcease. Lucien should die, then, when the action demands it, and his eventual death in prison is only the first suicide postponed. The life that passes in between only repeats the folly of old, and Lucien gets another chance that he does not deserve, one that is not called for by his character and behavior, or by his fictional role in Balzac's created universe. He will fail again, that is, and for the same reasons as before, combining guilt, ill luck, weakness of will, and lack of special force at decisive moments. He seems guilty both in his clandestine departure with Louise and on his return when he hopes that no one will see him. He hoped that no one would see him go because he was guilty in the manner and circumstances of his going, guilty of treason on behalf of his illusions, the *avenir* so totally false that he deserves the bitter punishment visited upon him for pursuing it. But when he comes home, he is guilty rather of defeat, and wounded pride, here, may be only the other side of his former guilt. If he were returning from Paris, a success, he would not steal into town afraid of being seen, for neither Lucien nor anyone else would ask or care what a man had been guilty of on his way to the summit. Nonetheless, Lucien engenders a measure of sympathy as his fatal bad luck pursues him to the end of *Illusions*, and the money that would have saved David arrives just after the irrevocable papers have been signed, so that

Cointet, the kind of man who is lucky, is able to remark on his own narrow escape. The malice of fortune then combines with other elements to achieve Lucien's ruin, as later, when the message of rescue comes after his death in *Splendeurs*.

Guilt and bad luck join with an inner weakness that makes Lucien an easy prey to temptation, an easy mark for his enemies, an easy victim of the world as it is. M. Laubriet compares Lucien with Wenceslas Steinbock of *La Cousine Bette*, also a gifted youth of many excellent qualities, but also ruined eventually through failure in resolution, in coolness, in force of will and character. Lucien is seducible, like Eve before the serpent, by words persuading him to actions he already wishes to perform, temptation being always self-engendered in such a nature. True, every poor young man is allied to the criminal by resentment against a society that excludes them both from fortune and success, and this helps to account for the ease of Lucien's response. But Vautrin offers him hard cash and a most persuasive discourse. The money enables Lucien to pay off David and so free himself from his suicidal despair. The discourse revives his spirit and ambition, setting him back on the road to Paris. Thus Vautrin both inspires the desire to return and enables Lucien to do so.

But as M. Milner has pointed out, temptation proceeds also from the needs of the tempter, and Vautrin is in desperate need of Lucien, making their union logical and inevitable. Vautrin will find someone, and it turns out to be Lucien because he corresponds to what Vautrin has planned to satisfy his needs. Lucien becomes "la chose," the instrument of Vautrin's revenge on society. We know, as Vautrin does not, that Lucien's disastrous fate has already been decided, that this is a doomed enterprise, based on illusion even less justified than before. In signing his pact with Vautrin, Lucien gives up nothing; he remains what he is, a creature destined for ignominy. He admits that he himself cannot achieve his ambitions, that his ambition is allied more than before to sentiments of revenge. He will use Vautrin to punish those who drove him out of Paris, but this too is an illusion, for he cannot overcome his enemies without paying a price that must again defeat him. To have his revenge, he becomes the passive instrument of Vautrin's revenge, his mask in fact, emphasizing the unreal, illusory quality of the action to come. Their agreement has other implications that Vautrin himself seems not to fear. As Vautrin's embodiment, his means of returning to the *Comédie*, Lucien makes a prisoner of Vautrin: if anything happens to one it happens to them both, and neither can succeed without the other. If each shares the other's life, he must also share his death, and when Lucien is dead, so in effect is Vautrin as such, who then turns into Bibi-Lupin, policeman. Yet for the first time in his life, Lucien seems to render something equal to what he has accepted from another. Vautrin is now vulnerable, since he has allied himself with a doomed creature. He can no longer dominate circumstances or events, and is helpless when at last Lucien's fatal career drags him likewise into the abyss. Their pact gives Lucien the greater liberty, offering another chance with freedom to act.

We shall find them in *Splendeurs* inhabiting a fantastic universe, a world of mutually sustained dreams lived more intensely than their truer preceding lives. Their agreement is a variation on that in *Le Pacte* (1822), a work in the Satanic tradition. A man sells his soul to Satan, and in return he is allowed to emigrate into the bodies of persons or beings that he will designate. But Lucien agrees to let the devil inhabit his body. It is Satan who passes into another body, not the one whose soul has been sold, removed to make way for the devil's presence. In effect Lucien gives up his entire being: his soul to get Satan's help in achieving his ambitions, as in the standard "pact" myth; his body so that the devil may occupy it, using it to carry out his promise of success to Lucien, and to inflict his own revenge upon the world.

7

Splendeurs et misères
des courtisanes

The narrative of Lucien's second career in Paris begins with ominous praise of his striking beauty. At the last Opera ball of the year, he walks about evidently in search of someone, while many gaze in astonishment at this extraordinarily handsome "jeune dandy" of irreproachable manners, the picture of assured elegance and worldly poise. His appearance belies the sordid truth of his recent past and the fatal weakness of his character, his youth and beauty, like clothes, hiding "de profonds abîmes." Lucien deceives everyone without exception at first, and now Balzac quickly reestablishes his controlling themes and images in remarking Lucien's appearance: the "abîmes" within him, which correspond to those awaiting him in the world, and the illusion that a change in his name will transform his destiny.

Lucien is seen by Châtelet and Mme d'Espard, who is astonished at the changed manner of the "fils d'apothicaire." When Châtelet approaches and calls him M. Chardon, however, Lucien coolly rebukes his enemy for using this ridiculous name, now changed to Rubempré by the king's ordinance. Lucien is happy to prevail at the Opera, the scene of his first humiliation in Paris by Mme d'Espard, to whose cruel smile of that occasion he now speaks with the *sourire* of a man not wishing to compromise good fortune that is secure. Meanwhile Vautrin, in a mask, planning to obtain the Marquise as Lucien's mistress, hovers in the background, a Satanic master of ceremonies. He draws Rastignac aside and, recalling their days at Pension Vauquer, forces him to befriend Lucien. When the poet is accosted by his journalist friends, he lacks the sustained nerve to cut them dead. He loses a chance to rise above an odious aspect of his past, for he is still corruptible, too tolerant of hypocrisy and moral indifference. As he refuses to divulge the source of his new prosperity, Lucien suddenly leaves the group to join a masked woman. Bixiou recognizes her as the courtesan La Torpille, and it is assumed that Lucien derives his support from her.

We learn the story of Esther, who, in despair after being recognized at the Opera, also attempts suicide, is interrupted and returned to the world by Vautrin. Having met Lucien three months ago, she fell so passionately in love with him as to deify him. Once a common "fille à numéro" in the house of Mme Meynardie, to conceal her past she has given Lucien the address at which Vautrin finds her, a friend's room where she has tried to live by honest work as a needlewoman. Lucien loves her and believes her virtuous; she will soon be nineteen years old, just the same age as Coralie was at her death. The simple fact of her age seems to be a prophecy, for it recalls Coralie, whose place Esther will now take in Lucien's life, and whose sacrificial end she must share. So Balzac's courtesans, despite the freedom of their lives, are caught up in the *Comédie* and go on to predetermined destinies. Both Coralie and Esther must love Lucien, and each in turn must be destroyed by her love.

Vautrin undertakes to rehabilitate Esther, and places her in a religious school for girls of good family, where she is educated and transformed until Vautrin relents on seeing that she is literally dying of her love for Lucien. Vautrin has established him in a luxurious apartment with all the features demanded by the elegant life of a dandy, a "poète, écrivain, ambitieux, vicieux, à la fois orgueilleux et vaniteux, plein de négligence et souhaitant l'ordre," an incomplete genius who conceives but cannot execute. But with Vautrin to support him and to supply what is lacking in his character, their union seems to flourish until Lucien's intense passion for Esther threatens to disrupt the new *avenir*. After a violent quarrel it soon becomes clear that he is aware of Vautrin's clerical disguise while not yet knowing the criminal's true identity. To insure the continuity of his plans, Vautrin sets certain conditions for the two lovers. They are not to consider marriage. Esther must live in the place provided for her as if in prison; she may go out only at night and must never be seen by anyone. Vautrin explains why this must be done: Lucien will achieve the title of Marquis through marriage to a girl of high birth, and then go on to a career in diplomacy, ending as a peer of France. For all this, Esther, like Coralie before her, must lay down her life. When she asks Lucien whether it is his will that she accept the power of Vautrin over her life now, that she be supervised and guarded by two hideous women, he nods in silence, accepting as always the sacrifice of others in the cause of illusion.

And yet, the *avenir* seems less a folly when outlined by Vautrin. It is more specific than before, when Lucien's unsupported dreams were vague and shifting. Actual steps are to be taken, stated positions to be gained one after another until the goal, equally clear, is attained. One step is already taken, the king's ordinance permitting the change in name: we are not told when or how this was done, but this move, once impossible, gives the impression that the remaining steps upward are within Vautrin's resources. Further, Lucien has Vautrin with him to supply the forms of energy whose absence had caused his previous failure. Lucien himself seems to have learned from experience; he has a convincing air of success like one making all of the right moves, sensible enough to conceal what once he flaunted openly. He has always had ability, as is universally admitted, but is now more stable, with more sense and control. As Rastignac points out, Lucien has to be taken seriously.

He now spends four happy years, secure under the direction of Vautrin and blissful in the love of Esther. He is outwardly discreet, cool, and reserved, so that on the surface his life displays the right tone. He rarely goes anywhere on foot, and so avoids meeting people he no longer wishes to know. By mid-1829, his marriage to Clothilde de Grandlieu is being discussed, the union that will assure the title of Marquis and establish Lucien's political and diplomatic career. His secret love affair is a sound basis for a correct visible life, since it prevents the need for pursuing other women and avoids unwise connections. Lucien's happiness with Esther is totally unsuspected in the middle of Paris, "un poème, une symphonie de quatre ans." The controlling metaphor of Lucien's submission to Vautrin is again military: complete obedience to orders without trying to understand them, proper terms derived from the laws of combat on the battlefield of Paris. Lucien lets himself be coerced into actions that horrify him: he shuts his eyes and obeys, while only Vautrin is free.

How much the Rubempré cycle is a *carrefour* of the *Comédie* comes to mind when Lucien is invited for Sunday dinner at Delphine de Nucingen's house. He sees the elite of the Balzacian world assembled there, and his own degree of success emerges in the hypocrisy and forced amiability that people feel obliged to show him. As he enters the room, more handsome and stunningly dressed than ever, Rastignac, de Marsay, du Tillet, and Bianchon discuss Lucien's present and future, recalling the obstacles in the way of his ambitions. At dinner Nucingen tells of the strange beauty he has seen at night in the forest, and now Lucien commits the blunder of letting his knowledge of Esther emerge in a fleeting smile. "Vous rêviez! dit en souriant Lucien," and Rastignac, seeing the smile, interprets it correctly. It is evident that Lucien realizes whom Nucingen has seen, for he quickly leaves the company, annoyed with himself for having smiled. Bianchon's interpretation of the event is that Lucien knows whom Nucingen has seen. His remark, so innocent and natural in this context, gives Nucingen the idea of having Lucien spied upon, thus disclosing "un abîme sous le bonheur d'Esther."

As a sign of his new prudence, Lucien confesses the episode of his smile to Vautrin, who responds instantly with a proposal to sell Esther to Nucingen and thus raise the money needed to pay existing debts and to finance the marriage to Clothilde. As Coralie was sold by her mother, so Esther is to be sold into the control of a man she will hate. Lucien realizes that this will kill her. As always, his first response is decent, and he recoils in horror, but he bows his head weakly before Vautrin's fearful exposure of his position, from which crime alone will rescue him. His first ambitions were wrong because he was too weak to achieve them. Then after a while, when they seemed within range again, the ambitions become not only wrong but wicked because the means needed to attain them lay in crime and infamy. For the Devil, the chance sight of Esther is a stroke of luck upon which they must now capitalize, and the language borrows from images of gambling, luck, and infernal transactions. Lucien's ambitions are like a note made out to the Devil, who will collect when the note falls due. It promises that Lucien will commit whatever crimes are necessary to achieve his ambitions; it falls due if he refuses to pay, if he will not commit crime, that is, in order to succeed. The narrative makes allusion to Satanic pacts, undertaken to insure a "bel avenir" for Lucien, who is now drawn more inextricably than ever into his association with Vautrin, knowing perfectly well who and what lies under the disguise of Carlos Herrera. Since the day of Esther's kidnapping and imprisonment Lucien has known the horrible foundation of his happiness, and, as Balzac now identifies Vautrin, what had been the foolish but forgivable dreams of misguided youth are transformed, with Lucien's weak consent, into criminal ambitions. Vautrin corrupts Lucien gradually by drawing him into consent to infamous deeds under the increase of cruel necessities, under pressure of circumstances he cannot escape. He destroys the remains of Lucien's virtue, while letting him appear noble and pure in the eyes of the world. The final secret of his identity is not released to Lucien until the habits of life in Paris, the satisfied vanity of his success, have enslaved the poet's soul and body. The narrative pauses to contrast Rastignac and Lucien, using the last name for one and the first name for the other as if comparing man and boy. "Là, où jadis Rastignac, tenté par ce démon, avait résisté, Lucien succomba." Out of dramatic necessity Balzac seems for the moment to accept this as wholly true. He is, at any rate, at great pains to stress his meaning, lest its full diabolic implications escape us. "Le mal," he says, "dont la configuration poétique s'appelle le Diable, usa envers cet homme à moitié femme de ses plus attachantes séductions," still making a kind of excuse for his failing hero. Vautrin prevails, then, by placing Lucien under obligation for his very life, preventing his suicide, promising him a great future, drawing him into requirements that demand crime for their achievement, making him used to a position and life in the world which, unlike Pip, he cannot give up, subtly, slowly maneuvering and compromising him, seeming to give much and ask little, until Lucien has lost all will or power to resist. The Sophoclean dramatic movement of seeming failure, quick success, then rapid collapse, recurs throughout, and Lucien seems an assured success in Paris just before the revelation of what lies behind the façade he presents to the world, of what must destroy him in the end. To this moral revelation he must now add the knowledge of a growing financial crisis, for not only have Esther and Lucien spent the funds that Vautrin is supposed to be guarding as a banker for the criminal world, but all three have contracted huge debts with no hope of rescue until by chance Nucingen sees Esther. Vautrin's quick response to this stroke of luck shows how precariously he has based the fantastic edifice of his plans.

CLOTHILDE

Balzac, having shown us what lies behind Lucien's façade of well-mannered virtue, now turns to the world into which Lucien aspires to gain admission by his marriage to Clothilde-Frédérique de Grandlieu. The oldest of the Grandlieu daughters and the sister of the more fortunate and lovely Sabine, poor Clothilde is now twenty-seven years of age, unattractive, angular, bony, but deeply in love with Lucien. He would gladly endure a far more repulsive choice in order to gain access to her father's house. He is never more the incurably provincial arriviste than in those moments when the great door turns upon its hinges to admit his cabriolet: "Quoique mon père ait été simple pharmacien à l'Houmeau," he says to himself, "j'entre pourtant là." Crimes even worse than alliance with a forger would have been acceptable to Lucien in order to continue mounting these steps and to hear the announcement, "Monsieur de Rubempré." For in this house, second only to the royal court itself, one may see the greatest names in France—a grand salon indeed, into which even Léontine de Sérisy has never gained admission. But Lucien's beauty and style suffice, for the wicked and beautiful Diane de Maufrigneuse falls in love with him and manages, with the aid of Clothilde and others, to introduce the poet. Envious forces try to discredit Lucien with the Duke himself, but he is steadfast, ignores many affronts as he comes calling five days out of seven, while under the guidance of Vautrin's shrewd diplomacy he maintains a cool reserve in other relationships. The Grandlieu salon is now his main field of battle, for which he carefully saves his most powerful weapons until assured that Clothilde has fallen hopelessly in love with him. He plays the role of lover superbly, he writes glowing letters to Clothilde, he pretends to be a fervent Catholic and monarchist, he writes half-anonymous articles in support of church and throne, but so far the hatred of Mme d'Espard has prevented any official recognition, such as appointment as secretary to a cabinet minister. In fact, he has not yet dined in the house of Clothilde's father because of his uncertain income, which leaves him open to the insinuations of Mme d'Espard. This implacable enemy asks a number of questions of Clothilde's mother, but the girl herself cannot resist a youth who is "beau comme un rêve," an expression that recalls Lucien's own dreams of an *avenir*, which likewise rest on nothing more substantial than his physical beauty. As for the source of the million he will need to buy back the Rubempré estates and so be made a Marquis, Clothilde's mother can say that no dishonest man will be acceptable, though he may be, like Lucien, a poet, young and handsome.

After the conversation between Mme d'Espard and the Duchess, Clothilde makes a number of disclosures. She reports the prevailing gossip about debts of sixty thousand francs, and that the Duke has learned of the work done by his mother and sister. Lucien admits that they have been poor, as the tears come to his eyes, the first tears of his second coming to Paris. He mentions the death of his mother two years ago and insists on the present great wealth of his sister, explaining also the reasons for Mme d'Espard's hatred. Meanwhile Clothilde reassures Lucien, who is to remain away for a time until her father can change his attitude. In typical contrast, Lucien goes from Clothilde to Esther, now weeping, heartbroken, for fear of separation from him if she must accept Nucingen. Lucien thinks of the similar love he has inspired in Coralie, of the sensuous appeal he seems to have for such women. Unlike Coralie, Esther cannot endure the thought of Lucien's marriage, but sees that it is essential to his *destinée*, the associations of falsity around this term being now transferred to the marriage, a false means to a false end, part of a doomed enterprise. But Lucien's beauty continues to unite the most diverse possible elements through the love it inspires in women from the entire range of society. Léontine de Sérisy, also its victim, is joined by the pathetic Lydie Peyrade, daughter of the police spy to whom she confesses having fallen in love with Lucien as he walked in the Tuileries with Mme de Sérisy. Peyrade now warns Lydie against

Lucien, who has, through his beauty, a great initial advantage, only to find in the end that nothing can come of it. An agreeable exterior is so happily received by the world that handsome young men are easily misled; they do not have enough difficulty at the outset, when one should have it, and therefore troubles come later at higher cost.

Nucingen hires Peyrade and Contenson as spies to discover the whereabouts of Esther, now hidden in the forest of Saint-Germain after Vautrin has installed another woman in her apartment to mislead the spies. When he tells the two lovers that their dream is over and that Esther is not to see Lucien, Lucien weeps, she rushes to him, takes him in her arms, and drinks up the tear that falls upon his cheek. Balzac's technique of accumulated meanings for a given word here achieves a bitterly ironic force for *avenir* when Vautrin refers to Lucien's need to triumph at the Hôtel de Grandlieu, "et enfin la nécessité pour Esther de se sacrifier à ce magnifique avenir." Knowing that Lucien's marriage will destroy Esther, Vautrin outlines with relentless cruelty the entire plan that insures her doom. She will obey, for "mon amour est une maladie mortelle." Esther now becomes the means of getting enormous sums from Nucingen, but the money must seem to come from Lucien's family as if they had provided six hundred thousand francs to facilitate his marriage. When, after five months during which Nucingen's mounting passion has not been satisfied, the house acquired for Esther becomes ready, she cannot hope any longer to postpone her odious surrender. Vautrin confronts Esther with this continued prudery, whereby she is endangering her lover's happiness, when so little after all is being asked of her, only to go back in her past, to become La Torpille again, until the essential million is safely gained.

Lucien at last gets the money to pay for the Rubempré estates when Esther becomes owner of the house set up for her by Nucingen. All seems to go well; Lucien is cordially received by the Grandlieus amid smiles of contentment, Clothilde glows with happiness, and as Lucien leaves her house, he hopes to be married before the coming of Lent in 1830. But once again this is only apparent success before the counterattack of grim reality. The following day, Lucien is suddenly confronted by Corentin, who has discovered the liaison with Esther and the source of his recently acquired fortune. He demands a hundred thousand francs in blackmail, lest he disclose the truth to Clothilde's father. Lucien stares him coolly in the eye, denies all charges, and denies any dependence on Herrera, who has nothing to do with his affairs and is now on the way to Spain. The day of reckoning is not so readily ignored; Lucien appears one evening at the Hôtel de Grandlieu in a magnificent coupé with splendid horses, the fatal carriage that has so often conveyed him into disaster. A footman refuses him admittance, and to show that Lucien knows the meaning of this, the narrator need only tell us that "une petite sueur froide lui mit quelques perles au front." He goes to the Théâtre des Italiens, wandering in the foyer like a drunken man. The laws of the world apply themselves to his life and hopes, ironic as it is that Lucien, who has tried hard to live by these laws at terrible moral sacrifice to himself, should again suffer from their relentless application. Lucien is now embarrassed by Rastignac's congratulations on his coming marriage, compelled to hide his wretchedness "en souriant."

Lucien's hard-won gains seem rapidly to drain away as the hostile Duc de Rhétoré reveals the affair with Esther to Mme de Sérisy while Lucien, talking to Esther, relates the disaster at the Hôtel de Grandlieu. Mme de Sérisy's response, the narrator remarks, could not be placed in "la catégorie de ses sourires," but she will find it more difficult than she now imagines to overcome her infatuation. Vautrin has moved to undo the plot against Lucien by kidnapping Lydie Peyrade, demanding of her father that Lucien be reinstated and received as before. Thus Lucien, not himself a criminal, will find himself the beneficiary of such crimes as are needed for his *avenir*, not excluding kidnapping and murder. As in his "fatale semaine," he is caught up in circumstances, forces he has set in motion but which carry him to unforeseen commitments and actions. Unknown to Lucien, Corentin and the incorruptible Derville have paid a visit to Ève and David, there to determine whether they could have paid the money for Lucien's estate. The degeneration in Lucien's character would emerge from his behavior to Ève and David as now revealed, even if his second career in Paris were not so damaging. As in *Illusions*, their beautiful and tender life is presented in an ideal glow, their only trace of unhappiness caused by Lucien's shameful conduct. In six years he has written Ève only six times, and the last of his meager three visits had the wicked purpose of asking for a lie to assist him in his *politique*. If Ève can be said to have cherished any further illusions concerning her brother, the last now disappears as she listens in tears to Derville, who painfully reveals the impure source of Lucien's prosperity.

In Paris, events are proceeding rapidly toward fearful dénouements. Rastignac is sent as messenger from the Grandlieu family, announcing their irrevocable decision against Clothilde's marriage so long as the Duke himself remains alive. Clothilde herself, however, still loves Lucien and desires to see him. In the background the police-spy plot begins to break up with the murder of Peyrade by poison, the return of Lydie in a state of hopeless ruin, and the determination of Corentin to have revenge on Vautrin. On the last day of Esther's life, Lucien sees her in secret, overcome by her ravishing beauty yet knowing that she will kill herself rather than continue with Nucingen. When Lucien has to tell her that he plans to meet Clothilde at Fontainebleau, the unhappy girl cries out the ironic truth in her agonized question: "si j'avais sept ou huit millions, ne m'épouserais-tu pas?" Unknown to either of these doomed ones, Esther does have the enormous fortune she is to inherit from the usurer Gobseck, while Lucien is telling her of his love that would be for her alone if all were to be finished of his *avenir*. After Esther's death, the sum of seven hundred and fifty thousand francs is found under her pillow in an envelope addressed to Lucien, and Vautrin prepares a will in which Lucien becomes her sole heir. When the police arrive, however, the money in the envelope has disappeared, stolen by two servants with disastrous consequences.

Prison

Waiting to meet Clothilde in the forest, Lucien uses the future tense for the last time, as always to predict the utterly false. If he plays this comedy well, he reflects, "je serai le gendre du duc malgré lui." Clothilde arrives in the everlasting Balzacian carriage, an elegant berline, apparently intended to warn us of coming disaster and form a contrast to the dark vehicle in which Lucien is soon to ride for the last time. Clothilde herself ends a long interview with a true use of the future tense, we are sure, in promising Lucien "je ne me marierai jamais qu'avec vous." Lucien is suddenly arrested, and later the narrator describes the police wagon in which Lucien hides from glances of the passersby, this "sinistre et fatale voiture," replacing the dreamed-of equipage by which Lucien longed to parade his success before the world.

The arrest of Lucien and Vautrin for complicity in robbery and murder, as charged by Nucingen, creates a sensation that spreads, because of the celebrated beauty of the victim, through all the five worlds of Paris: the *grand monde*, the world of finance, of the courtesans, and of the young men, and the literary world. Balzac, by way of summary, reminds us of the scope of his vision and the universality of his fictional means in the body of a prostitute. For Lucien himself the hour of expiation sounds, and his person presents only an image of defeated guilt. He knows nothing of the events at Esther's house, but he knows that he has been linked with an escaped criminal, that from this may come catastrophes worse than death. For four hours now he weeps continuously, utterly through as a human being, his coming suicide inevitable. In a magnificent paragraph Balzac brings Lucien's *Bildung* full circle, repeats for summary the various terms applied to Lucien throughout, since he clearly intends these to have a cumulative force and to show the career of Lucien as bound together by the use of language in various ways. As Lucien enters his cell, he finds there an image of the first poor room he had occupied in Paris. But the difference between his first entry and this end is dramatic. Then he was still innocent, but now he is utterly fallen. He weeps over his broken hopes, over the defeat of every one of his personae, as Balzac says, "dans tous les moi que présentent l'ambitieux, l'amoureux, l'heureux, le dandy, le Parisien, le poète, le voluptueux et le privilégié, tout en lui s'était brisé dans cette chute icarienne." The use of Greek mythology again stands for the total unreality and folly of Lucien's attempt to succeed in the world. Like Icarus, he refused to see things as they were; he tried to rise by means that would not sustain him, that would not, indeed, survive the heat of the sun.

At the same moment Vautrin's mind is active, knowing as he does that if the police question Lucien first, the poet's weakness will betray him. But Camusot the judge is fortified by detailed notes on both Vautrin and Lucien prepared by Corentin, in which Herrera is clearly identified as the criminal who used to live at the Pension Vauquer, who has furnished money to Lucien for several years and so implicates him in his crimes, including the murder of Peyrade by poison. The notes on Lucien himself estimate that he spent, in the first three years of his second sojourn in Paris, the sum of three hundred thousand francs, which he must have obtained from Vautrin, and that the money to purchase his estate was obtained from Nucingen through Esther, from whose prostitution the two partners drew their resources. Vautrin frantically tries to reach Lucien with a note directing him to admit nothing of his true identity, and enlists the aid of Mme de Sérisy, whose passion for Lucien is awakened. To explain his own involvement with Lucien, Vautrin desperately insists that he is the poet's natural father, convinced that he can still save Lucien if he can prove himself only the priest Herrera, for the charge against Lucien is merely that he was associated with a criminal.

But a new document enters the case in the form of Esther's farewell letter to Lucien, one worthy of a place among Balzac's many superb letters of avowal, sacrifice, or adieu. We recall the exquisite letters to Eugène from his family, the messages of steadfast devotion to Lucien himself from Ève and David, the moving pathos of Eugénie Grandet's simple reply to the insensitive Charles. Esther reflects bitterly on the false values of society; while seven million francs await her, she thinks what money would have done for her in life. She laments the fate of a girl like herself and the world's attitude as she lies in the mud, but let her have millions, and all is forgotten. We wish now that Esther could know of her inheritance, millions assembled from all over society, including the wealth of those who despise her when penniless but respect her when she has money, no matter what its source, a doubly intense irony if it is the money of such as these that would make Esther rich. With heartrending pathos she bids farewell to her deity on earth, "Pauvre Lucien, cher ambitieux manqué, je songe à ton avenir," that terrible future yet able to command so great a sacrifice. For Esther, too, the carriage is a sign of success that will command the world's approval, the carriage in which men have come in search of her body, the carriage that would insure her respectful salutation if, instead of walking the streets, a prostitute, she were to pass by in her *voiture*. She urges Lucien to remember the two beautiful creatures who have died for him, and then go his way. She dies blessing the man who has caused her death, and as Camusot finishes the last pitiful words, he can only wonder how a man can be so beloved. It is a question naturally raised by Lucien's career: he is only what we see, for the depths of his nature scarcely change. He goes to the end of his young life accepting the gifts and sacrifices of others. If he had found the will to live, he might have taken the wealth of others on an enormous scale, considering the source of Gobseck's money. Vautrin himself is in tears on seeing Esther's letter, and bursts into tribute to this beautiful, poetic child, Lucien, who irresistibly inspires the necessity for others to sacrifice themselves to satisfy his least desire. Vautrin begs that Lucien be freed now, since clearly Esther's letter proves him innocent. He continues to fear Lucien's weak, inconsistent, half feminine nature and hopes to spare him further interrogation. Let him see Esther's letter, tell him that he is heir to her money, let him be free, rich, and married to Clothilde, and Vautrin's task is accomplished.

But Camusot remains suspicious. Clearly an important secret is being concealed, to be learned only through Lucien. Brought before the judge, he seems half dead, pale and defeated, his eyes red and swollen, his whole posture one of absolute despair. Camusot even feels a measure of pity on seeing how facile his victory must be over a man so bereft of moral courage. When shown Esther's letter, Lucien sobs uncontrollably, incapable of speaking a word for some fifteen minutes. Are these tears of genuine love or simply the same tears he has always wept over his own defeat? Did he love this beautiful girl after all, so that if entirely free to do so, he would have married her, as he implied on the last day of her life? If so, their story draws nearer the dimensions of tragedy.

Camusot deceives Lucien by adopting a kindly, paternal manner, assuring the poet that he may go free if he will answer a few questions. These questions bring out the facts of Lucien's first Parisian adventure, and later the false report on the source of his money. When Camusot exposes this lie, Lucien seems to lose what force he has remaining, and is quickly maneuvered into admitting that Herrera is an escaped convict, Jacques Collin, alias Vautrin. On hearing that Vautrin has said he was Lucien's father, the poet is astonished and horrified; he weeps again, but now for his mother's memory. The term *poète* continues to explain whatever makes Lucien the failure in life that he is. When Balzac uses such a term for important reasons, he is careful to tell us at some point its meaning so that his use of it in the immediate narrative will be clear. Lucien thinks, but too late after his blunders under questioning. Reflection always comes too late to men who are the slaves of sensation. "Là est la différence entre le poète et l'homme d'action," and Lucien now finds himself at the bottom of the abyss into which Camusot had lured him, "à la bonhomie de qui, lui poète, il s'était laissé prendre." Lucien's failure of resolution is the more painful because Vautrin has in the meantime succeeded in defending his identity as Herrera, in saving, that is, both himself and Lucien. But his audacity saves what Lucien has lost, and as Camusot lets the full implications of his blunder descend on Lucien, he sees drops of sweat form on his countenance, to grow, and fall, and mingle at last with the poet's tears. The final blow comes when Camusot reveals Lucien's inheritance of Gobseck's millions, and the narrator reminds us of Lucien's vulnerability to the malice of fortune: ten more minutes of resolution before Camusot and he would have gone free, rich and the husband of Clothilde. When his testimony is read to him, only one formality remains if he signs it: he must confront Vautrin and then be released. But this demand hardens Lucien's resolution, and he will now kill himself: he cannot face Vautrin after betraying him, he cannot testify at Vautrin's trial, having constantly feared that his alliance with Vautrin would be made public. In his cell, as he waits for delivery of writing materials, he is obsessed with suicide to the point of mania, and Balzac describes his condition "d'une aliénation mentale." Now Esther's letter, reread several times, confirms the desire to die, just as Romeo desired to rejoin his own dead love.

But like Julien Sorel, Lucien is the object of frantic efforts to save him, which at the last moment are about to succeed. Beautiful women, ministers, and magistrates combine their efforts, as Diane de Maufrigneuse, Mme de Sérisy, and de Granville demand the freedom of Lucien and Vautrin. De Granville cannot allow Lucien to be ruined, because his best friend's wife, Sérisy himself, and the Duchesse de Maufrigneuse would all be dragged with him into disgrace. Ironically, as Lucien longs for death in his cell, he is free of charges of theft and murder, his only problem that of association with an escaped convict. But the efforts of two women and de Granville combine to free him even of this charge, so that despite the folly, the monstrosity of his behavior, he might still escape its consequences. Now Lucien makes his last will, naming the children of Ève and David as principal heirs. Let Gobseck's money enrich the good and the pure in heart. He repays debts to Vautrin and Nucingen, establishes hospitals for prostitutes and debtors, orders a tomb for Esther and himself, leaves his library to M. de Sérisy, and his "toilette en or" to "Monsieur Eugène Rastignac." To de Granville at last he confesses the shame of his behavior before Camusot, so that even if totally exonerated, life would be impossible for him.

His last words are written to Vautrin, addressed as "Abbé." Lucien simply cannot live after what he has done; he admits his own betrayal of a benefactor, his own inadequacy when Vautrin wished to make him glorious only to plunge him into "les abîmes du suicide." Vautrin is a demon, coming down in a line of descent through Cain, one of those beings powerful enough to attract and then destroy the more tender spirits of weak men. To make amends for his own offense in betraying Vautrin, Lucien attaches a retraction of his replies to Camusot, denying that Herrera was identical with Jacques Collin. Then he says farewell to this "grandiose statue du mal et de la corruption." Vautrin has kept his promises, but Lucien is only what he was on the shore of la Charente. Alas, the scene of his death cannot be the beautiful river of his youth, but an ignominious cell in the Conciergerie of Paris.

"Le Jour sans Lendemain"

We have kept, on the whole, to our early resolution against the extremes of biographical criticism, and have read Balzac's work for its own sake, without searching for Balzac himself or trying to explain events in Lucien's career in terms of the author's own experience. Yet the role of lost illusions has often been remarked in the life of Balzac, and a work such as the *Prométhée* of Maurois abounds in the language, so familiar to us, of "belles espérances," "rêves déçus," or simply "espérances balzaciennes." The illusions lost in *Illusions* are like those lost by Balzac in his own life with its violent extremes, its mass of absurdities and contradictions beyond hope of resolution. Such a valuable work as the study of *Illusions* by Mme Bérard takes the general position that Balzac the man is the same as Balzac the author, that the sufferings and humiliations of his young heroes are those of Balzac himself, that his life and his text are therefore interchangeable as evidence, since he creates his work out of himself and his own experience. He is specially equipped to deal with the theme of *Illusions*, his own life having been strewn with the defeated schemes and foolish enterprises of an incurable dreamer, the *enfant* that Lucien never ceases to be. Further, his own life so nearly resembles that of Lucien himself that *Illusions* becomes in large measure an autobiography, though at times its subject matter extends well beyond the character of Lucien himself. The theme of a young man facing the world gets its fullest treatment in *Illusions*, which Balzac uses as a crossroads for the careers of four young men: Lucien, David, d'Arthez, and Lousteau, enabling him to explore the tragic history of the youth of France in his time more fully than anywhere else. Balzac himself had been all four of these young men in turn: the young provincial in Paris, the printer, the unknown philosopher working in a garret, and the unscrupulous journalist. He had also been Finot and Dauriat in his roles as editor and publisher.

When all the biographical parallels have been listed and the numerous incidents interchanged between Balzac's life and his work, we are not fully assisted either in reading the Rubempré cycle itself or in coming nearer to an understanding of the terrible dilemma that Balzac had imposed on his own brief existence. Jules Romains, among others, has pointed out that Balzac had to make his time count and that most of his defects as a writer were due to an imposed haste; he thus reduced the little time that he had by making it count so fully. In the narrative of Balzac's early twenties one is aware of growing tension as the years pass. As tension mounts, the pressure on his genius to burst forth into its proper fulfillment becomes daily less bearable. He reads, observes, thinks, talks, accumulates, absorbs the world, to what end? Every year now passing is taken from the other end of his life. Does Balzac "know" this? Yet he cannot begin until he is ready, and *Eugénie Grandet* cannot appear before the right moment. But the day comes when the synthesis has taken place and the masterpieces spring into being, poured forth in a torrent of creative energy, the more powerful and compelling for having been so long delayed, for both the quantity and the essential strength to increase.

The long suicide begins, not willed but somehow imposed, as Balzac sets an impossible task and destroys himself trying to achieve it. All that he has done is only a first step toward all that he has imagined, and Balzac contracts a debt that can never be paid, reflecting the perpetual bankruptcy in which his life was spent. His financial obligations are contracted in readily explainable ways, but why are they never paid from Balzac's considerable earnings? One thinks of the comic treatment of debt in Dickens' masterly portrait of Micawber, who must never pay his debts because payment would deprive him of the immense pleasure he takes in lamenting them. For Balzac, are the debts necessary to insure his doing the work necessary to pay them? Work has to be compelled, and in doing it life is consumed. In turn the work must be conceived on an impossible scale so as to remove any fear of its ever being finished. As the debts must never be paid, so the work must be impossible to complete in Balzac's lifetime, thus insuring that his life will be entirely consumed. Balzac finds himself delivered into the hands of his own demon. He gives up his real life as a man for another kind of life, as M. Picon says; he exchanges his possibilities as a man for those of a creator when he undertakes the task of writing the *Comédie*. So he gives up the daily life of other men, which is spent in the light of day, and becomes the nocturnal prisoner of his demonic vision. If in Lucien he lives over again the experience of his own life, his suicide is one of which Lucien, now quickly preparing his own death before anyone can prevent it, would be incapable, lacking the Promethean energy and will of his creator. Balzac's long suicide is more often likened to that of Raphaël Valentin in possessing the *Peau de chagrin*, in which the quantity of remaining life is constantly diminished by the effort to live it.

The indispensable M. Lotte has surveyed Balzac's treatment of suicide, and unlike M. Wurmser, who seems disappointed on being able to recall only five examples in the *Comédie*, he arrives at the figure of twenty-eight attempted suicides, of which twenty-one are successful. Only two of these are by hanging, Lucien himself, in his headlong desperation to quit the world, taking the most obvious means available to him. His mood is clearly different from normal, having changed completely from weakness to resolution, possessed now by monomania as he moves in a trance-like state to the end. Men who, in despair, are bent on killing themselves, develop a kind of exalted, concentrated spiritual condition, and Balzac establishes clearly, throughout his complex treatment of suicide, a connection between the deed and mental alienation. Lucien, then, appears obsessed, seized by hallucination, and in recalling his first move toward suicide by the river, Balzac shows that the final act has roots in the past, deriving from a former disposition, from a latent but chronic imbalance. He is not one more repetition of Werther or Chatterton, whose example in real and imagined life had inspired among youth a longing for heroic-melancholy death. Lucien has not endured the same kind of suffering in unrequited love. His reasons for wishing to die are clear when we realize that life was simply too much for his human powers. As Mr. Affron observes, his suicide comes as a relief; the law would permit him to live, but "in the eyes of the Balzacian universe he is unfit to survive." Also, despite M. Fouqueure's remark to the contrary, he executes a form of justice upon himself for what he has been guilty of: crime, betrayal, weakness, and folly compounded beyond any other expiation.

So the day that has no tomorrow has come at last for Lucien, and we remember *Les Chouans* and lovely Marie de Verneuil murmuring, "un jour sans lendemain." Shedding his ordinary indecisiveness, Lucien now acts quickly, with a determined energy and efficiency. There will be no tomorrow, the future tense is about to end, the *avenir*—so long at the center of his folly—is to be no more, he will see to that. When all is ready, he mounts the table, standing there for a while to gaze at the prison courtyard, admiring the architecture, recalling much of French history, forgetting his immediate purpose. The narrator pauses to explain the frequency of hallucination in men of intense passions or sentiments. The specters and fantasies now present to Lucien's mind, however, seem no more insubstantial than his lifelong dreams of future success. He sees the palace of Saint-Louis in all its original beauty, and, just before the end, his creator returns to an inescapable dualism:

> Il accepta cette vue sublime comme un poétique adieu de la création civilisée. . . . Il était deux Lucien, un Lucien poète en promenade dans le Moyen-Age sous les arcades et sous les tourelles de Saint-Louis, et un Lucien apprêtant son suicide.

A newspaper notice is carefully worded to exonerate the poet and conceal the stain upon justice that would be visible if the truth were known. An autopsy has proved that death was the result of an aneurism, and so had nothing to do with his arrest. We think of the role that "clothing" of so many varieties played throughout Lucien's life. He could not live, and he cannot die, it seems, without some "clothing" of reality, some untruth being told on his behalf, some illusion once more created around him, so that others will think him to be what he was not.

Vautrin's response to the death of his creature, his son, his other embodiment reveals the full measure of his absorption, human and diabolical, in Lucien. In agonies of grief, he asks the doctor to cut a lock of the poet's hair. In the cell he reads Lucien's letter, now reprinted for us to read, before and after the death it foretells. Holding Lucien's dead hand, Vautrin reads on. It is half past five on a May afternoon. When, at one in the morning, the body is removed, Vautrin is found kneeling beside the bed, still holding Lucien's hand, having wept for seven hours. To aid the pretense that Lucien died at home a free man, his body is moved from the prison at night so that the funeral may proceed from his own address.

But in death Lucien has the power to save Vautrin after all, since the three women of noble rank involved with Lucien— Clothilde de Grandlieu, Diane de Maufrigneuse, and Léontine de Sérisy—are necessarily at Vautrin's mercy. Granville sees that, if Vautrin is exposed, these women are ruined for having been connected, through Lucien, with the former convict. The compromising letters from all three women, still in Vautrin's possession, place their great families in peril. Vautrin uses the letters to compel the law to his bidding, and when he is exonerated, his status changed, and his future succession to Bibi-Lupin on the police secured, he goes to Saint-Germain des Prés just as the mass for Lucien is being finished and holy water sprinkled on the bier. Some dozen mourners appear with the body at Père-Lachaise, among them Rastignac, and we recall the burial of Père Goriot, a friend whom Rastignac betrayed as he betrayed Lucien in revealing his origin. He sheds no tear now, having no remnant of his youthful innocence or honor to inspire it. As Lucien is lowered to the grave beside Esther, Vautrin himself falls into a faint and so does not hear the light sound of the pellets of earth thrown upon the body by the gravediggers, "pour venir demander leur pourboire."

The lingering connection of Lucien's life with others who remain in the world continues to the final page of the Rubempré cycle. Vautrin seems finally to have knotted all possible loose ends, but after the funeral Granville reminds him of a promise to save Léontine de Sérisy, who is in a state approaching madness. He returns to his old quarters for a letter written to her by Lucien after she had repulsed him from her box on seeing him with Esther at the Italiens. In despair, Lucien did not send it, but Vautrin preserved it as a sacred document in the pages of his clerical breviary. Léontine suffers from feelings of guilt, thinking that Lucien killed himself over her cruel treatment of him. On reading this old love letter, she will recover in the belief that Lucien still loved her. As she holds the curative letter to her breast, Vautrin reflects on the power of women over men and his own conquest of the world at last. "Il se mit à sourire superbement," the narrative simply remarks. On this word, which has played with countless nuances over the surface of Lucien's career, his unhappy tale is to end, not to the sound of Vautrin's hideous and booming gaiety, but in the silence of the devil's smile.

8

The Hero as Failure

A summary glance at the Rubempré cycle reveals an uneven distribution of power and effect, especially in the less controlled masses of *Splendeurs*. The order of composition had left Balzac with some embarrassing problems of anachronism and false perspective when, in 1843, he wished to produce a clear and consistent narrative leading to a logical continuation of Lucien's career in *Splendeurs*. *La Torpille* had been published in 1838, between Parts I and II of *Illusions*. M. Pommier's study of the problem isolates a number of different Luciens and Vautrins, divided into subdivisions A and B. If Lucien I is the youth of *Illusions*, Part I (1837), and Lucien II the provincial in Paris of Part II (1839), then Lucien III is the one in *La Torpille* (1838) seen at the Opera as a new success. Thus Lucien III is known to the reader before Lucien II, who is going toward a future that he has already lived. Likewise, people who knew the hero well in the earlier stages related in *Illusions*, Part II, seem not to remember details of the very action in which they themselves were once prominent. Balzac's assorted grapplings with these problems were not wholly successful and help to account for the effect of a work whose enormous variety was never brought under perfect control. A. G. Lehmann has called *Splendeurs* a pessimistic metaphorical statement on society and mankind, a nihilistic study of human institutions that condemns the world for its lack of moral order. The novel as we read it now seems to have gotten away from Balzac; it became something he had not foreseen or planned, for Vautrin so commanded Balzac's imagination that he turned the work over to this demonic force in a kind of surrender of his own artistic function. Balzac seems to admit this when on two occasions he explains to the reader why he continues the book after Lucien's death. He must go on in order to complete, in the *Comédie*, the study of morals, of which the history of Lucien and those involved with him are only a part. Vautrin then takes over the book, as he does in *Père Goriot* whenever he is on stage. But now Balzac completely removes competing figures, to pursue to the end this supreme effort of his imagination. Vautrin is now for the first time a separate protagonist himself, not part of another's story.

If not inferior to *Illusions* at all levels, *Splendeurs* shows marked differences in tone and manner. The ending of *Illusions* is quite different from that of other large works in the *Comédie*. The hero's story is not concluded, for the last line tells of a coming sequel. Yet this seems against the inner logic of *Illusions* itself, whose movement demands the end to which Lucien himself sees no alternative. Balzac has interfered with the logic established by his own creation, and Lucien seems right, his creator wrong. He should die and remove himself from further defeat in a world that has already shown him, past any dispute, that he has no chance of prevailing. A man who kills himself has a higher estimation of his worth than the world does; when the difference between his own and the world's judgment of him becomes more than he can bear, he avoids the problem by ending it. M. Bardèche feels strongly, too, that the attempt being made in *Splendeurs* is wrong to begin with, that the stakes are now too high, and the consequences more extreme, since Balzac has chosen something impossible in the *donnée* of his novel. It is impossible for Lucien to become the son-in-law of one of the great nobles of France. So great a family would never, without inquiry, give its daughter to a parvenu. In launching this enterprise, Vautrin himself is bound to attract the attention of the police and others to his affairs, and hence to his identity. Further, the plan is futile and unnecessary because Lucien could make his fortune in many other ways. It is based on the foolish idea, which is nonetheless just Vautrin's limitation, that skillful crime or some act of effrontery can be the source of great fortunes.

M. Picon sees the return of Lucien from the grave as leading to a life above reality, in which Lucien passes from the reality in which he has lost his illusions into a fantastic revery. When we see him again at the Opera he is no longer the man who has lived through what *Illusions* asked him to suffer—a life that he could not, in fact, endure, so that he preferred to die rather than go on with it and intended to kill himself in such a way that he would simply disappear from the face of the earth. Vautrin snatches him from the grave and he returns. But no one escapes death save by some supernatural arrangement, something imagined or dreamed, since no one in fact ever escapes the end awaiting him, whatever it is. The pact with Vautrin, then, is not supposed to suggest a possible reality or to correspond to anything that could take place in the world as it is. Who has not longed to die and return, to reenter, as the spacemen say, or to go like Dante and Aeneas or the Gulliver of Voyage III into the next world while yet alive, to find instruction there and so come back to a wiser life? But Lucien returns in a kind of trance, unaffected by visions of a higher wisdom, having learned nothing from the countenance of death, to repeat only with less justification than before the same follies and to pursue the same illusions. He has no longer the excuse of ignorance and inexperience, for nothing in *Splendeurs* is done "pour la première fois" save, perhaps, the obscenities of Nucingen's passion for Esther.

Splendeurs is based, then, on a series of improbable fictions, not on the possibilities of life as it is, however fantastic or terrible these are shown to be throughout the *Comédie*. Clearly, Balzac has changed his fictional genre and is now writing not a true *Bildungs-roman* but a "roman policier" with all the melodramatic trappings of masked faces, disguises, mysterious identities, underworld fig-ures, prostitutes, and creatures of the night. Lucien has already lost in the world as it is; therefore the Devil creates an artificial world for his new adventures, with the action of *Splendeurs* be-ginning at the Opera, the theater farthest from reality. Lucien moves amid aliases, changed names, divers identities associated with crime or criminals, anyone, that is, with a need for conceal-ment. His life is joined to that of a criminal of multiple identities, who, when Lucien meets him, is going under a name different from that of Eugène's tempter. If *Illusions* was a daylight world familiar to ordinary men, in the world of *Splendeurs*, as it opens, Lucien is a mask among other masks. His changed name is a mask for the apothecary's son. Vautrin is wearing a mask, and when he removes it he merely shows another in his clerical garb. Other disguises proliferate: the prostitute Esther, in a totally unconvincing and artificial transformation, becomes an angel and puts on false airs to deceive Nucingen, who in turn tries to conceal his age. Jacqueline Collin is disguised as Asie, and later assumes four different identities. Vautrin appears as priest, as William Barker, and as a police officer. Peyrade and Contenson likewise adopt other poses, and the Rue de Langlade wears a disguise which it casts off only at night.

The coming of night releases the prostitutes whose lives and activities establish one of the principal themes of *Splendeurs*. M. Béguin has remarked on the manner in which Balzac endows them with intuitive knowledge, as if he desired to delegate a measure of his power and knowledge to them. They are more headlong in their response to life, to its dangers and lucky chances, so that their destiny embraces the largest possible variety of dé-nouements. They leap over the various social hierarchies, like the ambitious young of the *Comédie*, enabling Balzac to join society from top to bottom on a line that runs from the king himself, whose favorite is the Duc de Grandlieu, through the world of riches and finance, down at last to the prison cell where Lucien dies, having himself lived from the prostitution of others and from his own.

M. Jean-Louis Bory has written effectively of Balzac's employment of three sources "de la poésie noire: l'espace, l'obscurité, la terreur." He sees the proliferation of crime, of secret and other societies after the empire, the increase in police numbers and activity, the disguises, pretenses with their resulting fear and suspicion—all having the effect, on Balzac's writing, that he placed much of his action at night. Certainly *Splendeurs* is heavily shrouded in darkness and mystery, with alleys, dead ends, dark recesses, dim gaslit streets as in Dickens and Wilde, with shadowy figures gliding mysteriously into sinister houses. Darkness, obscurity, silence itself all seem intent on hiding something, covering a nameless menace, especially when we know that the obscurity is not the same for everyone. We are led into the infamous city of Paris, the inferno once again where one who enters must indeed abandon hope. Balzac takes us ever down, and, just as with Dante, always plunges us more deeply into night: we descend from the beau monde, the world of business and money, through the police and justice, to the circle of criminals and prostitutes below. Even a large part of the daytime action in *Splendeurs* is in courts and prisons, leading finally to death and the grave. As crime has its way in the deserted and sleeping city, and Esther is permitted to go abroad only at night, we see this atmosphere as one only intensified here from its frequent use elsewhere in the *Comédie*. The miser Grandet counts his gold at night; after Paul and Natalie are married, they attend midnight mass where "les ténèbres, image de mort, attristent." At night Eugène learns of the ominous other life of Vautrin and the mystery of old Goriot's personal life. The Duchesse de Langeais is kidnapped and buried at night. Balzac seems to find men and women released, freer to be themselves in the night, which at once conceals and brings out the truth, for people behave as they really are when less clearly visible to others. We remember, too, that the *Comédie* itself was written in the dead of night—Balzac alone in a dark and silent world.

This atmosphere with the many trappings of melodrama inseparable from the genre attempted in *Splendeurs*, helps to account for the change in tone from the more immediately real, vivid impressions of *Illusions*. M. Henry Mitterand has made a number of useful distinctions in proposing more attention to Balzac's style. If style means the use of words for a certain result, we should look to the effect of Balzac's writing, considering where a given expression comes in the narrative and how it is used, its function in the novel and how this has been prepared for, so that the expression may attain its full emotional power. In this sense the "style" of Eugénie's letter to Charles is complete perfection; the "style" of Ève's response to David's proposal beside the river, while Lucien is being crucified on high, is that of a lyric poem radiating its ideal throughout the narrative by use of the single phrase "sans avenir"; she is a worker without a future, the poem says, not an idler living on doomed illusions.

Splendeurs is not so rich in happy perfection, in a style that arranges a rare union between means and ends. Having changed his genre and removed his action to a more artificial realm, Balzac is less able to give us the best of his clear vision of an imagined reality, one so vivid in its result that Balzac and we ourselves mistake it for daily life. In *Splendeurs* we are uneasy as the narrator strains to persuade us of the immediate truth of something that has to be explained to us, as M. Picon rightly says, rather than simply shown. The reality has to be documented to prove that it is in fact what Balzac says it is, and this effort permits the narrator less rather than more control. A certain verbose, inflated tone is not offset by the imaginative framework which seems insufficient in later stages of the novel. We do not speak here of the disproportion in weight given to different parts of the narrative, which in *Eugénie Grandet* and *Le Père Goriot* accounts for so much of their power. Nor do we have the same situation as in the unsatisfactory final pages of *Béatrix*, for example, where Balzac glosses over an action inadequately prepared, by writing an explanatory, theoretical essay. Lack of preparation cannot justify the haste in which he finishes *Splendeurs*, and we see that Balzac has imagined what the book will not contain so that he cannot fulfill the action within the work as planned.

In *Splendeurs* at its worst we have, rather, a simple failure of means. The success of Asie's maneuver in gaining access to Camusot and seeing Vautrin being led out by gendarmes seems too easy as against the impregnable obstacles so painstakingly described when the action entered the penal and judiciary world. Asie is a cause unworthy of this effect, and the imagined framework seems too thin, spun out, and exaggerated to carry the action convincingly. What is the underlying metaphor to sustain the human drama that unfolds? It becomes uncertain and frail amid a long discussion of legal procedures, for the processes of espionage and police conduct all submerge the human beings themselves. To return to these we must proceed through a dense structure of disguise and intrigue, which seems artificial and contrived, insufficient to satisfy the drama's needs.

It is difficult to say, finally, whether Lucien himself is a cause or the victim of those qualities that make of *Splendeurs* a less convincing work than *Illusions*. If we glance again at the terms or synonyms that accompany him, it seems at first that *dandy* is to replace *poète*, since he appears to be a success in Paris with the style, the clothes, the airs and manners of a worldly man of the city. But as his fortunes decline, the term *poète* returns, and its cumulative effect from *Illusions* through to the end is to emphasize Lucien's difference from, and irrelevance in, the world he tries to conquer. But also, while he remains much the same, his role in *Splendeurs* changes; the book does not seem to need Lucien, for all its more diffused and far-flung purposes make him less prominent in its action, and he seems more passive, acted upon, more feminine,

indecisive, fickle, vain, intuitive, and submissive. As Balzac had
established a series of clearly defined stages for the decline of
Eugène's character into Rastignac, so we might discover a set of
devices to follow the line of Lucien's defeat. These would include
the various temptation scenes, the periods of flattery that increase
his vanity, times of temporary loss or defeat that increase his ambition at first, times when he accepts the sacrifice of others, the
moments of decision to change his name, the experiences of shame
following this, and all the occasions in the later stages of his life
that show him as passive, feminine, kept by others. M. Barrière
finds Balzac more interested in showing the gradual degradation
of his characters than in their ascent to virtue. He relates a number of steps leading to Lucien's fall, but then seems to beg the
question in saying that thus "une âme pure mais faible arrive à la
corruption définitive." It is hardly enough to say that Lucien was
weak, for this kind of "weakness" itself is precisely what makes a
soul "impure" rather than "pure." What is corruption of this kind
but weakness? Mr. William Troy similarly defends Lucien, finding
him also a victim or "scapegoat" of society. He is "essentially a
noble soul in the most sentimental tradition" but is undone "by
his need for fame, luxury and social position," for which he sacrifices love, family and devoted friends. Yet if Lucien so desperately
needs the trappings of success in money, fame, and power and is
willing to sacrifice love and friendship for them, he is not a noble
soul, but a decidedly ignoble one. His betrayal of all that he should
cherish is not only a phase through which he passes on his way
toward maturity, as with Pip, but proceeds from a trait of his
nature that cannot be dismissed as "weakness," and for which he
is not responsible. The defeat and death of such a man will rarely
affect us so profoundly as it moved Oscar Wilde's Vivian, for
whom it remained one of the greatest tragedies of his life.

   Lucien is dead long before the end of *Splendeurs;* likewise he has
been less prominent in the action once the sale of Esther to
Nucingen has been decreed by Vautrin and shamefully accepted

by Lucien. The criminal element advances with the maneuvers of Vautrin and his creatures. The sense that Lucien is a cause inadequate to the effect increases, not only because he collapses into an instrument of Vautrin's will as if hypnotized or somnambulistic, but simply because he does and says so little outside of his planned conquest of Clothilde. After his repulse from Clothilde's door, when a footman shows him that he is rejected by the world, he sees, in the mindless face of the servant, the visage of destiny itself. After his arrest he seems to give up entirely, devoid of any resources of defiance or revenge against the world such as he was once capable of in his youthful anger. Despite all the lessons taught him by the *Bildungsmächte*, Lucien seems not to develop new powers, seems never to know more, unlike Dante, than the man who is teaching him. He is less than Joseph, who finds at a critical moment that his psychological insight is equal to interpretation of the king's dream. Lucien has no such special gift whereby to confound the wise and the learned. Unlike David before Goliath, or Roland, who did foil the sinewy Charles in *As You Like It*, Lucien has no special courage or adroitness with which to overcome a threatening danger, seemingly irreversible, at the last moment— no resource unsuspected by others. Lucien has nothing beneath his beauty, his clothes; he cannot call up from hidden reserves the strength to overcome the forces arrayed against him.

Mr. Fanger remarks that when Lucien yields to Vautrin at the end of *Illusions*, he carries out a symbolic death and rebirth. Lucien is then reborn, but as what or who? The question of his true identity, never fully answered, now continues as he lives an expensive life on unknown resources, occupying a disputed position in the world. He now has three persons helping to support him, Esther, Vautrin and Mme de Sérisy, all of whom love him devotedly, for they do not seem to feel themselves cheated or given something inadequate when Lucien sells himself to each in turn. He is the beneficiary of a theme recurring at least four times in the *Comédie*, at the beginning, middle, and end of Balzac's career, that of a

woman with a lurid past from which she hopes to escape through
love of a man far above herself. Marie de Verneuil of *Les Chouans*
begins this and other motifs, Coralie and Esther continue in their
devotion to Lucien, and Diane de Maufrigneuse in *Les Secrets de
la Princesse de Cadignan* survives the past by concealing it from
d'Arthez or at least making him believe that it is not so. Thus two
noblewomen and two prostitutes are the vehicles of Balzac's
theme, the noblewomen desiring in each case men of superb
virility and character, the prostitutes desiring the hero as failure, a
man who lives from them and takes their gains until his own trade
resembles their own. In *Splendeurs*, Lucien is kept by women. Behind
them is another man with a criminal record, and behind him in
turn there extends a line of assorted figures, some of shady character and others rich and well-connected men who have arrived and
who give Lucien assistance in their world. Before such a spectacle,
opinion has been divided. Some evidently share Balzac's own
weakness for Lucien and his tendency to excuse the beautiful
youth, despite some evidence to the contrary, seeing him more
misled and unlucky than culpable, more to be pitied than con-
demned, one who illustrates the terrible problems facing the
youth of France, which had to endure the gradually corrupting
influences of Paris, one who, despite the dreadful surface appearance of his behavior, is neither odious nor unsympathetic as he
goes down before a world that is too much for him. M. Pommier,
however, takes a more severe view of Lucien's incorrigible *fatuité*,
and Mme Delattre, discussing Lucien's suicide, is certain that
Balzac abandons him to his fate without regret. In his "Introduction" to *Splendeurs*, M. Adam sees Lucien as a weak, inadequate
instrument, convincing enough in *Illusions* but in the end a kind
of flabby mistake, incapable of inspiring horror despite his odious
behavior.

Certainly the text of *Splendeurs* continues to emphasize Lucien's
beauty, femininity, and more than a hint of homosexuality with
Vautrin; he appears to suffer only what is coming to him, seeming

at last to represent so much weakness and error as to be a kind of mistake in judgment on Balzac's part. The narrator specifically allows for a connection between Lucien's beauty and his weakness of character, saying that perfect physical beauty is almost always accompanied "de froideur ou de sottise." Vautrin himself, who keeps his illusions about Lucien beyond a point endurable by anyone else, tells Granville that no mother ever loved an only son as he loved Lucien, "cet ange," weak and tender, finally "une femme manquée" says Vautrin, who thought women an inferior species of being. M. Bardèche has remarked that every age produces a virile and a feminine aspect of the same idea. Julien Sorel follows the virile line of the nineteenth century with its freedom, energy, ambition and revolt. But Lucien has succumbed to the feminine poisons of poetry, romanticism, and vanity, willing in the end to accommodate himself to anything for the sake of his desired position. Mme Bérard dwells on the details of Lucien's physical beauty to explain his half-woman's nature and feminine seduction; physically, he resembles Esther herself, is beautiful in the same way. Contemplating Lucien just before his death, M. Bory compares him with Dorian Gray, who likewise suffered the misfortune, as a man, of being fantastically handsome. Beauty is an instrument of power, but of concealment as well; it seems, as the narrator has said, inseparable from weakness, and encourages its possessor to make capital of it quickly, for, since it fades rapidly, it must be made to yield what it can while it lasts.

And Lucien, we are sure, will not hesitate to give way to another's abnormality if need be. Despite his passionate affairs with women and the years of his love for Esther, he must at some point have yielded to Vautrin, whose love for Lucien is shown by M. Mauriac and others to have been homosexual. There is no specific reference to this trait until Part IV of *Splendeurs*, when de Calvi bears such a relation to Vautrin. In the final horror that Lucien seems to feel over his association with Vautrin, there is a mingling of guilt, disgust, and physical repulsion that might well follow from a homosexual relationship.

This form of love is only one sign of the devoted adulation showered upon Lucien from all sides all his life, which contributes to our sense of a cause inadequate to Balzac's effect, since everyone who has ever loved him ends in disillusion. The theme of love for an unworthy object is common in the *Comédie;* the most obvious examples are in *Eugénie Grandet, Le Père Goriot,* and *La Rabouilleuse.* But Lucien defeats everyone who has loved or believed in him: his mother, Ève and David, the great Daniel d'Arthez, three noble-women, if we count Louise with Léontine de Sérisy and Diane de Maufrigneuse, Coralie and Esther, who die for him, and Vautrin himself. We recall that Lucien is so bound together with Vautrin that when he kills himself, he kills his protector as well, who ceases to be and joins the police as someone else. M. Citron has said of Balzac himself that he died "à Paris, de Paris." Should we not say, likewise, that Vautrin dies of Lucien, as Père Goriot died of his ungrateful children?

If Lucien succeeds only in disillusioning everyone who cares for him, we have to consider how far his guilt affects his stature as a tragic figure. He can be seen as an abstract type simply used by Balzac to castigate the times, just as all satirists have used such types since the beginning of the genre. But he is a more vivid human creation as a separate individual, whose fate is at once that of all men of his kind and of himself alone. He is a tragic figure in-sofar as Balzac has us believe in his essential qualities of talent and character, which are wasted and lost in a futile pursuit of the world's values. But is he so guilty that he ceases to be a truly tragic figure? Does he commit such sins as to make of him only a weak or bad man who is punished as he deserves? There is then no tragic qualm, no sense of injustice or grievance against the gods. His denial of his father, betrayal of family and friends, his degradation at the hands of Vautrin become such a weight of offense that no fate is too extreme for his misdeeds. In his warfare with the world,

he succumbs to the danger common to all warfare against a terrible foe, that one must resemble the enemy in order to conquer
him. Lucien responds to the cruelty and falseness of the world as
if there were no other course than to accept the world's laws and
standards. He sees that the world is despicable for what it is, false
in what it honors and admires, yet he only redoubles his effort to
attain a place in it. He has to become what the world is; to gain it
he must indeed sell his own soul. Unlike Rastignac, who never
looks back and never sheds another tear, Lucien lacks the cold
ruthlessness demanded by the logic of his choice. Mr. Affron is
somewhat misleading in his remark that people in the *Comédie* who
live by moral principles such as "honesty, generosity, and trust are
doomed to failure." People who lack such principles fail also. In a
sense, Lucien fails because he lacks these virtues, not because he
lives by them. No one ever tried harder to obey the world's laws
than he, no one was more willing to pay the cost of success in
degradation, dehumanization, and submission to the worst in a
corrupt society; yet he fails. The error, then, was certainly not
virtue alone, or depravity alone. Lucien remains unbalanced as
the conflict within him weakens his strength for the fight against
the world without, and he cannot entirely rid himself of his virtuous impulses. He remains not wicked enough to succeed by force
of depravity, nor virtuous enough to fail solely from his own goodness. His final ignominy, in Mr. Lukacs' view, comes of a "mixture
of instability and ambition, the combination of a hankering for a
pure and honorable life with a boundless but erratic ambition."
Thus Lucien should either have been a much worse or a much
better man. Having once given in to the laws of the world, he
should have pursued them more consistently, with more calculation, presence of mind, adaptability, more cynicism, more resolute
calculation, to whatever conclusion his ambition might demand.
Failing this, he should equally have been true to his young ideal-
ism, and, like his friends David and d'Arthez, he should have
accepted such a life as he might attain on his merits. The careers

of men like Lucien and Pip make us think of Macbeth, likewise not coldly wicked enough to prevail. There is a sequence of ambition, shame, and remorse. One is tempted to achieve grandiose aims, leading to shame at the means needed to achieve them and remorse after having done what ambition calls for. Self-accusation appears like the ghost of Banquo to remind the ambitious one of the price to be paid for progress to his goal, a price that he is not resolutely wicked enough to pay.

The reader of *Béatrix* may well think that Calyste is too much of a fool to be worth the trouble Balzac takes to expose him, just as we say of Lucien that he will not bear the weight of Balzac's commentary on the world. As a character in this one story of a man's career he does seem inadequate, yet as metaphor he stands for all the follies of his kind. He must seem inadequate in his own single story if, as metaphor, Lucien is to include all the deluded young who fail to understand themselves and the world. Yet he seems worse than merely deluded in an excusably youthful way. In *Le Cabinet des antiques*, Victurnien thinks of suicide but tries a crime instead, whereas Lucien finally kills himself when there are no crimes left for him to try. We must also ask whether Lucien was such a deluded fool after all when we see how close he came, just before the end, to achieving his *avenir* and its components of riches, a title, and marriage to the highborn. All this might have been his, with a few more minutes of resolution. Are we then to suppose that, after all, his *avenir* was no illusion but a true possibility, within his grasp save for a cruel blow from the malice of fortune that might well have been the opposite? Yet surely Balzac is deliberate in showing the accidental and capricious cruelty by which Lucien finally loses all; we see that somehow this particular man will be doomed no matter what, that he is certain to end in failure, if not now, in this way, then at some other time in some other way. For amid the clashing dualisms, the bitter choices, the relentless temptations of the Balzacian world, Lucien's resolution has not sustained him. He has employed the perpetual *voiture* for the journey to Paris at the height of his illusions, he has paraded before his enemies in a sumptuous carriage, only to make an ignominious return in Louise's *voiture*. In the devil's own equipage he has consented to the sale of his entire being, has then driven a handsome coach to the doors of high nobility in pursuit of further illusions, but has made the final journey to prison in the dark, hearse-like wagon of police arrest. The *clothing* that was his beautiful body repeatedly assumed the luxurious garments that inspired admiration and illusion in others; the young poet of the provinces changed for a time into an elegant dandy, remaining in the end a symbol of futile irrelevance, a poetic dreamer unequal to the demands of combat on the battlefield of Paris. More fatally than Rastignac before him, Lucien had stepped into the abyss, but no miracle intervened to rescue at the last possible moment a weak and hapless youth. The *sourire* that had played over many a countenance showing the stupidity of M. de Bargeton, the sad admission of Ève, the growing discernment of Louise, the cynical realism of Châtelet, the malicious contempt of Henri de Marsay, the tender sacrifice of Esther and the foolish self-revelation of Lucien himself, had turned at last into confident mockery on the lips of the devil.

Our reading of Lucien's story must now break up into half-rhetorical questions concerning his status as a tragic figure. Is Lucien's *Bildung* complete in the final words, self-knowledge and accusation having come too late? Might he not live, once having admitted truths that nothing can efface? No, his creator must give way to Lucien at last, for he is right, as he was right beside the river Charente. He is no Euripidean Heracles who can go on accepting life to the end as punishment for the mindless folly of conduct that fell so heavily upon those who loved him.

Notes

The titles most frequently cited throughout are given in full on the first mention in each chapter. Thereafter *Illusions perdues, Splendeurs et misères des courtisanes,* and *La Comédie humaine* are referred to with the short titles of *Illusions, Splendeurs,* and *Comédie* respectively. Depending on the context, *Illusions* has three meanings, referring to the single work so titled, to the Rubempré cycle taken together, or to Balzac's fictional universe in general.

It has not seemed necessary to annotate most of the quotations from Balzac himself. As a rule these consist of brief passages, expressions, or words so often repeated that the particular page is not important. Not only are they found everywhere to carry Balzac's underlying meaning, but they could readily be replaced by other synonymous or related expressions with the same effect. They could, then, as well have been invented by the reader as by Balzac himself, and so are intended to promote a harmony between the reader's response and Balzac's own imagination.

Other passages or references are generally acknowledged in the notes under the appropriate page number of the text. Such a minimum of unobtrusive documentation should allow the reader to follow Lucien's career without interruption, the notes remaining for support, for whatever use or interest they have to offer. Names and titles are abbreviated from the fuller references in the Bibliography.

PAGE 1

On the *Bildungsroman* in French and German, Baldensperger, *Goethe en France*, 193–94. On the lack of "Entwicklung" in Balzac, Rudolf Murtfeld, *Balzac*, 60. The theme of *Illusions*, P. Barrière, *Honoré de Balzac et la tradition*, 109.

PAGE 2

On universality of theme, G. Picon, "Les 'Illusions perdues,' " 73. Proust on the title, *Contre Sainte-Beuve*, 206. Freud, *Civilization and Its Discontents*, 7, 36–39. H. Levin, *Gates of Horn*, 52, 85.

PAGE 3

On the freedom allowed to Balzac's characters, E. J. Oliver, *Honoré de Balzac*, 175, and A. Wurmser, *Comédie inhumaine*, 389. On Balzac's acceptance of their fate, A. Béguin, *Balzac lu et relu*, 67. The "Parcae" are cited by D. Fanger, *Dostoevsky and Romantic Realism*, 38. For the scope of *Illusions*, R. Mortimer, *Channel Packet*, 11, and Ethel Preston, *Recherches sur la technique de Balzac*, 16–17. On the physical centrality of *Illusions* in the *Comédie*, B. Guyon, "*Illusions perdues*," 1.

PAGE 5

On Balzac as creator and poet, A. Béguin, *Balzac lu et relu, passim;* B. Croce, "Balzac," 20; P. Laubriet, *L'Intelligence de l'Art*, 120–43; Henri Mitterand, "A Propos du style de Balzac," *Europe*, 145–63. On Balzac's precision, Samuel de Sacy, "Les Deux univers de Balzac . . . ," in *Balzac*, ed. P. Bertaut, 235. His imaginative power, R. A. Sayce, *Style in French Prose*, 61–63. On various aspects of Balzac's literary and imaginative power, see R. Fernandez, *Messages*, 72; Gilbert Sigaux, "Balzac enfant et père du siècle," in *Balzac*, ed. P. Bertaut, 68, 79; Hugo Friedrich, *Drei Klassiker*, 108–9; William Troy, "On Rereading Balzac," 207–19; E. Auerbach, *Mimesis*, 482; Proust, *Contre Sainte-Beuve*, 207–10.

PAGES 5–6

On French criticism, H. Levin, *Gates of Horn*, 3–23. On various aspects of recent study of Balzac, A. Pugh, "Ten Years of Balzac Studies," 91–97; C. Gould, "The Present State of Balzac Studies," 299–323. On the requirements of realism, B. Weinberg, *French Realism*, 126–27.

PAGE 6

On Balzac's fiction and pamphlets, M. Iknayan, *Idea of the Novel in France*, 100.

PAGE 7

For M. Bardèche's reading, see his *Lecture de Balzac*, 132. For the alliance of things and people, J. O. Fischer, "Réalisme et procédés," *Europe*, 222–23. On Balzac as "le grand coupable," M. Iknayan, *Idea of the Novel in France*, 160–61. On Balzac's writing, A. Bellessort, *Balzac et son œuvre*, 270–71; A. Wurmser, *Comédie inhumaine, passim*.

PAGE 8

See the "Introduction" of M. Adam to *Illusions*, p. xxxii. Albert Cook, *The Meaning of Fiction*, 79.

PAGE 12

Balzac mentions the "trente ans" in his "Préface" to Part III of *Illusions*. On the future, G. Poulet, *Interior Distance* . . . , 123; J. Duvignand, "L'Homme d'affaires . . . ," *Balzac*, ed. Bertaut, 176.

PAGE 13

On the novel theme, I. Watt, *Rise of the Novel*, 186–87. On provincials coming to Paris, R. Girard, *Mensonge romantique* . . . , 125; J. Vallès, *Les Réfractaires*, 182. On Wertherism and related topics, F. Baldensperger, *Goethe en France, passim.* On "mal du siècle," Alfred de Musset, *La Confession d'un enfant du siècle* (1836). See also G. Hourdin, *Balzac romancier des passions*, 78–80, and P. Moreau, *Romantisme*, 335.

PAGE 14

Balzac speaks of the lure of Paris in the "Préface" to *Le Cabinet des Antiques.* Cf. R. Caillois "Balzac et le Mythe de Paris," Edition *Club Français du Livre*, 4 (1962):2–6. On youth, new opportunities, money and related themes, M. Ferguson, *La Volonté dans la Comédie*, 155; M. Bardèche, *Lecture de Balzac*, 106; A. Bellessort, *Balzac et son œuvre*, 197; J. Bertaut, *Le Père Goriot*, 95–98. On the rush of youth into literature, V. Brombert, *Intellectual Hero*, 37; P. Martino, *Le Roman réaliste*, 5; R. Giraud, *Unheroic Hero*, 8; cf. de Tocqueville on Paris, *Old Regime*, 76, and *passim* on effects of democracy. On loss of happiness, C. Affron, *Patterns of Failure*, 38.

PAGE 16

On Napoleon, B. Guyon, *Pensée politique*, 8; H. Levin, *Gates of Horn*, 59. Balzac's female correspondent is in Bonteron, "Lettres de Femmes," *Cahiers Balzaciens*, 3:36. On Julien Sorel's un-Napoleonic nature, R. Alter, *Rogue's Progress*, p. iii. The passages from Stendhal are from the Pléiade edition, 1:304, 1083. Vautrin's warning is near the end of *Illusions*, 712. On Napoleon's brutal dreams, F. Marceau, *Balzac et son monde*, 32.

PAGE 17

On loss of the Napoleonic illusion, J. Lucas-Debreton, *Le Culte de Napoléon*, 25–26. The passages from Balzac are from "Préfaces" to Parts I and II of *Illusions*, 758, 763.

PAGE 19

For Bellessort, see his *Balzac et son œuvre*, 301 n. A. Béguin, *Balzac lu et relu*, 31. Cf. M. Bardèche, *Balzac romancier*, 364, where he plans to analyze "la composition intime et le jeu des échos intérieurs." See also Proust, *Contre Sainte-Beuve*, 210, and H. Levin, *Gates of Horn*, 176.

PAGE 20

On Balzac's apparent knowledge, Henry James, *French Poets and Novelists*, 82; O'Connor, *Mirror in the Roadway*, 85; Willa Cather, *Not Under Forty*, 19.

PAGE 21

For Balzac's nonsense, R. Mortimer, "Introduction to Balzac," *Horizon*, 4 (1941):408. For other pejorative comment on Balzac's faults, see Aldous Huxley, *Vulgarity in Literature*, 43–54; J. Carrère, *Degeneration in the Great French Masters*, 82; Proust, *Contre Sainte-Beuve*, 215–16; E. Auerbach, *Mimesis*, 478–79. M. Turnell on Balzac, *The Novel in France*, 222.

PAGE 22

For another use of the "cold sweat" image, see Balzac's *Sarrasine*, Pléiade ed., 6:89.

PAGE 22

On the structural approach, D. Lodge, *Language of Fiction*, 78–79. On vehicles and the conditions of their use, M. Bouteron, "Anthologie de la vie provinciale," 5–18; R. A. Sayce, *Style in French Prose*, 122. On the coach in Balzac and Dickens, H. House, *The Dickens World*, 26. On movement of the young, G. Poulet, *Interior Distance*, 116–17. Cf. A. Ponceau, *Paysages et Destins*, 49.

PAGE 25

Balzac dwells often and at length on the "high world," as I have called it here and throughout this work. Although he at no time uses the expression *haut monde* himself, I am, I feel sure, rendering with special force his intended meaning. In the chapter called "Madame de Bargeton," pages 36–80 in the Classiques Garnier edition of *Illusions*, Balzac takes great pains to develop the idea that the world to which Lucien aspires is physically above the place of his own origin and becomes as well an object of his ambition toward a *higher* place in life. In these pages the word *haut* or *haute* occurs some ten times. The object of Lucien's dreams lives in "la ville haute," or "Haut-Angoulême," and specifically "en haut la Noblesse et le Pouvoir" is distinguished from what is "en bas," where Lucien comes from. The idea of something "on high" is further developed in references to the "hauteur" of Mme de Bargeton, "le haut rang de cette femme," and Lucien's desire to "conquérir cette haute proie." As with Julien Sorel, the idea of actually mounting to a *higher* place is made inseparable from Lucien's illusions. Balzac speaks of "l'échelle par laquelle il devait monter à l'assaut des grandeurs."

PAGE 26

Stendhal quotes Napoleon's remark as motto for Part II, chap. 22, *Le Rouge et le Noir*.

PAGE 27

For Lucien on foot, G. Picon, "Les 'Illusions perdues,'" 72–73. On clothes, J. Reboul, "Balzac et la Vestignomanie," 210–33; H. Garrett, *Clothes and Character*, *passim*. On the various "laws" of Paris, N. W. Stevenson, *Paris dans la Comédie humaine*, chap. 5, "L'Enfer Parisien."

PAGE 29
P. Lock, "Hoarders and Spendthrifts," 40–41.

PAGE 30
On postponement of names, G. Mayer, *La Qualification affective*, 116.
R. Fernandez, *Messages*, 73, G. Mayer, *La Qualification affective*, 140.

PAGE 31
On concepts of the poet, Pedro Salinas, "Les Pouvoirs de l'écrivain,"
Unesco: Hommage à Balzac (1950), 379. G. Lukacs, *Studies in European
Realism*, 52. G. Mayer, *La Qualification affective*, 70.

PAGE 32
C. E. Schorske, "The Idea of the City," 102–4. P. Citron, *La Poésie de
Paris*, 2:184–85.

PAGES 32–33
On the poetry of Balzac's mythical Paris, H. Friedrich, *Drei Klassiker*,
102–3; cf. articles by Jules Bertaut and Michel Butor in *Balzac*, ed.
Bertaut, 166, 270. On contempt of man but not of money, *Splendeurs*, 183.
On ruin of the victor's joy, Roger Caillois, "Balzac et le Mythe de Paris,"
Edition *Club Français du Livre*, 4 (1962):11. C. Affron, *Patterns of Failure*,
29. On Père Goriot as dying of Paris, M. Bardèche, *Balzac romancier*, 334.

PAGE 33
On *abîme* and related terms applied to Paris, P. Citron, *La Poésie de
Paris*, 2:215 and n.; G. Mayer, *La Qualification affective*, 180–81.

PAGE 35
André Wurmser, *La Comédie inhumaine*, 414. H. Levin, *Gates of Horn*,
107.

PAGE 36
G. Mayer, *La Qualification affective*, 357. G. Poulet, *Interior Distance*,
99–100.

PAGE 37
On the present and future in Lucien's career, G. Picon, "Les 'Illusions
perdues'," 70–73. Cf. G. Jakob, *L'Illusion et la désillusion . . .* , 18. Similar
meanings are attached to *avenir* and its synonyms, including expected
sacrifice from others in *Les Chouans, Sarrasine, L'Illustre Gaudissart*, and *La
Muse du département*.

PAGES 38–39
On the range and importance of temptation, D. R. Howard, *Three
Temptations*, 4, 44–46; M. Bardèche, *Balzac romancier*, 340–41. On pacts
with the devil and other Satanic references, A. Prioult, *Balzac avant la
Comédie humaine*, 159; M. Milner, *Le Diable dans la littérature*, 2:29–36.

Page 39

On the Melmoth theme, H. Crampton, "Melmoth in *La Comédie humaine*," 42–50.

Page 41

On the role of luck or chance, H. U. Forest, *L'Esthétique du roman balzacien*, 93–94.

Pages 41–42

On Balzac's view of "homo duplex" like a coin, E. J. Oliver, *Honoré de Balzac*, 129, 141. On various aspects of Balzac's dualism, A. Maurois, *Prométhée*, 150; A. Béguin, *Balzac lu et relu*, 93; B. Guyon, *Pensée politique* . . . , 730; Philippe Bertault, "Le Dualisme religieux de Balzac," in *Balzac et la religion*, 143–67. On adversaries in two camps, H. U. Forest, *L'Esthétique du roman balzacien*, 183.

Page 42

The passage on "la sottise" is from *Pierrette*, Classiques Garniers, 182. C. Affron, *Patterns of Failure*, 16.

Page 43

On the contrasts in small towns and their economic problems, Jeanne-Marie Bourdet, "La Petite ville de province," *Europe*, 18; J. H. Donnard, *La Vie économique*, 156.

Page 45

On the type of arriviste hero, J. Bertaut, *Le Père Goriot*, 101. A. Wurmser, in *La Comédie inhumaine*, 159–60, discusses Dumas' d'Artagnan as an ambitious provincial coming to Paris to "arrive."

Page 46

J. Carrère, *Degeneration in the Great French Masters*, 83–84, 94–95.

Page 47

A. J. George, *Short Fiction in France, passim*. On the change from sentimental love, F. Baldensperger, *Goethe en France*, 88.

Page 48

On Julien's ability to develop, H. Friedrich, *Drei Klassiker*, 56. R. Alter, *Rogue's Progress*, 31–32; cf. H. Levin, *Gates of Horn*, 93.

Page 49

H. Friedrich, *Drei Klassiker*, 51.

Page 51

On the hero's climbing, descending, or falling, H. Levin, *Gates of Horn*, 144.

PAGE 54

For comparisons of Julien with Balzacian heroes, A. Wurmser, *Comédie inhumaine*, 162–63; Paul-Emile Cadilhac, "A la Poudrerie d'Angoulême," *Illustration* (Nov. 5, 1938), 307–12; P. Castex, "Introduction," *Le Père Goriot* (Garnier, 1960), p. xxl.

PAGE 56

On Balzac's failure to mention Julien, G. Delattre, *Les Opinions littéraires*, 364. For Raphaël's anticipation of Rastignac and Lucien, F. Marceau, *Balzac et son monde*, 49.

PAGE 58

On abysses, M. Bardèche, *Balzac romancier*, 215.

PAGE 61

On de Marsay, M. Bardèche, *Balzac romancier*, 341–42.

PAGE 62

C. Affron, *Patterns of Failure*, 58. P. J. Yarrow defends Balzac against Turnell, "*Le Père Goriot* Reconsidered," 363–73.

PAGE 64

J. Bory, "Balzac dévoile le dessous . . ." in *Balzac*, ed. Bertaut, 120.

PAGE 65

Freud, *Civilization and its Discontents*, 109.

PAGE 66

On Lucien's future betrayal of Vautrin, see P. Castex in his edition of *Le Père Goriot*, 132, n. 2. D. Adamson reassesses the novel in *Symposium*, 19:101–14.

PAGE 71

J. Pommier, "Naissance d'un héros," 193–202. For other valuable comment on Rastignac and Père Goriot, G. Mayer, *Balzac et la Touraine*, 131; A. Le Breton, "Le Pessimisme," in *Balzac: L'Homme et l'œuvre*, 242–50; E. P. Dargan, *Studies in Balzac's Realism*, 136–50, and the last chapter of M. Bardèche, *Balzac romancier*. On Lucien and Rastignac, N. W. Stevenson, *Paris dans la Comédie . . .* , 172–81; D. Fanger, *Dostoevsky*, 56–57, 71; C. Mauriac, *Aimer Balzac*, 225.

PAGE 72

On the devil and related themes, M. Milner, *Le Diable dans la littérature*, 11, 12, 18, 33. A. Béguin, *Balzac lu et relu*, 119.

PAGE 72

On Félix and Mme de Mortsauf, C. Mauriac, *Aimer Balzac*, 189.

PAGE 73

F. Marceau, *Balzac et son monde*, 43. On connections with Vautrin and Nucingen, G. Hourdin, *Balzac romancier des passions*, 93.

PAGE 74

On Rastignac as "arriviste sans scrupule," M. Ferguson, *La Volonté dans la Comédie*, 159. On his future, M. Bardèche, *Lecture*, 109–10.

PAGE 75

On times of publication, *Correspondance de Balzac* (Garnier, 1964), 3: 4–6.

PAGE 77

On Victurnien's departure, A. Ponceau, *Paysages et destins*, 49.

PAGE 78

Victurnien is compared with Lucien by F. Marceau, *Balzac et son monde*, 71.

PAGE 82

Béguin, *Balzac lu et relu*, 169–72; B. Guyon, "Illusions perdues," 3–4. On the order of publication, M. Bardèche, "Sur *Illusions perdues*," in Edition, *Club de l'Honnête Homme*, 8:22. On revisions, Mme Bérard, *La Genèse d'un roman*, 2:119–22, and A. Adam, "Introduction" to *Illusions perdues*, pp. xxx–xxxl.

PAGE 83

M. Bardèche, "Sur *Illusions perdues*," in Edition *Club de L'Honnête Homme*, 8:36–37.

PAGE 84

On future action and unfulfilled illusion, G. Picon, "Les 'Illusions perdues,' " 70–72. On forms of disillusion, G. Jakob, *L'Illusion et la désillusion* . . . , 17–18. Writing here in English, we seem to take the English and French words spelled the same, "illusion," as the same in meaning. Prof. Hoffmann quite rightly warns against this, and the reader should be referred to Robert, *Dictionnaire de la langue française*, where the several meanings of the French word "illusion" will intensify the ambiguity of Balzac's title.

PAGE 86

D. Fanger, *Dostoevsky*, 63. On the physical and moral atmosphere created by Balzac's descriptions, E. Auerbach, *Mimesis*, 472–73; R. Fernandez, *Messages*, 77.

PAGE 87

Alain, "Le Style de Balzac," Edition *Club Français du Livre* (1964), 2:v.

PAGE 88
On Séchard as miser, H. Forest, *L'Esthétique du roman balzacien*, 220; M. Bardèche, *Lecture*, 128.

PAGE 92
P. Abraham, *Créatures chez Balzac*, 109‑ 22.

PAGE 93
M. Beebe, *Ivory Towers*, 186.

PAGE 94
B. F. Bart, "Balzac and Flaubert," 198–200.

PAGE 98
On the poet-genius who owes nothing to others, E. Seillière, *Balzac et la morale Romantique*, 48–53.

PAGE 102
On the soirée in French fiction, Mme Bérard, *La Genèse d'un roman*, 2:63.

PAGE 110
H. James, *French Poets and Novelists*, 103.

PAGE 111
Jean Cayrol, "Preface to *Illusions perdues*," 340.

PAGE 113
Mme Bérard, *La Genèse d'un roman*, 2:56, 165, 304.

PAGE 117
On the change in attitude wrought by Paris, G. Lukacs, *Studies in Realism*, 57; G. Mayer, *Qualification affective*, 231.

PAGE 118
Lucien's sufferings in the Opera box, W. H. Helm, *Aspects of Balzac*, 135–36. G. Lukacs and G. Mayer both discuss this painful scene with respect to Lucien's clothes and their role in his humiliation, *Studies in Realism*, 58, and *Qualification affective*, 289–90. Lucien *is*, then, the clothes he has on.

PAGE 119
G. Mayer, *Qualification affective*, 135; G. Poulet, *Interior Distance*, 114.

PAGES 119–20
On de Marsay and the lorgnon, C. Affron, *Patterns of Failure*, 82.

Page 120
On the effect of the passage of time as noted in Lucien's letter to Ève,
S. Rogers, *Balzac and the Novel*, *passim*.

Page 122
On Rousseau in Paris, P. Citron, *La Poésie de Paris*, 2:211–12, n. 8,
G. Lukacs, *Studies in Realism*, 49.

Page 126
On the arriviste as writer, P. Martino, *Le Roman réaliste*, 6.

Page 144
On Balzac's pity being mingled with contempt, G. Mayer, *Qualification
affective*, 115.

Pages 144–45
On the death of Coralie, A. Beguin, *Balzac lu et relu*, 118. On Lucien's
writing of songs, J. Vallès, *Les Réfractaires*, 19–20.

Page 146
On Balzac's preparation for the fate of Lucien, G. Lukacs, *Studies in
Realism*, 56–57; A. Allemand, *Unité et structure*, 186–87; F. Marceau,
Balzac et son monde, 36–37. On Lucien's relation to prostitution and
Bérénice, C. Affron, *Patterns of Failure*, 100. For other aspects of prostitu-
tion in *Illusions*, see H. Levin, *Gates of Horn*, 206; G. Lukacs, *Studies in
Realism*, 49–53.

Page 147
P. Citron, "Les Affreux du Miroir," *Europe* . . . , 101. On adoring
families, G. Mayer, "Introduction," *Les Illusions Perdues*, p. xv.

Page 147
On Lucien's illusions, G. Jakob, *L'Illusion et la désillusion* . . . , 24–26;
J. Cayrol, "Preface to *Illusions perdues*," 338. W. Van der Gun, *La
Courtisane Romantique* . . . , 79–81, 97–101. Cf. C. Mauriac, *Aimer Balzac*,
81–82, who, despite Van der Gun's reading, prefers the love of Lucien
and Coralie to the dull romance of Ève and David.

Page 150
J. Cayrol, "Preface to *Illusions perdues*," 333.

Page 155
On the changes in Ève, G. Mayer, *Qualification affective*, 140.

Page 164
On passing the house of Rastignac, Proust, *Contre Sainte-Beuve*, 218–19.

Page 165
G. Lukacs, *Studies in Realism*, 61–62.

PAGE 166

On Vautrin's various roles, W. Troy, "On Rereading Balzac," 212; M. Beebe, *Ivory Towers*, 187–88; G. Poulet, *Interior Distance*, 146; G. Lukacs, *Studies in Realism*, 61.

PAGE 167

M. Bardèche, "Sur *Illusions perdues*," Edition *Club de l'Honnête Homme*, 8:36–37. On Lucien's spiritual death, C. Affron, *Patterns of Failure*, 107.

PAGE 168

On Lucien's weakness and imprudence, A. Ponceau, *Paysages et destins* . . . , 228. The comparison to Wenceslas, P. Laubriet, *L'Intelligence de l'art* . . . , 206–8. On Vautrin as Satan, H. Forest, *L'Esthétique du roman balzacien*, 173. On youth allied to the criminal, G. Hourdin, *Balzac romancier des passions*, 91. On temptation, M. Milner, *Le Diable dans la littérature*, 2:39. M. Milner also points out that if Vautrin corrupts Lucien by showing the truth about reality, there is a sense in which illusion is good and reality evil.

PAGE 169

On the "pact," A. Prioult, *Balzac avant la Comédie humaine*, 159. On the consequences of Lucien's meeting with Vautrin, A. Allemand, *Unité et structure* . . . , 219–31.

PAGE 171

On the love of Coralie and Esther for Lucien, D. Furber, "The Fate and Freedom of Balzac's Courtesans," 348.

PAGE 173

On the discussion of Lucien's coming marriage to Clothilde, Proust has a delightful parody, which suggests the smallness and intimacy of Balzac's "world." La Marquise d'Espard invites the leading figures of the *Comédie* to an evening, and it is Mme de Beauséant who mentions Lucien's engagement, saying, however, that the affair is not to be generally known lest Léontine de Sérisy fall into despair. See Proust, "Pastiches et Mélanges: L'Affaire Lemoine: dans un Roman de Balzac," *Œuvres Complètes* (1933), 8:11–18. Mr. Levin has also remarked on how the smallness of Balzac's "world" makes it seem more real, *Gates of Horn*, 183.

PAGE 187

On the autobiographical element in the Rubempré cycle, Mme Bérard, *La Genèse d'un roman*, 1:151–97; G. Picon, "Les 'Illusions perdues,' " 65–66; A. Maurois, *Prométhée, passim;* B. Guyon, *Illusions perdues*, 4–5.

PAGE 188
On Balzac's own "suicide" in life, J. Romains, "Introduction," *The Short Novels of Balzac*, 14–16; G. Poulet, *Interior Distance*, 111–12.

PAGE 188
G. Picon, "Les 'Illusions perdues,'" 66. F. Lotte, "Le Suicide dans *La Comèdie humaine*," 12. A. Wurmser, *La Comédie inhumaine*, 217; cf. G. Limbour, "Préface" to "Splendeurs et misères . . ." in Edition *Club Français du Livre*, 5:11.

PAGE 189
On romantic suicide of Werther, F. Baldensperger, *Goethe en France*, 31–32; C. Affron, *Patterns of Failure*, 109–10. A. Fouqueure, *Balzac à Angoulême*, 59. On Lucien's mental state, M. Le Yaouanc, *Nosographie*, 312, 380.

PAGE 190
For the passage on Lucien's dualism, *Splendeurs*, 479. Cf. G. Poulet, *Interior Distance*, 105.

PAGE 193
J. Pommier, *L'Invention et l'écriture . . .*, 70–91. A. G. Lehmann, "Honoré de Balzac," 436–38. Balzac's reasons for continuing, *Splendeurs*, 485, 505.

PAGE 194
M. Bardèche, *Lecture de Balzac*, 145. Cf. his remarks in Edition *Club de l'Honnête Homme*, 11:25–26.

PAGE 195
G. Picon, "Les 'Illusions perdues,'" 58–68. Another defect of *Splendeurs* is that Nucingen seems to behave as he does because he is a banker, as if there were some connection between the way he has made his fortune and his unspeakable conduct. Nor is Nucingen corrupt because money and banking give him a chance for the monstrous and cynical maneuvers whereby he gets his wealth. He is corrupt in the order of nature, and expresses his corruption in banking because in his time it offers him, better than anything else, a chance to profit from his knavery. Banking in the *Comédie* does not itself make the corruption that profits from it, A. Wurmser to the contrary notwithstanding. The same corruption in another time would take another form.

PAGE 196
On masks and disguises, D. Fanger, *Dostoevsky*, 59–60. A. Béguin, *Balzac lu et relu*, 108–11.

PAGE 197
J. Bory, *Balzac et les ténèbres*, 11–101. Cf. E. J. Oliver, *Honoré de Balzac*, 172–73; G. Limbour, "Préface" to *Splendeurs et misères des courtisanes*, Edition *Club Français du Livre*, 5:8–9.

PAGES 197–98

On the sinister influence of the dark, see the episode of the marriage of Paul and Natalie as they attend a midnight mass in *Le Contrat de mariage*. Henri Mitterand, *Europe*, 149–50.

PAGE 198

G. Picon, "Les 'Illusions perdues,'" 63. For Asie's maneuver, *Splendeurs*, 405–11. Cf. the inadequacy of Balzac's explanation for the wild passion of Mme de Sérisy for Lucien. At this point in the narrative, 415–16, he has no time to explain it and simply tells us that it is so without convincing us.

PAGE 200

P. Barrière, *Honoré de Balzac et la tradition*, 153–54.

PAGE 200

W. Troy, "On Rereading Balzac . . . ," 214–15. Oscar Wilde, "The Decay of Lying," 17–18; cf. Proust, *Contre Sainte-Beuve*, 217–18. On Lucien's response to the repulse from Hôtel de Grandlieu, F. Marceau, *Balzac et son monde*, 50.

PAGE 201

D. Fanger, *Dostoevsky . . .* , 57.

PAGE 202

On excuses for Lucien's behavior, Ethel Preston, *Recherches sur la technique . . .* , 157–58; M. Bardèche, *Lecture de Balzac*, 133–34; F. Marceau, *Balzac et son monde*, 42. For condemnation of Lucien, J. Pommier, *L'Invention et l'Écriture*, 81; Geneviève Delattre, *Les Opinions littéraires*, 296; H. U. Forest, *L'Esthétique du roman*, 43.

PAGE 203

M. Bardèche, "Sur *Illusions perdues*," Edition *Club de L'Honnête Homme*, 8:36–37. Mme Bérard, *La Genèse d'un roman*, 2:30, 222, n. 2, 225. On homosexuality, C. Mauriac, *Aimer Balzac*, 64–72; M. Bardèche, *Lecture de Balzac*, 148; F. Marceau, *Balzac et son monde*, 38; A. Wurmser, *La Comédie inhumaine*, 627; H. Levin, "Balzac et Proust," 296 ff.; B. Griffith, *Balzac aux Etats Unis*, 190–200.

PAGE 204

P. Citron, *La Poésie de Paris*, 2:237.

PAGE 205

C. Affron, *Patterns of Failure*, 24; cf. *Ibid.*, 36–37, 81, and Norah Stevenson, *Paris dans la Comédie humaine*, chap. 5, *passim;* R. Giraud, *The Unheroic Hero*, 190, G. Lukacs, *Studies in Realism*, 52–53.

Bibliography

I

Illusions perdues (1961) and *Splendeurs et misères des courtisanes* (1958) have been read in the Classiques Garnier, published in Paris and edited by Antoine Adam. All references and quotations in the preceding essay to the Rubempré cycle are from this edition. Wherever possible, the Classiques Garnier have been used for other works of Balzac throughout: *Histoire des treize* ("Ferragus, La Duchesse de Langeais, La Fille aux yeux d'or"), *Le Médecin de campagne, Le Lys dans la vallée, Eugénie Grandet, Le Père Goriot, La Vieille Fille, Le Cabinet des antiques, Pierrette, Béatrix, L'Envers de l'histoire contemporaine* and *La Rabouilleuse.* Alfred de Musset's *La Confession d'un Enfant du Siècle* was also read in the Classiques Garnier, Paris, 1960. While the text of the Pléiade edition of Balzac, chiefly by M. Bouteron beginning in 1951, is not so satisfactory as the more accurate and finished product of the Classiques Garnier, it has the virtue of making easily available the less celebrated titles, with which every serious reader should be familiar. Besides Marivaux's *Le Paysan parvenu*, Stendhal's *Le Rouge et le Noir*, and *Lucien Leuwen*, the following works of Balzac to which the text refers may be found in the Pléiade edition: *Les Chouans, Melmoth réconcilié, Sarrasine, La Messe de l'Athée, La Peau de chagrin, L'Illustre Gaudissart, La Muse du département, Le Contrat de mariage, La Femme abandonnée, Les Employés, Un Début dans la vie, Les Secrets de la Princesse de Cadignan,* and *L'Interdiction.* Although the great summits of the *Comédie humaine* may stand separately, they gain enormously in richness and power the more familiar one is with preceding and following works.

Other editions of Balzac under the auspices of the "Club de l'Honnête Homme" (Paris, 1958) and the "Club Français du Livre" (Paris, 1962–64) are beautifully printed and bound, but have been used chiefly for a number of valuable introductions by MM. Bardèche, Cayrol, and others mentioned in the notes.

223

II

The following list of books and articles confines itself to materials actually used in the text. Despite the mass of existing commentary on Balzac, the student wishing to interpret individual works in depth is not greatly assisted, as already noted. The *Année Balzacienne*, which has been appearing every year since 1960, offers a useful survey of recent work on Balzac, but only an occasional piece like Mr. Hoffmann's article on beast imagery in *Le Père Goriot* employs the characteristic resources of modern literary study. At the end of the *Genèse* study, Mme Bérard devotes some six pages (2: 318–23) to "une bibliographie restreinte," which nonetheless offers most of the older works that bear on *Illusions perdues* or the career of Lucien. Her list contains many of the titles given here, in alphabetical order by author's last name.

Abraham, Pierre. ". . . . Comment Balzac décrit la figure humaine," pp. 109–22 in *Créatures chez Balzac*. Paris: Gallimard, 1931.

Adamson, Donald. "*Le Père Goriot:* Notes Toward a Reassessment." *Symposium* 19 (1965): 101–14.

Affron, Charles. *Patterns of Failure in "La Comédie Humaine."* New Haven: Yale University Press, 1966.

Allemand, André. *Unité et structure de l'univers Balzacien*. Paris: Plon, 1965.

Alter, Robert. *Rogue's Progress: Studies in the Picaresque Novel*. Cambridge: Harvard University Press, 1964.

Auerbach, Erich. *Mimesis*. Translated by Willard R. Trask. Princeton: Princeton University Press, 1953.

Baldensperger, Fernand. *Goethe en France*. Paris: Hachette et Cie, 1904.

Bardèche, Maurice. *Balzac romancier*. Paris: Plon, 1943.

———. *Une Lecture de Balzac*. Paris: Les Sept Couleurs, 1964.

Barrière, P. *Honoré de Balzac et la tradition littéraire classique*. Paris: Librairie Hachette, 1928.

Bart, B. F. "Balzac and Flaubert: Energy versus Art." *Romanic Review* 42 (1951): 198–204.

Beebe, Maurice. *Ivory Towers and Sacred Founts*. New York: New York University Press, 1964.

Béguin, Albert. *Balzac lu et relu*, with "Préface" by Gaëton Picon. Paris: Seuil, 1965.

Bellessort, André. *Balzac et son œuvre*. Paris: Perrin et Cie, 1924.

Bérard, Suzanne Jean. *La Genèse d'un roman de Balzac: "Illusions Perdues," 1837*. Two vols. Paris: A. Colin, 1961.

Bertault, Philippe. *Balzac et la religion*. Paris: Boivin, 1942.

Bertaut, Jules. *Le Père Goriot de Balzac*. Amiens: E. Malfère, 1928.

———. *Balzac*. Collection Génies et réalités. Paris: Hachette, 1959.

Bouteron, Marcel. "Lettres de femmes adresseés à Honoré de Balzac," in *Les Cahiers Balzaciens*, 3. Paris: La Cité des Livres, 1924.

————. "Anthologie de la vie provinciale d'après *La Comédie humaine.*" *Revue des Sciences Humaines*, 1950, pp. 5–18.

Brombert, Victor. *The Intellectual Hero*. Philadelphia: Lippincott, 1960.

Cadilhac, Paul–Émile. "A la Poudrerie d'Angoulême. . . ." *Illustration*, November 5, 1938: 307–12.

Carrère, Jean. *Degeneration in the Great French Masters*. London: T. F. Unwin, Ltd., 1922.

Cather, Willa. *Not under Forty*. New York: Knopf, 1936.

Cayrol, Jean. "Préface" to *Illusions perdues*. Paris: Club Français du Livre, 1962–64.

Citron, Pierre. *La Poésie de Paris dans la littérature française de Rousseau à Baudelaire*. Two vols. Paris: Editions de Minuit, 1961.

Cook, Albert. *The Meaning of Fiction*. Detroit: Wayne State University Press, 1960.

Crampton, Hope. "Melmoth in *La Comédie Humaine.*" *Modern Language Review* 61 (1966): 42–50.

Croce, Benedetto. "Balzac." *Adam: International Review* 17 (1949): 12–18.

Dargan, Edwin P. *Studies in Balzac's Realism*. Chicago: University of Chicago Press, 1932.

Delattre, Geneviève. *Les Opinions littéraires de Balzac*. Paris: Presses Universitaires de France, 1961.

Donnard, Jean-Hervé. *La Vie économique et les classes sociales dans l'œuvre de Balzac*. Paris: A Colin, 1961.

Europe: Colloque: Balzac 43 (1965).

Fanger, Donald. *Dostoevsky and Romantic Realism*. Cambridge: Harvard University Press, 1965.

Ferguson, Muriel B. *La Volonté dans la Comédie Humaine de Balzac*. Paris: G. Courville, 1935.

Fernandez, Ramon. "The Method of Balzac," pp. 61–88 in *Messages: Library Essays*, translated by Montgomery Belgion. Port Washington, New York: Kennikat Press, 1964, 61–88.

Forest, H. U. *L'Esthétique du roman Balzacien*. Paris: Presses Universitaires de France, 1950.

Fouqueure, André. *Honoré de Balzac à Angoulême*. Paris: Société Générale d'Imprimerie et d'Edition Levé, 1913.

Freud, Sigmund. *Civilization and Its Discontents*, translated by Joan Riviere. London: Hogarth Press and Institute of Psycho-Analysis, 1949.

Friedrich, Hugo. *Drei Klassiker des Französischen Romans*. Frankfurt: V. Klosterman, 1961.

Furber, Donald. "The Fate and Freedom of Balzac's Courtesans." *The French Review* 39 (1965): 346–53.

Garrett, Helen. *Clothes and Character: The Function of Dress in Balzac*. Philadelphia: University of Pennsylvania, 1941.

George, Albert J. *Short Fiction in France: 1800–1850*. Syracuse: Syracuse University Press, 1964.

Girard, René. *Mensonge romantique et verité romanesque*. Paris: Grasset, 1961.

Giraud, Raymond. *The Unheroic Hero in the Novels of Stendhal, Balzac, and Flaubert*. New Brunswick, N.J.: Rutgers University Press, 1957.

Gould, Charles. "The Present State of Balzac Studies." *French Studies* 12 (1958): 299–323.

Griffith, Benjamin. *Balzac aux Etats-Unis*, pp. 190–200. Paris: Les Presses Modernes, 1931.

Guyon, Bernard. *La Pensée politique et sociale de Balzac*. Paris: A. Colin, 1947.

———. "Illusions perdues." *L'Information Littéraire* 6 (1954): 1–6.

Helm, W. H. *Aspects of Balzac*. New York: J. Pott, 1905.

Hoffmann, Léon François. "Les Métaphores animales dans *Le Père Goriot*." *L'Année Balzacienne*, 1963: 91–105.

Hourdin, Georges. *Balzac, romancier des passions*. Paris: Les Temps Présents, 1950.

House, Humphry. *The Dickens World*. London: Oxford University Press, 1960.

Howard, Donald R. *The Three Temptations: Medieval Man in Search of the World*. Princeton: Princeton University Press, 1966.

Hunt, Herbert. *La Comédie Humaine*. London: The Athlone Press, 1959.

Huxley, Aldous. *Vulgarity in Literature*. London: Chatto and Windus, 1930.

Iknayan, Marguerite. *The Idea of the Novel in France: The Critical Reaction 1815–1848*. Geneva: E. Droz, 1961.

Jakob, Gustave. *L'Illusion et la désillusion dans le roman réaliste français (1851 à 1890)*. Paris: Jouve et Cie, 1912.

James, Henry. *The Art of Fiction and Other Essays*, edited by Morris Roberts. New York: Oxford University Press, 1948.

———. *French Poets and Novelists*. London and New York: Macmillan Co., 1919.

Laubriet, Pierre. *L'Intelligence de l'art chez Balzac*. Paris: Didier, 1961.

Le Breton, André. *Balzac: L'Homme et l'œuvre*. Paris: A. Colin, 1905.

Lehmann, A. G. "Honoré de Balzac." *The Listener* 75 (March 24, 1966): 436–38.

Levin, Harry. "Balzac et Proust," in *Unesco: Hommage à Balzac*. Paris: Mercure de France, 1950.

———. *The Gates of Horn*. New York: Oxford University Press, 1963.

Le Yaouanc, Moïse. *Nosographie de l'humanité Balzacienne*. Maloine: 1959.

Lock, Peter W. "Hoarders and Spendthrifts in 'La Comédie Humaine.'" *The Modern Language Review* 61 (1966): 29–41.

Lodge, David. *The Language of Fiction*. London: Routledge & Kegan Paul; New York: Columbia University Press, 1966.

Lotte, Fernand. "Le Suicide dans la Comédie Humaine." *Médecine de France* 53 (1954): 10–16.

Lucas-Dubreton, J. *Le Culte de Napoléon: 1815–48.* Paris: A. Michel, 1960.

Lukacs, Georg. *Studies in European Realism.* London: Hillway Publishing Co., 1964.

Marceau, Félicien. *Balzac et son monde.* Paris: Gallimard, 1955.

Martino, Pierre. *Le Roman réaliste sous le Second Empire.* Paris: Hachette et Cie, 1913.

Mauriac, Claude. *Aimer Balzac.* Paris: La Table Ronde, 1945.

Maurois, André. *Prométhée.* Paris: Librairie Hachette, 1965.

Mayer, Gilbert. *Balzac et la Touraine.* Paris, n.d.

———. "Introduction" to *Les Illusions perdues*, I, Édition Critique. Paris: Droz, 1946.

———. *La Qualification affective dans les romans d'Honoré de Balzac.* Paris: E. Droz, 1940.

Milner, Max. *Le Diable dans la littérature française: 1772–1861.* Two vols. Paris: J. Corti, 1960.

Moreau, Pierre. "Le Romantisme," vol. 8 of *Histoire de la littérature française*, ed. J. Calvet. Paris: J. de Gigord, 1932.

Mortimer, Raymond. "Introduction to Balzac," in *Channel Packet.* London: The Hogarth Press, 1943.

Murtfeld, Rudolf. *Balzac.* Berne: Francke, 1956.

O'Connor, Frank. *Mirror in the Roadway.* New York: Knopf, 1956.

Oliver, Edward J. *Honoré de Balzac.* New York: Macmillan Co., 1965.

Picon, Gaëton. "Les 'Illusions perdues' ou l'espérance retrouvée." *Mercure de France* 332 (1958): 60–75.

Pommier, Jean. *L'Invention et L'Écriture dans la Torpille de Honoré de Balzac.* Geneva: Droz, 1957.

———. "Naissance d'un Héros: Rastignac." *Revue d'Histoire Littéraire de la France.* 50 (1950): 192–209.

Ponceau, Amédée. *Paysages et destins Balzaciens.* Paris: Myrte, 1950.

Poulet, Georges. *The Interior Distance*, translated by Elliott Coleman. Baltimore: Johns Hopkins Press, 1959.

Preston, Ethel. *Recherches sur la technique de Balzac.* Paris: Les Presses Françaises, 1926.

Prioult, A. *Balzac avant la Comédie Humaine.* Paris: G. Courville, 1936.

Proust, Marcel. *Le Balzac de Monsieur Guermantes.* Neuchâtel: Ides et Calendes, 1950.

———. "Sainte-Beuve et Balzac," in *Contre Sainte-Beuve*, 19th ed. Paris: Gallimard, 1954.

———. "L'Affaire Lemoine: Dans un Roman de Balzac," pp. 11–18 in *Pastiches et mélanges: œuvres complètes* VIII. Paris: Nouvelle Revue Française, 1933.

Pugh, Anthony A. "Ten Years of Balzac Studies." *Modern Languages* 46 (1965): 91–97.

Reboul, Jeanne. "Balzac et la vestignomanie." *Revue d'Histoire Littéraire de la France* 50 (1950): 210–33.

Rogers, Samuel. *Balzac and the Novel*. Madison: University of Wisconsin Press, 1953.

Romains, Jules. "Introduction," to *The Short Novels of Balzac*. New York: Dial Press, 1948.

Salinas, Pedro. "Les Pouvoirs de l'écrivain," in *Unesco: Hommage à Balzac*. Paris: Mercure de France, 1950.

Sayce, R. A. *Style in French Prose*. Oxford: Clarendon Press, 1953.

Schorske, Carl E. "The Idea of the City in European Thought: Voltaire to Spengler," pp. 94–114 in *The Historian and the City*, edited by Oscar Handlin and John Burchard. Cambridge: M.I.T. Press, 1963.

Seillière, Ernest. *Balzac et la morale romantique*. Paris: F. Alcan, 1922.

Stevenson, Norah W. *Paris dans la Comédie Humaine de Balzac*. Paris: G. Courville, 1938.

Tocqueville, Alexis de. *The Old Regime and the French Revolution*. New York: Doubleday, 1955.

Troy, William. "On Rereading Balzac," pp. 207–19 in *The Critical Performance*, edited by S. E. Hyman. New York: Vintage Books, 1956.

Turnell, Martin. *The Novel in France*. New York: Vintage, 1958.

Vallès, Jules. *Les Réfractaires*. Paris: Bibliothèque-Charpentier, 1924.

Van der Gun, Willem H. *La Courtisane romantique et son rôle dans la Comédie Humaine de Balzac*. Assen, Netherlands: Van Gorcum, 1963.

Watt, Ian. *The Rise of the Novel*. Berkeley: University of California Press, 1963.

Weinberg, Bernard. *French Realism: The Critical Reaction, 1830–1870*. New York: Modern Language Association of America; London: Oxford University Press, 1937.

Wenger, Jared. *The Province and the Provinces in the Work of Honoré de Balzac*. Princeton: G. Branta, 1937.

Wilde, Oscar. "The Decay of Lying," in *Intentions*. London: The Edinburgh Society, 1911.

———. "Balzac in English," in *A Critic in Pall Mall*. New York and London: G. P. Putnam's Sons, 1919.

Wurmser, André. *La Comédie inhumaine*. Paris: Gallimard, 1964.

Yarrow, P. J. "*Le Père Goriot* Re-considered." *Essays in Criticism* 7 (1957): 363–73.

Index

Adam, Antoine, 8, 83, 125, 202
Adamson, Donald, 66
Affron, Charles, 33, 42, 62, 189, 205
Agathe, 60
Alain, 87
Albert Savarus, 92
Alençon, 78
Alter, Robert, 48
Anastasie, 70
Angoulême, 3, 22, 24, 29, 43, 55, 86, 104, 114, 117, 151, 152
Antoinette, 7, 22, 25
Argow le Pirate, 46
Armande, Aunt, 75, 78
Arnold, Matthew, 2
As You Like It, 201
Asie, 196, 199

Balthazar, 39
Balzac: biblical associations in, 39, 52, 124, 166; "circumstances" for, 141; criticisms of, 20–21; dualism of, 3; as essayist, 7–8; generalization by, 19–20; irony of, 31; life appearing in *Comédie*, 6–7, 186–87; mode of narration, 42, 127; morality of, 124; pessimism of, 3; postpones charac-ter's name, 30; purpose to warn young poets, 17–18; quality of work, 8, 20, 187–88; realism of, 5, 155; reality in, 37; self-imposed task of, 187–89; style of, 198; technique of, 10, 87, 102, 103, 106, 112, 113, 131, 175, 181–82, 184, 193–207; themes of, 24, 79, 96, 128, 135; typical structure of, 5; use of metaphor and simile, 20–21, 111, 206; use of "strategies," 9, 103; use of synonyms, 29–30, 37, 112, 117; work formed by 19th century, 12–31
Bardèche, Maurice, 3, 7, 61, 84, 167, 194, 203
Bargeton, Louise de, 21, 24, 25, 29, 33, 35, 36, 38, 39, 43, 49, 93, 103, 115, 119, 120, 132, 138, 139, 143, 145, 150, 159, 162, 204, 207; career of, 95–96, 116–18; origins of, 94–95; as tempter, 97–98, 101, 107, 109–11
Bargeton, M. de, 22, 29, 35–36, 102–3, 108, 109, 207
Barker, William, 196
Barrière, P., 1, 200
Bart, B. F., 94

229

THE HERO AS FAILURE studies Balzac as an author in the *Bildungsroman* genre, the novel of education which traces the career of a young man as he sets out in the world to win success.

Following a brief discussion of the historical circumstances which inspired great numbers of nineteenth-century French youth to flock to Paris in search of quick advancement, Schilling shows that Lucien de Rubempré was anticipated in Balzac's earlier works as well as in Stendhal's great *Le Rouge et le Noir*. He then traces Lucien's career as Balzac portrayed it in the two novels that lie at the very center of his achievement in *La Comédie humaine: Illusions perdues* and *Splendeurs et misères des courtisanes*. From impoverished provincial beginnings, Lucien makes his way toward hoped-for success in Paris. Failing dismally, he returns home, and, about to despair, he is taken back to Paris by Balzac's great creation, the criminal Vautrin, only to commit suicide in prison.